SOUTHERN INSURGENCY

Wildcat: Workers' Movements and Global Capitalism

Series Editors:

Peter Alexander (University of Johannesburg)
Immanuel Ness (City University of New York)
Tim Pringle (SOAS, University of London)
Malehoko Tshoaedi (University of Pretoria)

Workers' movements are a common and recurring feature in contemporary capitalism. The same militancy that inspired the mass labor movements of the twentieth century continues to define worker struggles that proliferate throughout the world today.

For more than a century labor unions have mobilized to represent the political-economic interests of workers by uncovering the abuses of capitalism, establishing wage standards, improving oppressive working conditions, and bargaining with employers and the state. Since the 1970s, organized labor has declined in size and influence as the global power and influence of capital has expanded dramatically. The world over, existing unions are in a condition of fracture and turbulence in response to neoliberalism, financialization, and the reappearance of rapacious forms of imperialism. New and modernized unions are adapting to conditions and creating class-conscious workers' movement rooted in militancy and solidarity. Ironically, while the power of organized labor contracts, working-class militancy and resistance persists and is growing in the Global South.

Wildcat publishes ambitious and innovative works on the history and political economy of workers' movements and is a forum for debate on pivotal movements and labor struggles. The series applies a broad definition of the labor movement to include workers in and out of unions, and seeks works that examine proletarianization and class formation; mass production; gender, affective and reproductive labor; imperialism and workers; syndicalism and independent unions, and labor and Leftist social and political movements.

Also available:

Just Work?: Migrant Workers' Struggles Today
Edited by Aziz Choudry and Mondli Hlatshwayo

Southern Insurgency

The Coming of the Global Working Class

Immanuel Ness

PlutoPress
www.plutobooks.com

First published 2016 by Pluto Press
345 Archway Road, London N6 5AA

www.plutobooks.com

British Library Cataloguing in Publication Data
A catalogue record for this book is available from the British Library

ISBN 978 0 7453 3600 8 Hardback
ISBN 978 0 7453 3599 5 Paperback
ISBN 978 1 7837 1708 8 PDF eBook
ISBN 978 1 7837 1710 1 Kindle eBook
ISBN 978 1 7837 1709 5 EPUB eBook

This book is printed on paper suitable for recycling and made from fully managed and
sustained forest sources. Logging, pulping and manufacturing processes are expected to
conform to the environmental standards of the country of origin.

Typeset by Curran Publishing Services
Text design by Melanie Patrick
Simultaneously printed by CPI Antony Rowe, Chippenham, UK
and
Edwards Bros in the United States of America

Contents

Maps, figures, and tables

Maps

Figures

Tables

Maps, figures, and tables

Preface and Acknowledgments

This book is informed by national and comparative studies of labor movements in the contemporary era. The overwhelming evidence suggests that existing labor structures are unable to challenge the hegemony of international capital, global production and commodity chains, and the oppression of the neoliberal state. This is not to say that organized labor has ever possessed a persistent power over capital, aside from interregna of revolution and ephemeral worker rebellions. The book suggests that the working class and peasants can only achieve a modicum of institutional and structural power and dignity inside the modern capitalist state. A central premise is that the early 21st century has vastly and irreversibly altered the geographic location of the working class to the Global South, where the majority of the world's population resides. The geographic location of the working class has followed in the tracks of the expansion of trade liberalization, neoliberal capitalism, and global imperialism from the 1980s to the present.

As in previous generations the modern working class is also primarily comprised of peasant workers migrating from rural regions. However, with severe exceptions where countries of the Global South (or Third World) border states in the Global North (Mexico to the United States, North Africa to Europe), the vast majority of modern industrial workers in China, India, Indonesia, Africa, and Latin America are internal migrants, just as the industrial working class during the emergence of capitalism in the 19th century were migrant workers from rural regions. In Europe and North America, migrant industrial workers often crossed international boundaries: for example Irish workers in England, and Southern and Eastern Europeans in the Americas.

But something new has happened that is based on the scale of commodity production. Today, commodity production is a global project and dominates the production of all products – from the extraction of iron ore to high-technology and biomedical and phar-maceutical goods.

This ethnographic and comparative book has been made possible through the incredible support of numerous people throughout the world, especially India, China, and South Africa, who provided accurate accounts of workers' movements in each country and assisted with ethnographic research. I endeavored to interview many specialists and participants from different orga-nizations so as to provide accounts ensuring the accuracy of the case studies in each region. These accounts have been reinforced by workers directly involved in struggles, their family members, and community leaders, together with labor activists who retold detailed descriptions of their specific struggles. Research and interviews were conducted in New Delhi and Haryana State in North Central India, the Pearl River Delta of south-east China, and the mining belt in North West Province, South Africa. In each case I was accompanied by legal experts, labor activists, and academics who were involved in the strikes and worker insurrections.

This book has also enjoyed the collective support of literally hundreds of colleagues and friends worldwide who helped me gain access to crucial locations and lent support in developing and framing the research project, and who have provided vital comments on the manuscript. Among them, I would like to extend my special thanks to Suzanne Adely, Peter Alexander, Robin Alexander, Judy Ancel, Apo Leung Po, Edur Velasco Arregui, Samantha Ashman, Maurizio Atzeni, Au Loong-yu, Amiya Kumar Bagchi, Susanna Barria, Patrick Bond, Amy Bromsen, Dario Bursztyn, Stephen Castles, Vivek Chibber, Héctor de la Cueda, Ashwin Desai, Rehad Desai, Sushovan Dhar, Jackie DiSalvo, Gérard Duménil, Madhumita Dutta, Steve Early, Silvia Federici, Doug Ferrari, Bill Fletcher, Jr., Ellen David Friedman, Atig Ghosh, Mike Goldfield, Tony Gronowicz, Lenin Gonzalez, Daniel Gross, David Harvey, Scott Horne, Dek Keenan, Rena Lau, Andrew Lawrence, Li Shing Hong, Rebecca Lurie, Staughton Lynd, Christos Mais, Simangele Manzi, Biju Matthew, Siphiwe Mbatha, Joe McDermott, Lori Minnite, Jeanne Mirer, Chere Monaisa, Patrick Neveling, Trevor Ngwane, Jörg Nowak, Benedicto

Martinez Orozco, Ed Ott, Ranjana Padhi, Fahmi Panimbang, Bill Parker, Prabhat Patnaik, Lee Pegler, Frances Fox Piven, Rakesh Ranjan, Merle Ratner, Dick Roman, Ashim Roy, Ranabir Samaddar, Jose Manuel Sandoval, Vishwas Satgar, Rakhi Seghal, Arup Kumar Sen, Bishop Joe Sepka, Sher Singh, Luke Sinwell, John Smith, Juliana So, Shelton Stromquist, Ashwini Sukanthar, Dominic Tuminaro, Lucien van der Walt, Achin Vanaik, N. Vasudevan, Eddie Webster, Michelle Williams, May Wong, Lu Zhang, along with many others who read and reviewed the manuscript.

Special thanks go to Zak Cope, among the leading thinkers of social class and imperialism today, who was of enormous help in reading, commenting, and critiquing this work. He was instrumental in developing the quantitative data and many of the tables which support the arguments of this book.

Vital logistical support was made possible through the research staff of the South African Research Chair in Social Change at the University of Johannesburg. Thanks are also due to the City University of New York Research Foundation for supporting some of the travel.

Finally, I thank David Shulman, acquisitions editor at Pluto Press, for his vision of the abiding significance of workers' and peasants' movements to radical transformation, and support in developing the new series which this book inaugurates, Wildcat: Workers Movements and Global Capitalism, edited by Peter Alexander, Tim Pringle, Malehoko Tschoaedi, and myself. I am impressed with the demanding review process at Pluto Press and a discernment to recognize and support outstanding works on the left.

Introduction

The New International Working Class

In the spring of 2014 a wave of unprecedented mass strikes in strategic industries in China, India, and South Africa defied the established wisdom among investors that low-wage workers pose no threat to corporate profit margins. Three years earlier, in 2011, came the first troubling indications that direct action by electronics, automotive, clothing, and mining workers could pose a risk to multinational investors and brands. In a growing range of industries, worker protests over wages and conditions could only be suppressed by armed state repression and violence. The spread of labor militancy across the Global South raises crucial questions about the revival of a global labor movement and the capacity of states and labor unions to contain dissent in such a way as to restore confidence in capital markets.

In the 2000s the labor insurgencies that have rocked the world economy have been set off by migrant workers and their children, who constitute a large share of the global working class. Migrant workers are constantly being recruited by contractors to replenish the supply of low-wage labor available to capital. Since the 1990s, the vast majority of migrant laborers working in China, India, and South Africa have been peasants and their families, who have moved to industrial zones and who typically lack residency and work privileges equivalent to those enjoyed by urban inhabitants.

The rapid industrialization that has occurred in the Global South over the past four decades now dominates global working patterns. The ascendancy of production workers in these new production centers today substantially overshadows the historical size of the working class of mass production in the Global North during its heyday in the 20th century. As debates on the left increasingly focus on the proliferation of financial investments, this book redirects attention to the profound significance of manufacturing and mining workers, who have been often disregarded in the mature economies of the Global North as investment has been redirected to factories and installations in the Global South, resulting in a new working class in education, the public sector, finance, and a proliferation of commercial jobs.

This book will show that the industrial working class has not disappeared but has been relocated and reconstituted in the South in larger numbers than ever before in history. Financialization and speculation are responsible for the closure of factories and the reduction in the number of middle-income jobs in mature economies of the Global North, while accelerating the expansion of a low-wage and insecure work force in the newly industrialized South. This contemporary system of neoliberal capitalist global accumulation distorts economies through investment in finance, real estate, derivatives, and other financial instruments, and has threatened the world economy to the point of disruption through speculative investments, increasing inequality worldwide as well as between North and South.

HERE COMES THE POST-INDUSTRIAL ECONOMY

As in the North, workers in the South face constraints imposed by workers' movements that are legacies of 20th-century capitalism, and are struggling to build new working-class institutions that will redefine the shape of class conflict for the next 50 years. In the 1970s the assault on the working class was in full swing, as capital and the state united in opposition to the representation of existing unions and the welfare state forged by the labor movements of the early 20th century. To capital, organized labor posed an obstacle to expanding corporate profits and restoring absolute hegemony in the workplace. Over the next four decades a resurgent capitalist class conducted a fierce war against labor unions in the West, turning them from a formidable force in major industries into a weak irritant at best.

At the same time, the very existence of a working class was also called into question by leading scholars on the right and the left. While the right wing declared the working class dead and a false construct, leftist scholars were also challenging the legitimacy of the working class as a force for social equity and transformation. Yet, more than 40 years after the onslaught of the economic, political, and intellectual offensive against organized labor throughout the world, the working class has a heartbeat and is stronger than ever before despite the dramatic decline in organized labor. This assessment is rooted in an empirical examination of workers' movements over the last decade which can no longer be contained by the state and international monopoly capital. While it may be the case that the labor movements in Europe and North America are a spent force, it is their very defeats that have marginalized their existing supine and bureaucratic order and regenerated a fierce workers' movement in the early 21st century.

Meanwhile the capitalist development of the South has regenerated Marxist debates about the nature of the working class, with industrialization for export stimulating the unambiguous presence of a class structure that traverses geographic boundaries. This book argues that the North applied models of representation in the South that contained the scope of worker representation within narrow boundaries, restricting worker mobilization. As the developing and emerging economies in the South have followed the pattern of the North, workers are choosing new means to advance their interests. It is in the South that workers have shaken off the shackles and restraints imposed by the labor movement.

Momentous and unexpected labor uprisings and mass strikes are unfolding today among migrant workers in urban industrial zones who to varying degrees are challenging the neoliberal capitalist project. The intensity of these class conflicts in mines and factories was not envisaged by foreign investors, multinational corporations, and private contractors – or by many leftist scholars and activists in the West. Labor scholars agonized about the relocation of well-paid manufacturing jobs and the rise of a post-industrial economy, and a consensus emerged among advocates of free markets on the right and progressives on the left that work was no longer relevant to society or to popular aspirations, human freedom, and revolutionary transformation.

As early as 1973 sociologist Daniel Bell and champions of free market capitalism attributed the inexorable decline of the American working class to the vanishing of key manufacturing industries in the United States and the growth of information and new technology, while neither appreciating the importance of minerals nor considering the ongoing necessity to produce clothing, cars, and electronics. Somehow every region of the world would have to shift from farming, mining, and manufacturing to reach the status of a post-industrial society.[1] While Bell dismisses the obvious class differences within Western societies he is indifferent to the necessity of industrial production under capitalism.

Leftists and postmodernists have adopted the identical language of free market apologists for multinational capital. *Farewell to the Working Class* was declared by French political theorist André Gorz in 1980, auguring a post-industrial socialism free of workers. To Gorz, the socialist aspirations of the working class are 'as obsolete as the proletariat itself', and they have been supplanted by a 'non-class of non-workers' who have been created by the 'growth of new production technology' and will abolish all classes 'along with work itself and all forms of domination.'[2]

Bell and Gorz concur that post-industrialism has replaced capitalism and class conflict, and that collective class unity is a figment of the imagination or an ideology that is dominated by the hegemony of a declining or unrepresentative class of workers in post-industrial society. Post-industrialism is a reality in the North principally because of the vast differences in wages and social benefits, and the growing dependence on highly exploited workers in the South who produce essential goods and services for multinational capital and also low-cost goods and services predominantly for consumers in the West. Meanwhile the well-founded assertion among labor unions and proponents of manufacturing workers in the North is that corporate relocation of production to low-wage regions and states in the South has been at the expense of good manufacturing jobs.

The case studies in this book investigate the developing labor militancy and direct action in the early 21st century among production workers in China, India, and South Africa, where employers exploit differences to create hierarchical systems of relative favoritism to promote lower wages and poorer conditions for all laborers. In each case, contractors and employers have hired young migrant workers with limited social ties to work in mines and factories. Employers also seek to divide workers on the basis of age, caste, ethnicity, and gender. Each case study demonstrates that industrial workers engage in a range of tactics and strategies to advance their collective interests both within and outside existing trade unions and organizational structures. The case studies, drawn from South African mines, Indian auto factories, and Chinese shoe producers, reveal that industrial workers mobilize around collective interests in order to improve their conditions. Although the particular workers in each struggle face dissimilar challenges and, at least in the case of India, have been defeated and imprisoned en masse for mobilizing collectively, they expose the growing activism among workers that is transforming itself into mass movements with unique characteristics in each country.

WHY GLOBAL SOUTH WORKERS?

In each of this book's case studies I examine the composition of workers, the nature of their struggle, and the relationship of emerging rank-and-file workers' movements to existing unions and the state, together with their outcomes. While factories continue to close in Europe, Japan, North America, and throughout the world, global production is growing dramatically. Yet for more than 40 years researchers and journalists have pondered the working class mostly without consideration of the vast majority of workers who are laboring in the Global South. At a time when public attention spotlights the integration of these developing and emerging countries into the world capitalist economy, little attention is paid to corporate repression and worker resistance in the modern factories and mines that are integral to the world economy. Most media coverage of mass labor disputes is in the international financial press, and is oriented to providing vital information on key industries to foreign investors.[3]

At a time when academics are struggling to locate any sign of life among amorphous working classes in Europe and North America, worker struggles are rampant throughout the South. Three areas of inquiry among sociologists of work and political economists mainly studying labor in the North at present are precarious workers, unpaid work, and affective (or emotional) labor. New research, meanwhile, looks at potential forms of work in unstructured and often unregulated labor markets that are filled by day laborers, domestic workers, sex workers, street peddlers and food cart operators, temporary laborers, and for-hire drivers, all mainly employed in the informal economy.[4]

The discovery of workers in the informal economy with few legal rights reveals their weakness and their dependency on non-governmental organizations (NGOs) and advocacy groups, and on political and electoral advocacy to defend and expand their rights. In the United States, campaigns to improve the conditions of fast-food outlet and Walmart department store workers are pursued primarily by advocates and by external union and community organizers to generate public attention for the purpose of raising the minimum wage, with the hazy prospect of organizing workers into unions down the road.[5] The reconstitution of the labor force in the Global North from manufacturing and production to services and commerce is weakening the ability of workers in the West to organize unions. It is far more difficult to organize part-time and temporary service, retail, and hospitality workers employed at Starbucks, Tesco, or Walmart with irregular hours and nebulous connections to the workplace than industrial workers at Ford or Nissan who work full-time in their factories.

Neoliberal economists and philosophers have only recently recognized the consequences of the capitalist neoliberal globalization that began in the 1980s. The development of the working class in the South is illustrated in Table 1.1, which compares total male and female employment in agriculture, industry and services from 1999 to 2009. Table 1.2 shows that although the workforce in the developing South is far larger, the developed North generates significantly higher value added in industry and services despite the expansive growth in foreign direct investment (FDI). In this way,

Table 1.1 Total male and female employment by sector, world, and regions (millions)

	Agriculture				Industry				Services			
	1999	2007	2008	2009	1999	2007	2008	2009	1999	2007	2008	2009
World	1,038.9	1,056.8	1,061.2	1,068.1	533.2	659.5	668.5	666.4	1,010.8	1,267.3	1,299.2	1,316.7
Developed economies and European Union	24.8	18.7	17.8	17.5	122	119.3	117.9	109.8	296.1	338.4	343.3	341.1
Transition economies	39.1	32	32.6	32.3	35.3	40.9	40.8	39.5	70.1	87.2	88.4	88.6
East Asia	354.3	314.2	305.1	299.7	176.1	219	222.3	226	209.5	273.7	281.3	287.3
South-East Asia and the Pacific	115.8	122.2	123.7	124.5	37.4	48.8	49.2	49.9	81.5	100.4	103.8	106.8
South Asia	299.7	330.4	339.3	346.6	77.7	117	119.7	122.2	126.2	170.6	175.1	179
Latin America and the Caribbean	43.4	41.7	41.4	41.2	43.3	55.5	57.3	56.1	115.5	148.9	153.2	155.9
Middle East	10.1	12.2	11.9	12	11.8	15.8	15.9	16.4	23.7	31.6	33.2	34.4
North Africa	14.4	17.9	18.2	18.4	10.1	13.7	14.4	14.9	24.7	31.3	32.3	32.9
Sub-Saharan Africa	137.5	167.5	171.2	175.9	19.4	29.5	30.9	31.7	63.4	85.3	88.7	90.7
Total for developing and transition economies	1,014.3	1,038.1	1,043.4	1,050.6	411.1	540.2	550.5	556.7	714.6	929	956	975.6
Share of developing and transition economies in world total (%)	97.6	98.2	98.3	98.4	77.1	81.9	82.3	83.5	70.7	73.3	73.6	74.1

Source: International Labor Organization (2011) *Global Employment Trends 2011: The Challenge of a Jobs Recovery*, Table A11: Employment by sector and sex, world and regions (millions), Geneva: United Nations, p. 68.

Table 1.2 Value added by activity in 2010 (US$ billion)

	Agriculture	Industry	Services	Total
Developed countries	400	12,400	31,700	44,500
Developing countries	2,100	5,000	10,600	17,700
World	2,500	17,400	42,300	62,200

Source: UN Statistics Division (2014) 'GDP and its breakdown at current prices in US Dollars' (http://unstats.un.org/unsd/snaama/dnltransfer.asp?fID=2).

Note: Agriculture includes farming, fishing, and forestry. Industry includes mining, manufacturing, energy production, and construction. Services cover government activities, communications, transportation, finance, and all other private economic activities that do not produce material goods.

the rate of labor exploitation is far higher in the Third World than in developed countries.

GLOBAL CAPITAL INVESTMENT AND CLASS STRUGGLE

Why does foreign capital dictate the conditions of work and the rise of corporate absolutism in the Global South in which workers are prevented from forming independent unions? State authorities collude directly with foreign corporations, often with the complicity or indifference of unrepresentative enduring unions, in order to ensure a friendly environment for investment that prevents workers from being able to form independent unions. As we shall see in Chapters 4, 5, and 6, independent workers' unions are opposed by governments in India, South Africa, and China. Since the 1980s, new export processing zones (EPZs) have been rapidly growing to create industrial regions near strategic urban agglomerations. These industrial production zones ban the formation of independent workers' organizations unless they are company unions firmly under the control of employers, to ensure the preservation of low-cost manufacturing.[6]

Workers in neoliberal states must deal with corporatist unions and antiquated labor laws that were created for workers in the Global North, while state capitalism in China prevents workers from creating independent unions. This research examines the similarities and differences between neoliberal and market socialist regimes for industrial workers employed in a global system, regarding class power, wages, and conditions. We will find surprising outcomes: official union bodies that are disconnected from workers (ACFTU in China) may lead to better outcomes than cases where workers are coopted through corporatist structures (COSATU in South Africa), or simply ignored by the state (India).

In the global world economy, monopoly capital promotes the export of migrant workers to strategic destinations in the Global South and Global North so as to expand reserve armies of labor and continue the conditions necessary for low wages and unsecure conditions among all workers. As unemployment grows exponentially through urban and international migration, labor and wage costs are reduced and restrained. As Foster and McChesney write in *The Endless Crisis*:

> The new imperialism of the late twentieth and twenty-first centuries is thus characterized, at the top of the world system, by the domination of monopoly-finance capital, and, at the bottom, by the emergence of a massive global reserve army of labor. The result of this immense polarization is an augmentation of the 'imperialist rent' extracted from the South through the integration of low-wage, highly exploited workers into capitalist production. This then becomes a lever for an increase in the reserve army and the rate of exploitation in the North as well.[7]

The immense inequality in wage costs across industries is demonstrated in Figures 1.1 to 1.4, which show international comparisons of hourly labor costs in the primary textile industry, labor costs in manufacturing industries in different countries, average hourly manufacturing wages, and hourly compensation costs in manufacturing in selected countries. Foster and McChesney marshal International Labour Organization (ILO) and UN Conference on Trade and Development (UNCTAD) data to demonstrate incontrovertibly that while industrial production contracted in the Global North from 1980 to 2007, production in the South has expanded, and global

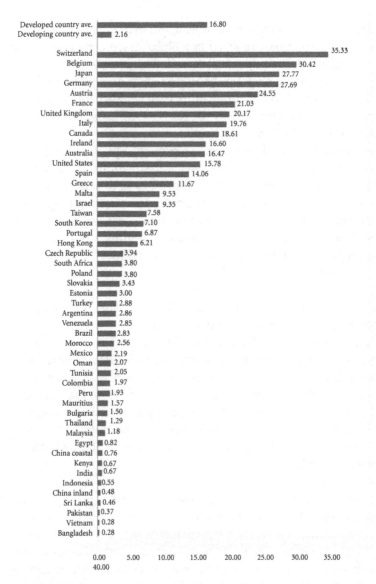

Figure 1.1 International comparison of hourly labor costs in the textile industry, 2011 (in US$)

Data source: Werner International Management Consultants Report, 2011, www.ukft.
org/documents/industryinformation/04-ASSOC-INDSTRAT-122-2012AII-Werner%20
Textile%20Labour%20Costs.doc%5B1%5D.PDF

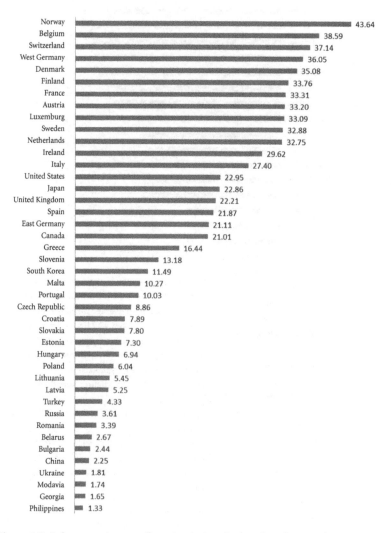

Figure 1.2 Labor costs in manufacturing industries in selected countries, 2012 (in euros per hour)

Data source: Rudolf Grünig and Dirk Morschett (2012) Table 9.1, 'Labor costs in manufacturing industries in different countries,' in *Developing International Strategies: Going and Being International for Medium-sized Companies*, Berlin: Springer.

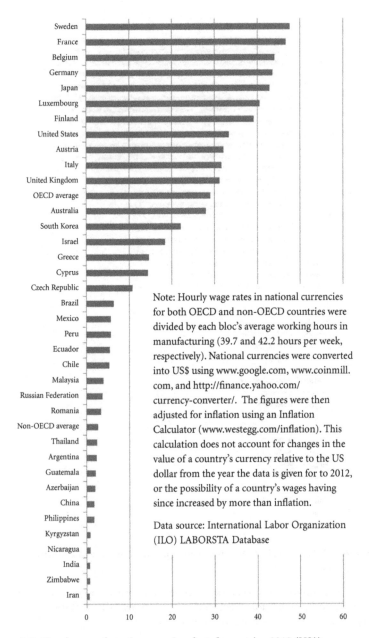

Note: Hourly wage rates in national currencies for both OECD and non-OECD countries were divided by each bloc's average working hours in manufacturing (39.7 and 42.2 hours per week, respectively). National currencies were converted into US$ using www.google.com, www.coinmill.com, and http://finance.yahoo.com/currency-converter/. The figures were then adjusted for inflation using an Inflation Calculator (www.westegg.com/inflation). This calculation does not account for changes in the value of a country's currency relative to the US dollar from the year the data is given for to 2012, or the possibility of a country's wages having since increased by more than inflation.

Data source: International Labor Organization (ILO) LABORSTA Database

Figure 1.3 Hourly manufacturing wage in selected countries, 2012 (US$)

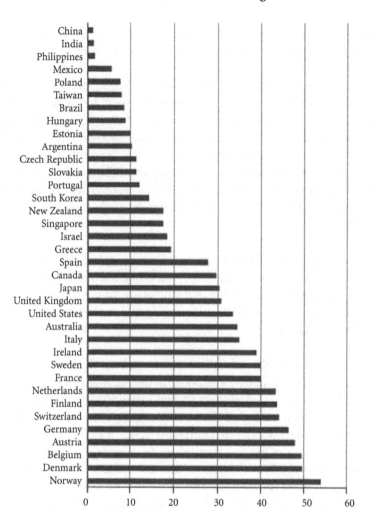

Figure 1.4 Hourly compensation costs in manufacturing in selected countries, 2009 (in US$)

Note: data for China and India refer to 2007 and are not directly comparable with each other or with data for other countries.

Data source: US Bureau of Labor Statistics.

production as a whole has grown from 1.9 billion to 3.1 billion workers – far more working people than at any time in the history of capitalism.[8]

The contemporary era of neoliberal capitalism in the early 21st century has replicated the earlier exploitative and dangerous forms of proletarianization that forced peasants from rural to industrial urban regions to work in commodity production and service sectors. This process bears striking similarity to the dangerous, unsanitary, and impoverished working and living conditions among workers in Manchester from 1842 to 1844, which were vividly depicted by Friedrich Engels in *The Condition of the Working Class in England in 1844*:

> But while England has thus outgrown the juvenile state of capitalist exploitation described by me, other countries have only just attained it. ... Their manufactures are young as compared with those of England, but increasing at a far more rapid rate than the latter.[9]

The expansion of the urban industrial working class in the Global South since 1970 is in part a response to the restructuring of financial capital. As finance capital seeks to avoid traditional unions, workers are forming new rank-and-file worker organizations to defend their collective interests even as compliant states seek to repress labor demands by blocking the establishment of worker collective institutions. Ronaldo Munck suggests that the modern labor movement resembles those formed in the late 19th century to provide a counterforce to the hegemonic dominance of finance capital:

> [T]he historical parallels of the late nineteenth century and the emergence of the contemporary union movement teach us is that this necessary shift will not be smooth and organic. It is more likely that alternative social forces (the 'informal sector' for example) and new geographical locations (China, India and the Global South more generally) will challenge and subvert the current structures and strategies. What is clear is that the

accelerated accumulation of capital generated by globalization has produced a massively increased global proletariat in the classical Marxist sense in China and India in particular. While perhaps up to twenty million of these new workers lost their jobs in China following the financial crisis of 2008 they have utterly transformed the nature of the global working class.[10]

In the post-Second World War era, mainstream economists predicted that the rise of the United States as the preeminent global power would be accompanied by the amelioration of world poverty and inequality through international development and investment. Through the support of the World Bank, the International Monetary Fund (IMF), foreign trade, private FDI, and foreign aid, new independent governments would direct development and economic expansion. However, import substitution policies in the immediate post-war era contributed to commodification of agriculture and natural resources, creating greater reliance on the global economy. As Michael Yates observes, the World Bank poverty indexes fail to consider that subsistence peasants living outside of the money economy have greater security than those who are forced into the formal economy:

> It should be noted that the World Bank has been instrumental in promoting large-scale export agriculture in poor countries. Many persons living below the World Bank poverty level are subsistence peasants operating outside the money economy. Their economic well-being is often greater than a dollar a day would indicate. As they are in effect dispossessed by Bank-promoted agriculture and move into urban areas, their money income may exceed the World Bank poverty level, but, in fact, they are considerably worse off than they were in the countryside.[11]

As peasants are forced off the land through commodification of agriculture, displaced rural peasants become urban workers who are unable to obtain the basic necessities for survival.

IMPERIALISM, GLOBALIZATION, AND
MULTINATIONAL CAPITAL

Successive financial crises affecting the Global South and North demonstrate the significance of understanding the contemporary era through the lens of imperial domination by multinational capital. Ronald Chilcote asserts that the neoliberal era of 'globalization' does not represent a break with imperialism, but an extension of capitalist extractive power worldwide on a regional and local basis, where economic and political benefits flow to the capitalist ecumene in the Global North. In the neoliberal era, extractive power has given rise to a global proletariat, documented in Paul Mason's comparative historical account of worker struggles extending from 19th-century Europe to the Third World in the present era.[12]

Ideological apologists for globalization and the application of market-based strategies ignore the growing importance of imperial and state violence that is used to support the system of economic inequality and exploitation.[13] The threat of military and economic violence through coercion or the withdrawal of financial capital is more prominent in the contemporary era of capitalist globalization than it was in the postwar era of independence in the Global South. Since the 1990s, states that failed to comply with the strict rules of the capitalist international financial system have been sanctioned and threatened with economic and military destabilization by the capitalist West.[14] In addition, the imposition of neoliberal reforms includes imperialist funding of police and private militias to suppress workers and peasants who oppose the new system, which is dominated by multinational foreign investments that redound to the benefit of the Global North.[15]

Rejecting the notion of capitalist globalization as a way forward, Samir Amin asserts the necessity to build a socialist form of globalization in opposition to the imperialist process which profits by reasserting colonial differences through the modern nation state:

The alternative solution would be to accept authentic popular changes, which are the only forces capable of putting an end to the yawning financial chasm which the colonial systems have become. The tenacious colonial prejudices of the West and the short-term vision of the Left, incapable of imagining North–South relations outside the framework of the imperialist tradition, straight away eliminate this choice. ... Capitalist globalization such as is being offered at this time of crisis, as a means of managing it, is not in itself a way of resolving the crisis. ... The historical limit of capitalism is found exactly here: the polarized world that it creates is and will be more and more inhuman and explosive.[16]

IMPERIALISM, MONOPOLY CAPITALISM, AND REPRESSIVE POWER

In the early 20th century V. I. Lenin identified monopoly capitalism as the dominant force in imperial subjugation. In his view, as profits in the industrialized West fell in response to the decline in profitability of local production that caused economic recession, finance capital sought new markets in which to invest profits. The global expansion of multinational banks representing the most substantial power of monopoly capitalism served as a fundamental intermediary in expanding capitalist imperialism.[17] The concentration of finance capital through speculative banking stimulated the expansion of monopoly capitalist investments and laid the basis for foreign expansion in new markets in the underdeveloped world. The expropriation of surplus labor in these new markets expanded the profitability of capital. Given the substantial financial investments required, only monopoly firms were capable of investing in the imperial world outside Western Europe and the United States.

According to Harry Magdoff, the shift from competitive to monopoly capitalism represents the new form of imperialism that expanded throughout the next century.[18] Economies characterized by competition between many firms were replaced by ones in which competition was limited to a handful of giant corporations in each industry. Further, during this period, the advance of transportation and communication technology and the challenge posed to Britain by the new industrial nations brought two additional features to the imperialist stage: an intensification of competitive struggle in the world arena, and the maturation of a truly international capitalist system where competition occurs in the markets of the advanced nations as well as in those of the semi-industrialized and non-industrialized nations. The struggle for colonial and informal control over economically backward regions for natural resources and low-wage labor is but one phase of this economic war against the Third World, and a distinctive attribute of the new imperialism.[19]

Following the Second World War, Magdoff argues, the emphasis of global imperialism continued to shift from competition among colonial states to the necessity for consensus among imperial powers possessing economic and technological advantages. The United States' emergence as the dominant military power[20] solidified the dollar as the world currency while expanding the foreign presence and profitability of industry and increasingly financial capital in monopoly form.[21]

FROM MARKET LIBERALIZATION TO WORLD BANK BENEVOLENCE?

The neoliberal reforms of the late 1980s prescribed by the IMF, World Bank and the US Federal Reserve aimed to persuade all economies, especially developing countries of the Global South, to abide by a strict system of privatization and economic liberalization. Countries were expected to accept a system of reforms that removed all forms of social insurance and protection, privatized national resources and companies, and allowed for the free flow of international and domestic trade, without government restrictions. These policies were applied indiscriminately throughout the world without regard for the traditions or poverty conditions of individual countries. Those nation states that opposed the system were threatened with expulsion from the international system.

However, even before the financial crisis of 2008 the World Bank, a leading architect of the imposition of global neoliberalism, challenged the system, recognizing its damaging consequences on those living in extreme poverty. Since the implementation of neoliberal reforms by governments in the Global South in the late 1980s, the Global South has suffered a series of financial, monetary, and ecological catastrophes that also intensified mass poverty and the inequality between the South and North. The passage of the North American Free Trade Agreement (NAFTA), for example, has undermined the quality of life for workers and peasants in Canada, the United States, and Mexico, as monopoly capital shifted production to the lowest-cost producers, and forced Mexican peasants off the land through the dumping of low-cost agricultural goods from corporate farmers in Canada and the United States. In 1997–98, South-east Asian and East Asian economies, viewed as the engine of growth in the Pacific Rim, collapsed as financiers withdrew capital from the region. The global financial crisis that occurred in 2008 in the wake of the speculative housing bubble in the United States and Western Europe sent shockwaves throughout world economy while insulating banks and the financial masterminds of the schemes.

Further, global economists recognized the imbalance created by a uniform system of neoliberal standards. Branko Milanovic, the World Bank's lead research economist, asserts that the West bears some responsibility for the poverty conditions in the Global South, saying that economists and policy makers cannot 'seriously believe that colonization, or, more recently, the Cold War had nothing to do with furthering civil wars and adding to the misery of the poor countries' and that Europe would 'be in a state of permanent war today if its borders were drawn as arbitrarily by foreign powers as the African borders were.'[22]

Milanovic advocates redistribution, or supplying foreign aid in the form of loans only to poor countries with pervasive poverty or widespread deprivation and underdevelopment. While acknowledging that inequality and poverty are consequences of market-driven policies, Milanovic fails to address the historical consequences of the imperialist and monopoly capitalist domination that has continued and expanded for two centuries right up to the present day.

IMPERIALISM, MONOPOLY CAPITAL, POVERTY, AND WORKER RESISTANCE

The research developed in this book supports the Marxist theoretical tradition, which recognizes the unrelenting significance of modern imperialism. As Magdoff argues, new imperialism has not diminished in the postcolonial era but has in fact accelerated through the assertion of military power, the never-ending search for natural resources, and low-wage labor markets found in the Global South, where a large reserve army of labor increases labor competition and reduces the bargaining power of workers throughout the world.[23]

In the post-Cold War era, while capital investments have grown dramatically throughout the Global South, the United States has emerged as the hegemonic power in the world, which can employ military force to ensure the circulation of natural resources and industrial goods, and modern cyber-technology to control any threats to its dominance in the world system. Samir Amin designates the new form of imperialism as *generalized monopoly capitalism* supported by the leading financial powers of the Global North. The system both expands the power of the capitalist class in the North and pauperizes workers in the South:

This concept of generalized-monopoly capitalism enables us to specify the scope of the major transformations involving the configuration of class structures and the ways in which political life is managed. In the centers of the system, the United States/Western Europe/Japan Triad, generalized-monopoly capitalism brought about the generalization of the wage system. The managers, termed 'executives,' involved in the monopolies' administration of the economy, were thenceforward salaried employees. ... At society's other pole the generalized proletarianization suggested by the wage system was accompanied by multiplication of the ways in which the labor force was segmented.[24]

The financialization of capital has forced the Global South to develop manufacturing and production by turning from the development of local and national markets to generating export promotion, leading to the growth of a larger working class. Ostensibly, FDI is the lifeblood that provides the capital necessary to create manufacturing and jobs that will reduce economic insecurity, although often at the cost of uprooting peasants and by imposing harsh living conditions on those who migrate to work at FDI destinations. Although some developing countries have reduced extreme poverty, by and large big businesses in the imperial world are the primary beneficiaries of FDI, multiplying their financial leverage, reducing or eliminating public and balance of payments deficits, and supporting standard economic policies that do not prioritize the sustainable economic development necessary for human survival.

Through creating a flexible supply of labor through temporary, informal, contract, and migrant labor, capital therefore expands the share of workers employed under insecure and precarious conditions. As Tom Brass shows, the development of capitalism in the modern world is compatible with the forms of unfree and bonded labor that are entrenched in caste systems of exploitation, and these endure and grow as multinationals compete for cheaper labor: 'Ironically ... free markets that are global in scope mean that unfree labour becomes for capitalists not just an option but in some instances a necessity, as competition cuts profit margins which in turn force down labour costs.'[25]

Cities become the cradle of economic insecurity for urban dwellers and recent migrants. The degradation of labor is heightened by uneven development as precarious labor responds to fight economic insecurity and poverty. Ultimately, these precarious workers become the visible element of a system that reproduces economic insecurity for the majority of people, while it enriches the few at the national and global levels.

A critical examination of the inequalities in the system of trade and foreign investment shows that FDI has replaced foreign aid and social safety nets that were intended to reduce economic insecurity, and instead contributes to intensified exploitation. Further, the unequal effects of FDI demonstrate that new investment does not offset underdevelopment and structural poverty. FDI reduces indispensable skills through training workers to produce primarily for foreign consumers. The outflow extends to the system of migrant workers trained in IT positions necessary for the Global North while minimizing the needs of the Global South.

21

CHAPTER OUTLINE

Part I of this book analyzes the theoretical and historical under-pinnings of the financialization of global capitalism, representing the destructive human consequences of foreign investment, and examining the emergence of class antagonisms and resistance to capitalist exploitation and oppression through the development of rank-and-file workers' organizations in the Global South.

Chapter 2 examines the contemporary growth of economic imperialism through the expansion of monopoly and multinational capital on a world scale. Historical and contemporary Marxist inter-pretations attribute this expansion to the restructuring of finance capital and the commodification of agriculture, infrastructure, manufacturing, and services, contributing to the displacement of peasants to urban regions in both North and South. As FDI, where the majority of profits are repatriated by the economic imperial power, replaces foreign aid as the primary form of development finance, the chapter examines its influence on the new shape of imperialism. The chapter examines the technological investments of monopoly capitalist imperialism in low-wage regions for mining, manufacturing, and services that are capable of generating the highest level of surplus value. The chapter also considers financial-ization and monopoly capitalist development in the Global South arising from cross-border movements of people, and shows the deepening of inequalities across the world, focusing on capital flows and the insecure prospects for development in poor countries.

Chapter 3 examines imperialism, labor migration, and the expansion of the reserve army of labor. The chapter surveys worker exploitation under temporary migration, and assesses the challenges and opportunities that imperialism and monopoly capital pose for workers. Although the movement of workers across national boundaries might create divisions that undermine existing labor standards, it might also be a source of working-class and union revitalization, through active international solidarity.

Part II (Chapters 4, 5, and 6) examines labor developments in three industrial sectors: platinum mining in South Africa, auto manufacturing in India, and shoe manufacturing in China. These examples demonstrate the capacity for working-class insurgency and the establishment of independent unions in key industrial sectors, where workers seek to upend national development plans that accord with neoliberal efforts to erode labor unions and repress the autonomous organization of workers. Consideration of the changes in mining and other industries in South Africa, India, and China demonstrates not only the advantages of poverty wages, poor working conditions, and a capacity to apply technological innovations to produce considerably higher levels of surplus labor than in other regions, but also the magnitude of the problem.

The three case studies provide convincing evidence of the emergence and expansion of oppositional proletarian formations and organizational mobilizations challenging the power and control of economic imperialism and finance capital.

Chapter 3 examines the rise of the industrial working class in India in the wake of neoliberal reforms aimed at expanding corporate profitability and upper-class power. The state has encouraged FDI by reducing taxes and tariffs, and facilitating the development of duty-free zones where labor standards have been withdrawn and labor unions are unwelcome. The rapid growth of neoliberal capitalism has modernized India's industrial centers and brought them into the world economy. Widely regarded as a successful model of economic development, the country is firmly united with the capitalist imperialist economy as exploitation of the vast majority of its population grows. This chapter examines how independent rank-and-file workers' unions in India have arisen in direct response to rising FDI aimed at eroding the power of traditional labor unions. As multinational companies demand strict subservience and impose draconian conditions on precarious workers, new class-struggle unions are forming and expanding in India's industrial belts.

Chapter 4 examines worker insurgency from 2010 to 2014 in the Pearl River Delta, the largest export production center in China's Guangdong Province. Two major forces in the region's rapid industrialization are the migration of millions of rural peasants to work in the burgeoning production industries, and massive investment by foreign capital in the region's manufacturing industries, which supply brands for the world economy. The 2014 strike at Yue Yuen is the largest private-sector strike in China's history, and suggests that activism among workers in the private manufacturing sector is growing dramatically as laborers expand their struggles beyond local protests, which had previously circumscribed the growth of a broader movement of industrial workers. The chapter examines how workers are defending their collective rights and challenging the coercive and socially irresponsible conduct of foreign multinationals.

Chapter 5 examines the formation of new worker organizations in South Africa's mining sector from 1998 to the present. While the end of apartheid has conferred formal political rights on the Black majority, the post-apartheid state has not given them concomitant economic rights. In the mining sector, migrant and local workers who are paid low wages, live in poverty, and work in grueling and dangerous jobs are resisting by joining autonomous general assemblies and engaging in sit-down strikes, often without the support of the National Mine Union. The chapter chronicles the democratic workers' struggles that led to the 2012 massacre of 34 workers in Marikana. Mine workers have mobilized in workplaces and communities through workers' assemblies that are nurturing class-struggle unionism to resist monopoly capital's exploitation. Older unions thrash about for relevance among militant workers, constrained by outmoded government laws that once granted them legitimacy but now render official forms of militancy illegal.

The case studies here show that it does not matter whether workers have established democratic rights or state recognition. Factory workers in South Africa, India, and China demonstrate that the absence of official state recognition ironically gives workers greater freedom to pursue their appeals for justice and improved conditions. Workers in the Global South are paving the way for a democratic, inclusive, and participatory unionism that challenges the system of capitalist domination far more successfully than existing unions in the West that are advanced by sanctimonious advocates of liberalism and corporate social responsibility.

In the South, rank-and-file workers are challenging existing unions to demand more than a raise – in effect a restructuring of society for all workers. Each chapter in Part II asks why workers are rejecting equivalence and parity with the Western trade union model. The evidence suggests that workers are developing a class consciousness at their workplaces together with an understanding of the range of possibilities in short-term rather than long-term contracts. Instead of making a truce with capital, class-conscious workers are seeking an alternative or transcendence which rejects corporatist models of accommodation but takes advantage of what is possible.

CONCLUSION

The system of economic imperialism has been identified by Marxist political economists for more than a century, through rigorous historical analysis, as a product of the extractive policies of monopoly capitalism on peoples of the Global South with the support of imperial and local powers. The purpose of this book is to document how workers in the early 21st century are countering exploitative corporate labor practices in the Global South, challenging autocratic systems of control which work through FDI.

In the contemporary era of imperialism dictated by the logic of financial capital, the global industrial working class is larger than at any time in history. In regions of the Global South that have become crucial locations and sources of labor supplies, capital investment, and emerging market economies, military and police power has been exercised in support of compliant national governments dependent on the foreign investment that has become ever more integrated into the world economy through advances in new technology.

In the neoliberal era of financialization, Third World countries are compelled to integrate their economies into the world system of capital or risk exclusion from the international system of trade, dominated by monopoly capital. To gain entry into the World Trade Organization (WTO) and become eligible for funding from the IMF and World Bank, states must guarantee political stability through the establishment of comprehensive criminal justice systems aimed at removing any internal threats to manufacturing by worker organization that could lead to interruption of industrial production through strikes and insurrections.

However, workers are building bridges in workplaces and communities by struggling for the rights of newcomers and the outcast temporary workers, and seeking independent unions free of employer domination. Through direct action and worker assemblies, workers are pushing existing unions to act as oppositional forces to capital or seeking alternatives to the status quo. They are initiating concrete efforts at building workers' organizations through parallel structures that exist independently of older established unions, which are weakening everywhere.

As capital formation changes and old unions lose their relevance, industrial workers are struggling to defend and advance their collective conditions as they challenge capital on a new terrain.

Part I

Capitalism and Imperialism

Part I

Capitalism and Imperialism

1

The Industrial Proletariat of the Global South

In the 20th century manufacturing was deemed essential for national economic development and modernization. Today international economists consider manufacturing as a sign of the subservience of emerging and developing countries to global capitalists and financiers in the advanced economies of the North. The terminology of the World Economic Forum and multinational economic institutions that differentiates between advanced, emerging, and developing economies contains an underlying contradiction. Advanced economies provide high-technology inputs into the consumer goods, such as automobile global positioning systems (GPS), technology, and creative content determined by the tastes of affluent consumers in the advanced countries. A range of industries are now considered dispensable for advanced countries: automobile production, shipbuilding, electronics, and even manufacturing of high-tech products are outsourced to 'emerging' and 'developing' countries that can produce commodities at a fraction of the cost in wages, while the profits are realized by firms in the North.

The shift of most industrial production to the South from 1980 to the present is a fundamental feature of neoliberalism in which monopoly capitalists in the North gain advantage over workers in the imperial world. The economies of the South, which were once considered to be developing, are in a position of permanent subordination to the advanced countries. Profitability is expanded and a higher surplus on investments is produced using inputs from the South, where newly proletarianized workers are being impoverished.

In the three decades from 1980 to 2011, the share of industrial employment in the Global South expanded from just over 50 per cent to 80 per cent of the world's 3.27 million workers in the formal sectors of the economy.[1] The shift of foreign direct investment (FDI) to the South for industrial production has dramatically enlarged a class of especially oppressed and exploited industrial workers that far exceeds the development of mass industrialization in Europe and North America in the 20th century. Foreign companies thrive on a workforce composed primarily of migrant contract laborers whose rights to strike are limited. Independent unions are banned or opposed. Contract and temporary workers deprived of rights keep wages down for all and expand profit margins which are appropriated by multinationals in the Global North. These are the New Industrial Proletariat.

As states in the South have competed for capital, they have also succeeded in removing the fangs of traditional unions that formed and consolidated in the postwar era of independence and national liberation struggles. The forces of organized labor formed in the image of their European colonial predecessors have adopted policies that demobilized workers in exchange for dispensations to union members employed in industrial sectors in key industries. Today's mobilization of workers in the South is challenging not only national and international capitalists, but also the institutional regime responsible for co-opting unions into a system that protected a small proportion of the urban working class. Worker assemblies and newly formed independent workers' organizations in the South are making demands reminiscent of those made by the mass industrial organizations advanced by rank-and-file workers who formed the Industrial Workers of the World (IWW) a century ago.

POVERTY NORTH AND SOUTH

The focus of media and academic research is on poverty in the North, in response to growing recognition of the generalization of destitution worldwide, as popularized by the Occupy movements in 2011. Poverty and inequality is indeed endemic in the North, above all in states that have eviscerated the social welfare protections that emerged in the mid-20th century in Europe and North

America. Growing disparity and indigence intensified in the wake of the economic shocks of 2008–09 through government policies that allowed industrial producers to declare bankruptcy in order to restructure wages while banks foreclosed on the homes of the working poor. The divergence was particularly marked in the centers of finance capital, London and New York.

Yet despite the decline of industrial jobs and the growth of poverty and inequality in the North (especially among racial minorities, immigrants, and youth), wages and material conditions in the imperialist core in Europe and North America remain far better in the era of neoliberal capitalism than those of almost all unionized workers in the South.

The expansion by multinational conglomerates of foreign investments in extractive and production industries in the South has in many ways contributed to a divergence of interests between workers in the North and South. While workers in the North may seek to keep commodity, food, energy, and natural resource prices low, capital is financing investments in the South designed to increase profitability through extracting higher levels of surplus labor, impoverishing industrial workers in poor countries, and threatening the remaining production workers in the North.

An enduring feature of existing trade union leadership in the auto industry of Europe and North America has been opposition to investment in low-wage factories in the global South. Organized labor in the North has only sought to improve conditions in the South with a view to advancing its own organizational interests. Raising the cost of labor in the South has always reduced the propensity of capital to export production, and redounded to the benefit of union members in the North. Given the concentration of mass production in North America, Europe, and Japan during the 20th century, existing trade unions unfailingly aligned with big business in their industrial sectors to prevent free trade. These efforts to preserve industrial production in the North failed miserably, as trade unions typically became allied with national manufacturers to defend shrinking industrial turfs from further outsourcing of production to the South.

THE 21ST-CENTURY 'FORCES OF LABOR'

A leading interpretation of the rise and fall of workers' movements is Beverly Silver's *Forces of Labor*.[2] Silver posits that in response to worker militancy in locations of industrial development, capital undertakes two primary fixes in the workplace: spatial and temporal.

Drawing on the development of capitalism in Europe and North America from the 1870s to the 1930s, Silver asserts that the expansion of capitalist production in a specific state and region inevitably leads to a concomitant intensification and strengthening of working-class organizational power, creating a crisis of profitability. The centralization of production tends to stimulate the organization of the working class through the mobilization of workers and the consolidation of labor unions. Successful unions rooted in rank-and-file militancy typically organize and strike to improve wages and working conditions, forcing capital and nation states to mollify worker demands through wage concessions and the establishment of social safety nets. However, higher wages and welfare states undermine the stability of capital and are likely to produce economic crises. Thus capital is forced to consistently identify strategies to reduce labor costs through the reversal of social gains and reduction in wage costs, and 'intensifying the commodification of labor'.[3] In turn, the likelihood that measures that discipline the working class also weaken social harmony and legitimacy forces capital to seek out lower-cost regions for production.

The growth of labor movements and the consolidation of trade unions in the 19th and 20th centuries gave rise to higher wages, improved working conditions, and state labor laws which standardized the relationship between organized labor and capital. While capital retained control over workplaces, collective bargaining agreements with unions tended to increase wages and states expanded social welfare protections to the broader working class. The contradiction between capital accumulation and worker militancy creates a historical crisis for capitalism. When a mobilized working class inhibits capital from reasserting hegemony to expanding profits, over the past 140 years capital has consistently relocated to new low-cost production regions with more docile labor forces. Silver argues that the propensity toward crisis in the 'temporal dynamic' contributes to an effort to recover profitability through 'fixes in the spatial dynamic'. Thus capital seeks to identify geographic regions with a higher intensity of labor commodification in order to offset higher wage standards and welfare regimes that increase the cost of production and reduce profitability, and to assure that 'profits can be made – even with the partial de-commodification of labor and the establishment of expansive social contracts – as long as these concessions are made to only a small percentage of the world's workers.'[4]

While capital unceasingly seeks to pursue spatial fixes by the continuous relocation of production geographically to new regions, these initiatives only temporarily postpone crises, which reappear as militant working classes emerge in these new regions and challenge profitability by demanding higher wages and social benefits. Silver observes that the 'successive geographical relocation of capital constitutes an attempted spatial fix for crises of profitability and control that only succeeds in rescheduling crises in time and place.'[5]

Despite the growing labor militancy in the South, capital has preserved the dominance of the imperialist core by recapturing profits and material gains in the financial centers of the North.[6] Silver views the monopoly over trade and investment by capital in the North as a tendency rather than a structural feature of the world economy, but one that nevertheless accentuates inequality and poverty. This tendency has now become an essential feature of monopolistic firms which earn higher profits selling products in the North than can be obtained in the South. The emergence of a middle-income urban stratum in the South who can afford consumer goods also advantages firms in the North which own the financial assets of firms in poor countries, and has turned peasant and rural workers into highly exploited impoverished semi-proletarian laborers. South–South industrial trade is captured by financial firms which control FDI, commerce, and distribution systems, and which repatriate profits in the North.

To corroborate the North–South inequality that rests on imperialism and capital flows, Tables 2.1 to 2.4 demonstrate that, despite developing countries' low share of world gross domestic product (GDP) and FDI, globally Northern capital is completely dependent on the super-exploitation of low-wage Southern labor.[7]

Table 2.1 FDI inflows and outflows by major regions, 1990–2013 (US$ million)

	1990		1995		2000	
	Out	In	Out	In	Out	In
World	240,900.4	207,618.3	363,170.5	344,255.3	1,241,226.5	1,415,016.9
Developed economies	229,583.2	172,514.4	306,898.4	222,582.3	1,090,662.2	1,142,383.2
Developing economies	11,317.3	35,033.0	55,655.2	117,674.5	147,372.4	266,646.1
Transition economies	0.0	70.9	616.9	3,998.5	3,191.9	5,987.5

	2005		2010		2013	
	Out	In	Out	In	Out	In
World	904,270.2	996,713.8	1,467,579.6	1,422,254.8	1,410,695.8	1,451,965.4
Developed economies	743,475.3	622,866.5	988,769.3	703,474.1	857,453.5	565,626.5
Developing economies	141,040.7	341,433.3	420,919.4	648,207.6	454,066.9	778,372.4
Transition economies	19,754.2	32,414.0	57,890.8	70,573.1	99,175.4	107,966.5

Source: UNCTAD (2014) *World Investment Report 2014. Investing in the SDGs: An Action Plan*, 'Annex table 01 – FDI inflows, by region and economy, 1990–2013'; 'Annex table 02 – FDI outflows, by region and economy, 1990–2013'; Geneva: United Nations.

Table 2.2 FDI inflows and outflows by major regions, 1990–2013 (percentage shares of total)

	1990 Out	1990 In	1995 Out	1995 In	2000 Out	2000 In	2005 Out	2005 In	2010 Out	2010 In	2013 Out	2013 In
Developed economies	95.3	83.1	84.5	64.7	87.9	80.7	82.2	62.5	67.4	49.5	60.8	39.0
Developing economies	4.7	16.9	15.3	34.2	11.9	18.8	15.6	34.3	28.7	45.6	32.2	53.6
Transition economies	0.0	0.0	0.2	1.2	0.3	0.4	2.2	3.3	3.9	5.0	7.0	7.4

Source: UNCTAD (2014) *World Investment Report 2014. Investing in the SDGs: An Action Plan,* Annex table 01 – FDI inflows, by region and economy, 1990–2013'; Annex table 02 – FDI outflows, by region and economy, 1990–2013'; Geneva: United Nations.

Note: For developing countries as a whole, profits repatriated from FDI investments grew notably between 1995 and 2008. Repatriated income from FDI in the developing world increased 747%, from $33 billion in 1995 to $276 billion in 2008. In other words, repatriated profits are growing faster than FDI inflows. In 1995, repatriated profits represented 29% of FDI inflows, but, by 2008, repatriated profits represented 36% of FDI inflows. (UNDP, 2011, *Towards Human Resilience: Sustaining MDG Progress in an Age of Economic Uncertainty,* New York: United Nations, p. 100).

35

Table 2.3 Gross fixed capital formation of developing countries (constant 2005 US$, millions)

	1990	1995	2000	2005	2010
World	6,731,810	7,087,020	8,899,560	10,421,600	11,345,100
Developing countries	911,006	1,186,331	1,531,615	2,343,238	3,522,715
Percentage share of world total	14	17	17	22	31

Note. Gross fixed capital formation (formerly gross domestic fixed investment) includes land improvements (fences, ditches, drains, and so on); plant, machinery, and equipment purchases; and the construction of roads, railways, and the like, including schools, offices, hospitals, private residential dwellings, and commercial and industrial buildings. According to the 1993 System of National Accounts (SNA), net acquisitions of valuables are also considered capital formation.

Source: World Bank.

PRODUCTION AND IMPERIALISM

By the 2010s, for the first time since the 1980s, the expansion of trade and finance had given rise to a new stage in labor–capital relations, which depends decisively on the exploitation by multinational corporations and local contractors of workers in the South, buttressed by the dominance of the imperialist states in the North.[8] There are several reasons for this.

Forced Migration

International capital, expanding through finance and banking, has invested in land and real estate in the South, inflating land and property prices beyond the reach of peasants and workers, and forcing them out of the countryside into industrial and urban centers where they become manufacturing, construction, and service workers.

Growth of Megacities

In the two decades from 1990 to 2010, the rapid and unending imposition of market liberalization expanded the population and

Table 2.4 FDI inflows as percentage of gross fixed capital formation, 1990–2013

Region/economy	1990	1995	2000	2005	2010	2013
World	4.2	5.2	18.0	9.5	9.7	8.2
Developed economies	4.2	4.3	18.6	8.4	9.0	6.7
Developing economies	4.0	7.9	16.2	12.1	10.2	9.2
Africa	3.0	7.3	9.6	17.0	12.0	12.7
Asia	3.9	7.7	13.9	10.9	8.3	6.2
Latin America and Caribbean	4.3	8.6	24.2	15.1	18.5	24.3
South-East Europe and CIS	0.5	3.1	11.9	12.5	18.9	17.2

Source: UNCTAD (2014) *World Investment Report 2014. Investing in the SDGs: An Action Plan*, 'Annex table 05 – FDI inflows as a percentage of gross fixed capital formation, 1990–2013,' Geneva: United Nations.

area of urban conglomerations to include areas that once formed part of the rural hinterland. The majority of the population of the new megacities in Africa, Asia, and Latin America consists of displaced rural peasants who have moved to shantytowns on the periphery of urban centers, many of which lack clean water, medical services, and sanitation.[9]

Industrial Production

Multilateral financial institutions determine the value added to industrial goods in each nation on the basis of GDP rather than the direct surplus value extracted from workers employed by the subcontractors of multinational corporations. As work is contracted out to low-price producers, calculation of corporate profits and contribution to the economy is concluded without acknowledging the labor input of Southern production workers who work for a fraction of the wages of the North. In addition, through establishing subsidiaries and relying heavily on labor contractors, multinational corporations seek to disown accountability for the impoverishment and dangerous and exploitative conditions that ensure profitability from enterprises employing the newly proletarianized labor forces.

The relocation of industrial production to the South compels us to reconsider the nature of global class relations in the early 21st century. As political economist John Smith asserts, 'What's involved here is not merely the globalisation of production but the *globalisation of the capital–labour relation,* in which capitalists in imperialist nations have become very much more dependent on value extracted from workers in the Global South.'[10] Smith sums up the dramatic shift in industrial production from North to South thus:

> In 1980 half the world's industrial workers lived in Europe, Japan, and North America, i.e. the imperialist nations. Since then, in just three decades, their numbers have declined in absolute terms by around a quarter, while the export-led expansion of the industrial workforce in low-wage countries has grown rapidly and now comprises 80 percent of the world's industrial workers. The scale and speed of this global shift, and even more so the form it has taken, are strong evidence of the significance of the outsourcing phenomenon.[11]

In a highly referenced report on the importance of low-wage labor to the world economy, Stephen Roach, former chief economist for the investment banker Morgan Stanley, confirms the strategic importance for finance capital to redirect and expand production to the South:

> In an era of excess supply, companies lack pricing leverage as never before. As such, businesses must be unrelenting in their search for new efficiencies. Not surprisingly, the primary focus of such efforts is labour, representing the bulk of production costs in the developed world. In the United States, worker compensation still makes up more than 75% of total domestic corporate income. And that's precisely the point. Wage rates in China and India range from 10% to 25% of those for comparable-quality workers in the United States and the rest of the developed world. Consequently, offshore outsourcing that extracts product and/or services from relatively low-wage

workers in the developing world has become an increasingly urgent survival tactic for companies in the developed economies. Mature outsourcing platforms, in conjunction with the internet, give new meaning to such tactics.[12]

The vast transfer in economic wealth and resulting inequality between developed North and industrializing South are demonstrated in the statistical tables. Table 2.5 shows the labor share of national income and Table 2.6 the capital share of national income around the world in 2008. Table 2.6 demonstrates that capital share of income for the developing countries is 22 percent higher than that in the developed countries, and the labor share of income is 12.4 percent lower in the developing countries than in the developed countries. Capital share is calculated by dividing gross operating surplus by the sum of gross operating surplus and compensation of employees based on data from 1992 to 2002 in developed and developing countries. Gross operating surplus is gross output less the cost of intermediate goods and services (to give gross value added), and less compensation of employees. It is a gross figure because it makes no allowance for depreciation of capital. The capital shares of Bolivia, Philippines, Poland, Tunisia, and Ukraine were obtained indirectly. In the UN source document (2004), gross operating surplus for those countries includes gross mixed income, which is the income of private unincorporated enterprises. However, in an earlier edition of the *National Accounts Statistics*, a ratio of gross mixed income to gross operating surplus is available.

Table 2.7 shows mergers and acquisitions (M&As) as a share of FDI inflows in developing countries, and Table 2.8 the number of FDI projects by destination from 2003 to 2013. These tables reveal that multinational corporations rely more than ever on M&As (representing the centralization of already existing capital by way of the takeover of monopolies by other monopolies) or profits generated from capital investments in the Third World, consisting in greenfield FDI (new capital investment in productive capacity without local restrictions).

According to UNCTAD's *World Investment Report 2014:*

Table 2.5 Labor share of national income around the world (percentages)

Country	1970s	1980s	1990s	2000s
Algeria	75.1	71.9	58.1	43.2
Armenia			89.9	94.6
Australia	84.8	76.2	75.3	71.2
Austria	76.0	80.5	78.9	74.1
Azerbaijan			45.6	45.2
Belgium	69.7	65.5	70.1	78.6
Botswana	58.5	52.1	42.9	34.7
Brazil			71.5	82.2
Bulgaria			51.0	53.2
Chile	68.5	64.1	64.5	68.2
China Hong Kong		51.7	52.8	57.7
Colombia	58.2	62.0	55.3	73.3
Cyprus			73.3	72.7
Czech Republic			68.2	68.7
Dominican Republic			67.6	63.9
Egypt			39.4	40.8
Estonia			70.0	64.1
Finland	72.4	75.3	74.4	67.7
France	65.3	78.4	72.6	76.3
Germany			76.5	71.5
Greece			67.1	65.2
Hungary		66.1	58.4	70.7
Iceland	86.9	86.4	81.9	89.3
Iran			45.0	46.1
Ireland	73.1	79.4	69.0	58.6
Israel			78.5	75.9
Italy	64.8	72.0	69.9	72.5
Jamaica		89.2	89.7	86.8
Japan	77.2	77.0	81.5	79.7
Kazakhstan			85.3	68.0
Kuwait			38.9	28.1
Kyrgyzstan			95.5	73.0
OECD average	74.5	75.7	72.8	72.3
Non-OECD average	65.1	65.2	62.1	59.9

Source: Marta Guerriero (2012) 'The labour share of income around the world: evidence from a panel dataset,' Appendix H, Labour share averages and trends, by decade, Institute for Development Policy and Management (IDPM), Working Paper Series WP No. 32/2012, University of Manchester, pp. 51–3.

Table 2.6 Capital share of national income around the world, 2008

Country	Capital share %	Growth rate (%)	GDP*
Argentina	0.529	1.13	10,466
Brazil	0.512	2.4	6,709
Bulgaria	0.525	-0.18	6,768
Chile	0.372	4.22	9,991
Columbia	0.455	0.96	5,683
Cote d'Ivoire	0.489	-0.58	2,195
Czech Republic	0.459	1.65	12,344
Dominican Republic	0.395	5.03	5,531
Estonia	0.342	4.64	9,154
Hungary	0.403	5.05	10,057
Kazakhstan	0.566	2.19	6,235
Kyrgyzstan	0.258	3.15	3,173
Latvia	0.380	4.61	8,043
Lithuania	0.414	3.4	8,046
Mexico	0.565	1.16	2,345
Moldova	0.420	-0.34	7,097
Mongolia	0.502	1.01	1,462
Nicaragua	0.438	-0.38	3,187
Slovakia	0.358	2.33	8,578
Poland	0.274	3.99	7,286
Tunisia	0.354	3.15	6,085
Mozambique	0.554	1.8	1,014
Philippines	0.460	1.26	3,241
Portugal	0.313	4.5	15,245
Ukraine	0.297	-0.87	5,108
Australia	0.291	4.59	23,027
Austria	0.293	3.58	24,145
Belgium	0.309	3.35	22,334
Canada	0.303	4.58	22,942
Denmark	0.375	4.03	24,515
Finland	0.396	5.12	19,495
France	0.328	3.7	22,347
Germany	0.378	2.96	22,944
Greece	0.611	4.21	12,547
Iceland	0.391	4.53	22,260
Italy	0.411	3.17	20,604
Japan	0.371	2.07	22,562
Korea, Republic of	0.254	4.58	14,020
Netherland	0.340	4.12	23,152
Spain	0.313	4.69	17,101
Sweden	0.307	3.89	22,204
United Kingdom	0.326	4.64	21,615
United States	0.268	4.29	30,048
Average for developed countries	0.348	4.006	21,548
Average for developing countries	0.425	2.211	6,602
Average for world	0.393	2.962	12,858

• per capita, US$

Table 2.7 Mergers and acquisitions as share of FDI inflows in developing countries

Year	2007	2008	2009
In US$ billion:			
M&A	130	125	46
Non-M&A FDI	526	628	502
FDI	656	753	548
Annual change in %:			
M&A		-4	-63
Non-M&A FDI		19	-20
FDI		15	-27

Source: UNDP (2011) *Towards Human Resilience: Sustaining MDG Progress in an Age of Economic Uncertainty*, New York: United Nations, p. 101.

Developing and transition economies tend to host green-field investment rather than cross-border M&As. More than two-thirds of the total value of greenfield investment is directed to these economies in the Third World, while only 25 per cent of cross-border M&As are undertaken there. At the same time, investors from these economies are becoming increasingly important players in cross-border M&A markets, which previously were dominated by developed country players.[13]

Meanwhile, Hoffman reports that 'M&A accounted for more than 89% of FDI in developed countries and for about 76% in the world for the period from 1998 to 2001 with a steady increase in these shares since the 1980s.'[14] Well over half of FDI inflows into OECD countries represent cross-border M&A rather than companies setting up factories or offices from scratch. Thus there is a distinct difference in the pattern of FDI in the imperialist and the semi-colonial countries of the world economy.[15] According to the World Bank:

[M]ore than one-third of FDI inflows to developing countries now originate in other developing countries: of the 11,113 cross-border M&A deals announced worldwide in 2010, 5623 – more than half – involved emerging-market companies,

Table 2.8 Number of greenfield FDI projects by destination, 2003–13, share of total (%)

Year	Developed economies	Developing and transition economies
2003	44	56
2004	46	54
2005	49	51
2006	50	50
2007	52	48
2008	46	54
2009	47	53
2010	49	51
2011	48	52
2012	49	51
2013	50	50

Source: UNCTAD (2014) *World Investment Report 2014. Investing in the SDGs: An Action Plan*, 'Annex table 22 – number of greenfield FDI projects, by destination, 2003-2013,.' Geneva: United Nations.

either as buyers or as takeover targets by advanced-country firms.[16]

A NEW INDUSTRIAL PROLETARIAT
UNDER NEOLIBERAL CAPITALISM

In *The Crisis of Neoliberalism*, political economists Gérard Duménil and Dominique Lévy contend that the concentration of income and wealth is generating a privileged ruling class which controls economic and political power through imperial hierarchies that concentrate wealth in the North as a 'permanent feature of capitalism.'[17] The dominant class, centered in the United States and Europe, attains profits and wealth through foreign trade realized primarily from the control and increasingly the possession by monopoly capitalists in the North of land, natural resources, and capital in the Third World:

Economically, the purpose of this domination is the extraction of a 'surplus' through the imposition of low prices of natural resources and investment abroad, be it portfolio or foreign direct investment. That countries of the periphery want to sell their natural resources and are eager to receive foreign investment does not change the nature of the relations of domination, just as when, within a given country, workers want to sell their labor power, the ultimate source of profit.[18]

Fundamental to the maintenance of the neoliberal capitalist system is the imperialist project to appropriate the resources and labor of the South. According to political economist Prabhat Patnaik, relocation of production to low-wage countries is facilitated through the capacity of finance to realize profits from investments in the Third World:

> the new finance capital is not necessarily tied to industry in any special sense. It moves around the world in the quest for quick, speculative gains, no matter in what sphere such gains accrue. This finance is not *separate* from industry, since even capital employed in industry is not immune to the quest for speculative gains, but industry does not occupy any special place in the plans of this finance capital. In other words not only does capital-as-finance function as capital-as-finance, but even capital-in-production also functions as capital-as-finance; capital-as-finance on the other hand has no special interest in production. This is basically what the process of 'financialization' involves, namely an enormous growth of capital-as-finance, pure and simple, and its quest for quick speculative gains.[19]

Why the Global South? Imperialist Globalization

The presence of an expansive reserve army of workers in the Global South has allowed managers to hire informal laborers, while systemic unemployment has diluted the power of conventional strikes and work stoppages. The informal sector has been a distinctive feature of the political economies of the South in the decades after the Second World War, especially tertiary workers in unregulated sectors of Africa, Asia, and the Americas. Sarah Mosoetsa and Michelle Williams, editors of the ILO's influential report on labor in the South, assert that existing unions must redirect organizing from traditional members to informal workers who are marginalized in the economies of the South:

> [T]rade unions' traditional forms of power – workplace bargaining and regulatory capacity – have also been eroded. These changes in the structure of the economy have had profound implications for labour. Labour in the traditional manufacturing sectors has had to find new forms of power and leverage in an effort to combat job losses and the diminishing significance of the sector in the economy and in response to the changing nature of work. At the same time, the new importance of the service sector, in which trade unions were formerly less interested in organizing, has forced labour to think about new approaches to organizing and new tactics for mobilizing.[20]

Semi-proletarian workers have been neglected by unions in the South since the independence era. Given the growth of financial investments on a world scale, even if manufacturers in the South produce for sale in national or regional markets, foreign investors in the North can easily retrieve profits realized offshore by manipulating monetary and commercial instruments. Sam Moyo, Paris Yeros, and Praveen Jha describe the contemporary system of imperialist domination through financialization:

> A systematic transfer of surplus value from the periphery to the centre, far beyond the initial investment, has been intrinsic to this relationship, whose mechanisms have included the repatriation of profits, interest payments, and dividends, the imposition of monopoly rents, as well as unequal exchange. Moreover, through these mechanisms, the centre has been able to displace its own contradictions of accumulation to the periphery, thereby curtailing class conflict in the centre

over a long period. The crisis that is now upon us, to the point of engulfing the centre itself, is arguably the terminal accumulation of systemic contradictions.[21]

The expansion of neoliberal capitalism has radically reshaped the composition of the industrial working class on a global level. The dominant mode of exploitation in Africa and Asia has been through the commodification of agriculture and mining, and the exploitation of the rural peasantry. Even mine workers were never fully integrated into the dominant urban industrial economies of major cities in the periphery of the Third World. In the South African mineral industry, the vast majority of workers were semi-proletarian migrants drawn from Mozambique, Swaziland, and other rural regions of the state to work for defined periods before returning home. The growth of global production units that are controlled by financial markets has closed out for almost all newcomers to industrial zones the possibility for the new industrial proletariat to return to rural regions.[22]

WORKERS' MOVEMENTS AND ORGANIZED LABOR

The welfare state accords in Europe and North America of the mid-20th century came about in direct response to the expansion of an autonomous workers' movement, formed among rank-and-file workers, that grew out of the Industrial Workers of the World and the socialist electoral blocs that emerged in the early part of that century. Since the 1970s, organized labor in the North has faced the inexorable erosion of working-class power among production workers, who have been the mainstay of worker insurgencies throughout the world since the origins of mass capitalist production in the early 20th century.

From the 1980s to 1990s the primacy of traditional unions representing industrial workers in the South came under attack from the emergence of militant unions galvanized by rank-and-file workers' movements in Latin America, East Asia, and Africa, notably Brazil, South Korea, and South Africa. In Brazil and South Africa, militant workers' movements aligned with left political parties and social movements to form national alliances that ultimately gained political power. In all three cases, the new alliances were unwilling to challenge, or incapable of challenging, the monopoly capital that dominated international finance and commerce.[23] These newly recognized unions in the developing world have been incorporated into state governing structures through neo-corporatist forms of institutional recognition of labor representation and collective bargaining rights that assented to the dominance of capital and the state in return for recognition and minimal economic gains for members.

As industrial investments have spread throughout the South, however, new independent workers' movements have emerged challenging the hegemony of capital, state, and union policies that have in many instances relinquished institutional power for the majority of the working class. Nevertheless, when workers' movements are transformed into formal bodies for organized labor in poor countries of the South, they are usually only able to represent a small portion of workers, and encounter significant limitations in extending wage and social protections to the vast majority of impoverished workers.

A fundamental question for labor unions and strategists at a time of deteriorating organizational power is how to challenge the hegemony of neoliberal economic institutions in the early 21st century. In view of the erosion of existing unions in the North, greater attention has been turned to workers' organizations throughout the South, where vibrant movements have emerged in Africa, Asia, and Latin America from the 1980s to the present. Four factors are behind the emergence of these movements.

A Move from Manufacturing to Services in the Global North

To serve demand in markets in the North and the expansion of markets in the Americas, Europe, and Asia for low-cost commodities, capital redirected the majority of its investments towards mining and production in the South between the 1970s and the 2010s. The transfer of financial investments to low-cost regions has eroded the bargaining power of organized labor in the North among workers in mass-production industries that had historically spawned the largest and most militant trade unions. Today's unions in the North are dominated by service and government workers who typically are not as militant as mining and production workers.

The Role of Production as the Epicenter of Militancy

As manufacturing has declined in the North, the concentration of labor union membership has eroded among workers who are committed to oppositional unionism, where the contradictions between management and labor are most clearly evident. In the absence of a base in production industries, trade unions representing manufacturing workers have sought to recruit service and government workers as well. United Auto Workers in the United States has failed to organize workers even in new factories, but instead has increased its membership among clerical, professional, and government workers. As a result, Gay Seidman's 1994 research of worker militancy among manufacturing workers in Brazil and South Africa is of enduring importance, demonstrating that new industrialization is a catalyst for broader sustained labor struggles that extend into working-class communities.[24]

The Exploitation of Labor

The level of labor exploitation as measured through the extraction of surplus labor in the Global South is far higher than any region of the developed imperial world. Modern factories and installations in the South are equipped with advanced technology but because of the use of labor contracting to informal workers, production quotas, and the speeding-up of the assembly lines, conditions cannot be conflated as equivalent with factories in any but the most avaricious firms in developed countries.

The Rise of New Workers' Formations

The capacity of most existing unions to represent workers has declined considerably in all regions of the world. However, the emergence of new unions is more prevalent in the Global South, where workers are prone to disregard traditional unions and labor authorities. Militant workers are establishing assemblies that represent rank-and-file associations, and new syndicalist-style unions are forming to represent workers in new industries. In some cases, existing unions are becoming irrelevant to workers even if they are recognized by the state and leading federations of labor.

TRADE UNION DECLINE: POVERTY AND INEQUALITY

The growth in FDI over the last two decades in manufacturing industries in the South that characteristically have higher levels of unionization has actually reduced the organizational power of workers. To lure multinational capital, local state managers and politicians either ensured that new industrial enterprise zones were union free, or permitted employers to form company-dominated unions. In most cases state labor agencies and trade unions throughout the South failed to enforce existing labor laws for the vast majority of workers who were contract laborers. As foreign capital investments in production and natural resources expanded in Latin America and South Asia, and total employment climbed sharply, existing trade unions have lost many members in absolute terms and also declined relative to the total workforce.

Powerful trade unions, some of which dated from the 1930s, have been declining dramatically in most regions of the world since 1975. The decline in trade union membership in both the North and the South is attributed to the rise of fiscally conservative governments, anti-unionism, neoliberal capitalism, deindustrialization in the North, industrialization in the South, and the growth of state capitalism in China, among countless other causes.

Whereas in the 20th century union leaders supported government labor legislation, unions in this century in the South have frequently negotiated corporatist arrangements with the state that have weakened the independent power of mass rank-and-file organizations. Table 2.9 presents an international comparison of trade union membership, revealing that the world's trade union movement is disproportionately composed of the world's best-paid workers employed in the

Table 2.9 International trade union membership

Country	Year	No. of TU members	Year	TU m'ship as % total paid employment	TU m'ship as % world total
Australia	2010	1,787,800	2011	18.0	0.46
Austria	2009	1,011,600	2008	28.1	0.26
Belgium	2003	2,723,000	2009	52.0	0.70
Brazil	2009	17,141,877	2009	16.8	4.43
Canada	2010	4,240,000	2009	29.4	1.10
Chile	2010	858,571	2009	15.8	0.22
China	2010	239,965,000	2000	90.30	62.01
Denmark	2011	2,042,529	2009	68.8	0.53
Estonia	2009	51,800	2009	7.7	0.01
Finland	2003	2,168,924	2009	69.2	0.56
France*	2009	8,676,900	2008	7.6	2.24
Germany	2009	11,356,110	2008	19.1	2.93
Hungary	2008	113,122	2009	16.8	0.03
India	2005	8,711,000	2005	32.90	2.25
Ireland	2008	561,000	2008	33.7	0.14
Japan	2008	10,065,000	2008	18.5	2.60
Korea, Rep. of	2009	1,640,000	2009	10.0	0.42
Malaysia	2008	805,565	2008	10.10	0.21
Mexico	2009	6,407,900	2009	13.9	1.66
Netherlands	2008	1,878,000	2009	19.1	0.49
New Zealand	2011	384,644	2009	21.4	0.10
Norway	2008	1,621,073	2009	54.3	0.42
Philippines	2008	1,941,727	2008	10.90	0.50
Poland	2009	2,548,500	2009	15.0	0.66
Portugal	2010	739,000	2009	20.1	0.19
Russia	2010	24,200,000	2009	31.9	6.25
Slovak Republic	2009	872,298	2008	17.1	0.23
South Africa	2008	3,298,559	1993	57.8	0.85
Sweden	2010	3,343,612	2009	68.4	0.86
Switzerland	2008	752,173	2008	22.5	0.19
Turkey	2008	3,205,662	2009	5.9	0.83
United Kingdom	2010	6,536,000	2009	27.2	1.69
United States	2009	15,327,000	2010	12.0	3.96
World (approx.)		386,975,946			100.00
OECD		108,054,095			27.92
Non-OECD		278,921,851			72.08
Non-OECD excluding China		38,956,851			10.07

* France data reflects the number of workers covered by trade union collective bargaining agreements.

Source: International Labour Organization LABORSTA Database.

services sectors of the developed economies. Unions in China today have a special status: most are linked to a single workplace (*dānwèi*) rather than to an occupation, and do not typically engage in collective bargaining. The All China Federation of Trade Unions (ACFTU) is the biggest trade union in the world since all Chinese workers are automatically enrolled as members. Without these Chinese members, trade union membership for the developing countries might comprise as little as 11 percent of the world total.

As Table 2.10 shows, in Europe, the following trends in trade union membership have been observed: [25]

- An increasing concentration of trade union members are employed in the **public sector** (an average 55.3 percent of union membership in Sweden, Slovenia, Austria, Slovakia, Italy, the United Kingdom, Latvia, Czech Republic, Germany, Netherlands, Hungary, Spain, Portugal and France as of 2002). In almost all countries the public sector is more unionized than industry, which in turn is more unionized that private sector services.
- Union membership is becoming increasingly **feminized**. In several countries women now comprise more than half of union membership.
- **Retired and unemployed** people form an increasing proportion of union membership. Recent data suggest that between 15 and 20 per cent of trade union members in the European Union are either unemployed or retired, with the range varying from under 1 per cent in Slovenia to 49.3 per cent in Italy.[26]
- In most countries there are reports of **young and ethnic minority** workers not joining unions in sufficient numbers, hence inhibiting the renewal of union organization. Furthermore, the average age of trade union members in many countries is markedly higher than the average age of the labor force.
- A rising proportion of trade union members are employed in **managerial, professional, or associate professional occupations**. Several of the unions and confederations that represent members from these occupations tend to highlight individual rather than collective membership identities, particularly on the issue of pay. Furthermore, relations between union and member are

51

Table 2.10 Trade union density rates and indices of membership composition in the European Union (in percentages, ordered by 2002 ratings)

Country	1980	1990	1995	2002	Female	Public sector
Sweden	78.2	80	83.1	78.0	52.7	47.9
Denmark	78.6	75.3	77	73.8*	48.5	
Finland	69.4	72.2	78	71.2*	50.5	
Cyprus				70.0		
Malta		54.4	56	62.8	27	
Belgium	53.4	53.9	55.7	55.8*		
Slovenia				41.0	49.4	76.2
Ireland	57.4	51	47.1	35.9	37.9	
Austria	58.4	46.9	40.7	35.4	31.8	39.7
Slovakia		78.7	57.3	35.4	49.6	70.9
Italy	54.5	38.8	38.1	34	38.3	53.1
Luxembourg		44.8	38.7	33.5*		
United Kingdom	55.1	39.3	34.1	30.4	43.7	47.4
Latvia				20.0	57.0	82.1
Greece		32.4	29.6	26.7*		
Czech Republic		78.7	46.3	25.1	57.9	44.5
Portugal		31.7	25.4			
Germany	34.9	31.2	29.2	23.2	31.2	39.3
Netherlands	34.8	25.5	25.7	22.1	34.2	28.8
Hungary			63.4	19.9	48.7	70.3
Estonia		90.6	31.6	16.6*		
Lithuania				16.0		
Spain	8.3	14.7	16.3			31.2
Poland			32.9	14.7*	55.1	76.6
France	17.1	10.1	9.8	9.7*	48.3	66.3

Note. Entries marked by * refer to 2001 rather than 2002. Density data for the EU15 are standardized and express trade union membership as a proportion of the employed, dependent labor force. The EU10 data follow national definitions and thus are not standardized. Blank spaces indicate that there are no reliable data available.

Sources: Jeremy Waddington (2005) 'Trade union membership in Europe: the extent of the problem and the range of trade union responses,' paper for ETUC/ETUI-REHS top-level summer school, Florence, July 1–2; EC (2004) *Industrial Relations in Europe*, Brussels: European Commission (for data 1990–2002); B. Ebbinghaus and J. Visser (2000) *The Societies of Europe: Trade Unions in Western Europe*, Basingstoke: Macmillan (for 1980 data).

different from those that characterize the 'traditional' organization of manual workers.

CORPORATISM AND TRADE UNIONS

In the early 21st century most states of the South grant trade union centers *de jure* power to represent members only after their general agreement to control rank-and-file militancy and pacify autonomous movements. Corporatism is imposed specifically to curb demands for higher wages and improved working conditions. Worker movements that succumb to corporatist relationships tied to state and capital tend to metamorphose into ineffective bureaucratic organizations. Because of this, while established trade unions consider corporatism to be the culmination of a struggle to achieve a social right, the system also institutionalizes class struggles by restricting bargaining and routing demands exclusively through state and capitalist institutions.[27]

As noted above, South Africa, South Korea, and Brazil have been viewed by labor scholars as exemplary models for transforming worker militancy into organized trade unions capable of influencing state policy and moderating the power of capital.[28] In all three countries, militant labor movements have contributed to the decline of authoritarian regimes and given way to neoliberal states that have promoted industrialization with the support of international capital. This expansion of monopoly capitalism in the South has contributed to a process of neo-corporatism – the recognition of labor unions and their co-optation by capital and state institutions that support the preservation and expansion of repressive labor policies. Labor unions, even those rooted in militant rank-and-file organizations, have become part of the neoliberal capitalist state through affiliated political parties. These new unions and parties, which often form part of governing coalitions, have encouraged foreign monopoly capital investments that severely exploit the working classes in the South. Through absorption into state-sanctioned systems of representation, collective bargaining, and electoral politics, the original workers' movements have been marginalized and disregarded, and are often under assault.

Neo-corporatism within structures of the capitalist state in the South provides marginal trade union influence over industrial and public policies.[29] However, ordinarily, while militant labor movements challenge the supremacy of capital to determine wages and conditions, the state's creation of a legal system through bargaining, accommodation, and incorporation culminates in the co-optation of labor organizations within the structures of the capitalist state by way of neoliberal social corporatism, as seen in Korea in the 1990s and 2000s.[30] However, in Mexico and in Southern states that depend on oil and natural resources, neoliberal policies have been adopted in response to a crisis of capital, which may withdraw corporatist structures to expand profitability, leading to an abrupt demise of the developmental state which had provided legitimacy and social cohesion.[31]

Incorporation may also come at the expense of working-class internationalism, as some relatively well-positioned workers within the global value chains are able to make gains for themselves at other workers' expense. Thus Cumbers, Nativel, and Routledge argue that the promotion of transnational labour rights 'is inevitably compromised by different subject positions in relation to broader processes of capital accumulation.'[32]

On the global level, the exploited workers of the South, whose surplus labor is indispensable for the growth and development of profits, are front and center in the expansion of the world capitalist system. Accordingly, the growth of working-class militancy in the South in opposition to European, Japanese, and North American investments is of fundamental significance to the development of transformative movements which may go on to challenge the capitalist system.

The neo-corporatist labor–state–capital accords have been frequently followed by mass disillusionment and the appearance of new working-class insurgencies for power on the shopfloor and in the community. While labor scholars tease out why workers take specific actions on the basis of industry and region to protest against the power of capital and the state and to mitigate severe labor conditions, what remains constant is the recurrence of labor militancy among workers mainly in growing industrial sectors.

Reliable conclusions on changes in worker union representation must recognize density rates and the comparative and historical capacity of labor unions in countries with growing manufacturing industries to represent and defend newly proletarianized industrial workers. A comparison of wages, conditions, and unions' capacity to represent workers will show a range of union structures that defend workers in distinct industries, regions, and contexts. In some cases, given the partial decline of traditional unions, dual unionism is appearing through workers' assemblies and syndicalist-style independent unions.

The new industrial proletariat is taking shape as inchoate worker organizations are fulfilling the forestalled functions of traditional unions. Workers are involved in rank-and-file militancy in three ways:

- **Worker assemblies.** These are organized in conditions where some or all of the workers lack independent union representation, or where an existing union is disengaged from some or all of the workers at a plant or facility. Workers form parallel unions that do not have official recognition and sometimes do not even have a name, but reflect the interests of unorganized workers.
- **Independent unions.** New independent unions represent workers who have not been absorbed into traditional unions through corporate arrangements with management. They form autonomously on a firm-level, local, and regional basis.
- **Pressuring traditional unions.** Unions use a repertoire of approaches, including, first, direct demands for official status as independent unions through state labor bodies, which would grant a measure of standing and authenticity among workers in the event that these frequently corrupt bodies deny workers representation status; and second, affiliating with traditional unions that are responsive to rank-and-file members, and in some cases forcing them to change their approach.

EXTRACTION AND PRODUCTION IN NEOLIBERAL CAPITALISM

Since the era of European colonialism in the 19th century, the South has been considered primarily as a source of raw materials for export to production markets in the North. During the Cold War era from the 1950s to 1980s, economies in most states of the South were dominated by mining, cash crops, and the extraction of primary resources. With few exceptions, the vast majority of manufacturing during the era was composed of import substitution industries for local and national consumer markets. In the late 1980s privatization initiatives in the South were directed at conferring ownership rights on informal businesses, a precursor to foreign investments and mass land grabbing by monopoly firms from the 1990s to 2010s.

The development of extractive industries from the 1980s to the 2010s required the expropriation and control of vast reserves by monopoly capital, with the eager support of rentier states that depend on selling the rights to mine natural resources in exchange for a share of profits. Profitability for monopoly capitalists in the North is reliant on the demand for the commodity in the world market and the cost of extracting or producing it. In mining industries with militant unions, the cost of the commodity will tend to increase, especially if demand is extensive and the mineral is scarce.

The application of new technologies for the profitable extraction of natural resources has expanded the mobility of mining and oil conglomerates. Since the 1980s, multinational firms have escaped the cost of labor and rent associated with mining in the South through the development of computer technology, fiber optics, and other substitutes for petroleum, coal, copper, and other natural resources. However, the importance of mining to multinational capital has increased in the early 21st century with the expansion in global production and the strategic requirement for minerals and energy to service technology across industrial sectors. The dramatic growth in direct ownership of land and minerals by food, mining, and energy conglomerates, from Monsanto, to Anglo-American, to Exxon-Mobil, reveals the value of land and natural resources to capitalism.

In situ mining requires a profitable means of extracting, transporting, and smelting minerals and ore. Profitability in the mining industry is also achieved through industrial consolidation and the development of cartels that monopolize the extraction, transportation, and processing of minerals by eliminating labor competition, dominating markets, and fixing prices. (See Chapter 5 on the South African platinum mining industry.[33]) Under neoliberal capitalism, multinational mining conglomerates have sought, with mixed success, to gain greater control over strategic mining sectors through capitalist investment and direct ownership. The production cost of primary products is almost always dependent on the cost of labor and the ability to exploit and plunder ecosystems without consequences.[34] The application of Silver's temporal-spatial approach confirms that labor costs are highly dependent on the organization of labor in a country or region over time and space. Mining conglomerates throughout the world have constantly sought to restrict union organization through technology, repression, and use of migrant labor.

CONCLUSION

Existing trade unions are an expression of the limitations of working-class organizations. They circumscribe the compromises achieved by past struggles and rank-and-file solidarity, and demarcate the boundaries of the limits of what capital and business consider acceptable and tolerable action. The rank-and-file insurgencies in mass production industries in Europe, Japan, and North America that made possible contemporary unions have been regarded by state authorities as illegal actions, and repressed by local police, national guards, and private security forces since the emergence of industrial capitalism.

The most effective forms of resistance were developed among mass production workers by IWW and other insurgent workers' movements that renounced the legitimacy of the state and opposed collective bargaining with business owners that suppressed class conflict. Branch unions of the IWW engaged in direct action in the workplace and within communities, and operated on the assumption that capital and the state would unceasingly oppose genuine class-based unions. Salient to the organization of militancy was the location of labor struggles in mining and manufacturing, where rank-and-file workers built bonds of solidarity in production industries dominating major urban centers in Europe and North America.

A century later, the industrial landscapes and the communities of industrial workers in the North have mostly disappeared, as rusting plants are displaced by empty desolate fields, or in major urban centers office and residential towers that generate profits through land speculation. Thus, if we are to understand the future of working-class militancy, we must follow the work rather than the workers.

Today the work has been repositioned from the North to the South. As more workers are employed in manufacturing than at any time in history, we are witnessing the embryonic rise of independent rank-and-file organizations formed by young laborers. These workers represent the new industrial proletariat. In more and more industries in Africa, Asia, and the Americas, this new proletariat is forming bonds of solidarity through independent organizations demanding improved conditions for all workers, pushing existing unions to represent and support members and non-members, and forming alliances within communities to improve the quality of life for all impoverished workers. The workplace and community demands that are now made by the new industrial proletariat reveal the motivations of workers rooted in solidarity, and a fundamental opposition to neoliberal capital, inequality, and poverty. The financial crisis of 2009 revealed the potential for the development of a militant working-class movement in the North. However it is mistaken to conflate the magnitude and consequences of counter-hegemonic movements against capital among workers in the South with those in the North.

Over the past 20 years, starting with the Zapatista peasant uprising in Chiapas in 1994, workers' movements in the South have been driven by anti-imperialism and opposition to the globalization of capital, and the destruction of peasant and rural communities and traditions. Workers' protests in the North, typically organized by the leadership and activists of traditional unions, such as the Battle in Seattle of 1999, were also aimed at defending the wages and jobs of industrial workers threatened by displacement by the reduction of tariffs and trade barriers. While struggles among peasants and workers in the South sought to counter involuntary proletarianization, workers in the North were concerned to reduce or staunch the commodification of labor and the erosion of standards.

This book is inspired by the rudimentary demands of the most exploited and oppressed workers of the world, who reside in the Third World and work in its production industries, and who are seeking to construct just societies in their communities through solidarity and direct action. The case studies in Part II are not set in the advanced countries, nor is the research necessarily connected to the financial crisis of 2009 or articulated through the Occupy movement. Instead it examines workers' movements in India, China, and South Africa, where workers are forming new organizations that are challenging the authority of capital, and fashioning new workers' organizations rooted in the same solidarity, equality, and fundamental opposition to capitalism that inspired and stimulated labor movements in mass production industries in Europe and North America in the 20th century.

2

Migration and the Reserve Army of Labor

The Marxist historical-materialist analysis of labor mobility from countryside to urban areas and across geographic boundaries is salient to an understanding of the history of human migration from antiquity to the modern neoliberal era, yet has until now been all but absent from mainstream contributions to this field. In spite of the rich Marxist literature on human mobility since the publication of Friedrich Engels's *The Condition of the Working Class in England in 1844*, bourgeois historians and social scientists have neglected to acknowledge its influence in their own work.[1]

In all phases of capitalism, agricultural workers have been pushed towards becoming wage labor in the cities where industrial jobs proliferated. In *The Great Transformation*, Karl Polanyi argued that agricultural peasants in mid-to-late 18th-century England resisted enclosure in the countryside, where they had worked for feudal estates and could rely on landlords for sustenance in times of drought and calamity.[2] At the same time as mechanization of agriculture by the capitalist class reduced the need for peasant laborers, proletarian workers were in greater demand in the urban centers of England. Friedrich Engels, in his famous account of the development of the working class in England, notes that deprivation spurred almost one million Irish to migrate to work in London, Liverpool, Manchester, and other major industrial cities in poverty, and unsanitary and marginalized conditions.[3]

Human mobility is also integral to the contemporary phase of imperialism, which is dependent on access to abundant and unrestricted non-union low-wage labor to work in new manufacturing facilities, and which offers capital the flexibility to invest and withdraw investments so that it can appropriate maximum profits. Cross-border migration allows multinational capital to expand labor markets using low-wage temporary and irregular workers with a range of skills to work in domestic services, construction, IT, services, and tourism, and to compete with higher-wage workers in advanced economies. Concomitantly, internal migration leads to the development of slack and informal labor markets where workers have few ties to local social institutions, and typically encounter isolation and marginalization.

This chapter looks at the history of migration, and assesses the weaknesses in both conventional neoclassical economic and liberal theoretical approaches that omit the distinct exploitative nature of labor mobility in the modern era. The former approach provides a celebratory and triumphant view, by ascribing motives to migrant workers, and the latter, with a view to ameliorating conditions, provides a familiar bleak portrait, without identifying the capitalist class and state as villains. Both persistently skim over and circumvent decisive evidence of the modern capitalist state displacing and exploiting migrant workers in new regions.

THEORIES OF LABOR MIGRATION

Since the 1950s, dominant assessments of labor mobility have been rooted in classical political economy, which analyzes the relative advantages and motivations for individual workers moving to a new location for personal gain. These calculations by working-class migrants, often referred to as push–pull factors, emphasize superior survival conditions in destination regions. The recurring perspective is that those individuals who are the most skilled laborers will migrate to improve their standard of living and advance developing economies. While the incentive to migrate ostensibly contributes to new working opportunities, training, and development, in classical economics no consideration is given to factors producing poverty in the regions of departure, or the genuine potential for poverty in the destination regions.[4]

Alternatively, consider workers living in countries where the pay-off to human capital is quite high. The rewards for those with in-demand skills are often substantial in many developing countries, such as Mexico and the Philippines. These high rewards partly account for the very unequal distributions of incomes observed in those countries, where the skilled earn substantially more than the less skilled. Highly skilled workers often enjoy far better economic opportunities than they would if they migrated to the United States, while less skilled workers can barely rise above subsistence level. As long as people migrate to countries that provide better economic opportunities, the skilled in these countries have little incentive to leave. It is the least skilled who want to emigrate, and the immigrant flow will thus be composed of workers with below-average skills.

George Borjas, the pre-eminent migration economist in the United States, contends that in the ideal capitalist society, migration creates a natural equilibrium by causing rural and foreign workers to move to urban industrial labor markets where they are in demand and will thrive:

> As long as economic considerations matter in the migration decision, skills tend to flow to those markets that offer the highest value. Immigrants originating in countries that offer relatively high rewards to human capital will tend to be less-skilled, while immigrants originating in countries that offer relatively low rewards to human capital will be relatively highly skilled. From the perspective of any potential host country, such as the United States, the country will likely attract highly skilled workers from some source countries (the countries where the returns to skills are low), and unskilled workers from other source countries (the countries where the returns to skills are high).[5]

The theory of personal economic choice neglects the mechanism by which labor migration is linked to structural economic forces that drive rural peasant workers from their homes and communities to new destinations out of poverty and economic necessity. Imperialism and labor migration are fundamentally interconnected: workers are driven from impoverished locations in the Global South to new locations of commodified capital accumulation in their home countries and the Global North, where capital seeks to increase the reserve army of labor. Thus the spaces of imperial expansion are spread out from the former colonial areas to locations throughout the world. In this way, profits generated in China, India, South Africa, and throughout the developing world are repatriated by banks in the Global North and converted into the US dollar, British pound, and euro.[6]

In sharp contrast to liberal theorists of migration, Raúl Delgado Wise contends that the vast majority of migration is an involuntary process brought about by the expansion of finance capital under contemporary neoliberal global capitalism, leading to international surplus labor with high levels of poverty and inequality: 'Migration has acquired a new role in the labor division of neoliberal globalization. Mechanisms of unequal development produce structural conditions, such as unemployment and inequality, which catapult the massive migration of dispossessed and marginalized people.'[7]

Drawing on abundant evidence of multilateral policies that cause dislocation of peasants into cities and impoverished urban-dwellers across borders throughout the world, Delgado Wise establishes that the vast expansion of migration is a consequence of the necessity for low-cost labor to move within the Global South to urban industrial zones, and to the Global North. 'Forced displacement' does not stimulate socio-economic mobility, but contributes to intensified urban blight, ecological crisis, poverty, and labor exploitation.[8]

In the neoliberal era of globalization, expanding economic inequality on the basis of race and national origin has led sociologist Rolando Munck to designate contemporary globalization as *global apartheid*:

[W]e are entering an era of global apartheid where ethnic and other divisions become entrenched and the basis for societal organization as apartheid did in South Africa before the free elections in 1994 led to the victory of the nonracial African National Congress. ... This argument flies in the face of complacent neo-liberal myths that the free market is race blind (as it was gender blind), and it also undermines claims for the universal applicability and even desirability of Western (read: United States) versions of democracy.[9]

While liberal economists, sociologists, government policy makers,

NGOs, and philosophers of social justice support migrants' rights by advancing mechanisms to improve conditions and wages, the complications inherent to accomplishing these goals often go unconsidered. Even the boldest efforts to restrain the flow of capital and prevent companies from seeking out the lowest wage labor they can find are ultimately doomed to failure if migrant rights advocates do not address the global economic inequalities that compel workers to relocate to new destinations. Most policy prescriptions, recommendations to improve the lives of migrants and their families in their countries of origin, and tangible efforts to reduce poverty and disease, however, do not deal with the foundation of global inequalities. For example, government and NGO efforts to eradicate the curable diseases prevalent among most of the world's population by disseminating needed medications are important and ethical endeavors, but do not address the causes of ecological degradation, famine, pandemic disease, state repression and violence that continuously afflict internal and cross-border migrant workers.[10]

In the late 20th century, MIT sociologist Michael Piore, Princeton sociologist Douglas Massey, and co-authors argued that migration occurs when an economic disparity is present between poor rural regions and industrial economies in which advanced economies seek low-wage labor. Taken together, their theories assert that migration is motivated not only by poverty but also by the demand of advanced industrial societies for labor from rural societies.[11] This discourse, however, is rooted in a received economistic ahistorical perspective that is applied universally to all societies and geographic locations. Capitalist society at any given moment is composed of a range of social formations with unequal and dissimilar political economies, cultural systems, and social structures. Therefore, workers' decisions to migrate are often not their own, but a product of the structural forces in society. Abstractions of historical and economic processes rooted in economic orthodoxy fail to recognize the imbalances – not only of wealth, but of power – that produce migration. Anthropologist Nina Glick Shiller contends that these dominant neoliberal hypothetical concepts and scientific generalizations fail to contend with authentic power relations that structure inequality and are causes of abject poverty among migrants who cross borders:

> The signing of NAFTA ... is not an abstraction. It represented the power of an imperial state – the US – instituting its agenda through its control of finance capital and military force. Capital is at its core a social relationship that links people both unequally within and across national borders. Notions of levels of analysis obscure this basic transnational aspect of daily life around the globe, which not only penetrates states but also shapes distinct migrant social fields across and within states.[12]

LABOR, MARXISM, AND THE SOCIAL FORMATION

Marxist theory includes a multiplicity of concepts that are essential for understanding labor migration, including the concept of the reserve army of labor and the reinvestment of surplus profits in new, more profitable enterprises with lower labor costs. In seeking to expand on Marxism's general conceptualization of migration under capitalism, this chapter distinguishes capitalism from its progenitors – especially feudalism in its diverse historical and geographic settings rooted in concrete economic relations of production and reproduction. Under this typology, urbanization is indispensable for the formation and expansion of capital in its earliest phases of development. Enclosure laws were essential to initial capitalist formation as they forced peasants off their land. Similarly, in the contemporary phase of capitalist globalization, transnational migration is indispensable for expanding the supply of labor while intensifying the problem of social reproduction in rural areas and less-developed countries. Until the late 20th century, it has been primarily men who have migrated from these regions to urban industrial areas and overseas, but since the turn of the century, more and more women are migrating to support their families.

The Marxist concept of *social formation* and of a global imbalance of power within contemporary capitalism is an important theoretical basis for comprehending the patterns of labor migration, which in turn are rooted in the material conditions within and between states.

An intrinsic feature of the capitalist mode of production is its uneven development over time and space, creating imbalances and discrepancies within and between advanced capitalist and developing regions, where profits are more easily extracted through lower wage and land costs. In the neoliberal era of capitalism, to increase surplus value and profitability, finance capital has shifted investment to production in the Global South, seizing on a large reserve army of labor, and vastly expanding manufacturing for foreign markets throughout the world. The social formations of the world economy permit the most advanced forms of capital to use low-wage labor in any region to their advantage in order to produce greater profits. Advances in productive technology in more advanced economic zones increase capital's capacity to produce more profitably when employing lower-wage labor.

MIGRATION AND LABOR OVER TIME AND SPACE: THE COMMODIFICATION OF LABOR

The advance of the colonial form of European imperialism into Africa, the Americas, and Asia was initiated not only by the search for natural resources but by the emergence and growth of mercantilism, a form of economic extraction that materialized in response to the rapid expansion of trade in commodities previously only accessible to monarchs and feudal lords. The development of sugar and spice plantations – followed by the mining of gold, silver, and other precious metals – was compulsory for the expansion of imperial states. Trade, linked to the maintenance of the imperial monarchy's power, was essential to colonial interests, and cheap slave and indentured labor was essential to extract and process the raw materials for that trade. Mercantilism, however, was oblivious to the catastrophic human and environmental toll it exacted. Indentured servitude and migration were imposed by colonial powers, and forced workers off their ancestral and common lands in both Europe and the colonies. Poverty-stricken undesirables were deported to desolate penal colonies in the Americas, Australia, and India, where they became a form of indentured labor for the empire. The majority of historical research and analysis work on European imperialism recognized the exploitative character of European domination and subjugation of colonial peoples, and the imperative of productive development to extract natural resources and grow cash crops for European markets. In each case labor in the colonial world was crucial for the capitalist enterprise. War and disease introduced by colonizers destroyed the lives of indigenous people and ecosystems throughout the world.

THE AMERICAS: COLONIZATION, CAPITALIST DEVELOPMENT, AND LABOR MIGRATION

When the first attempt at indentured servitude failed to generate enough labor, colonial powers turned to slavery, enslaving Native Americans and Africans to facilitate the process of commodity extraction. Significantly, the growth of the slave trade occurred at the same time that feudal systems of agrarian labor control were ending and capitalist demand for labor was growing. Following the abolition of slavery and indentured servitude, the next major phase of transnational labor migration was primarily from Europe to the Americas. Throughout the Americas, but particularly in the United States, industrial growth in the 19th century contributed to the demand for lower-wage workers from Europe. From the 1840s to the 1920s, mass migration from Europe and East Asia to the Americas was indispensable for constructing railroads and other transportation infrastructure, mining, agriculture, and the crucial food-processing industries. While migration was crucial for the development of capitalist states in the Americas, however, the systematic economic downturn during the Great Depression contributed to xenophobia and nativism in North America.

The exclusion of Chinese, Filipino, and other Asian migrants placed greater demands on the Southern and Eastern European workers who formed part of the new industrial work force in mass-production industries under grueling conditions. In the early 20th-century United States, European immigrant workers toiled in the most difficult jobs in garment sweatshops, meat-packing factories, steel production, and auto industries, as many craft industries that had provided working-class autonomy were replaced. Immigrants formed part of the growing service economy as well, working predominantly in restaurants, hotels, transportation services, and shipping.

From 1910 to 1970, the United States relied on the northward migration of African Americans and Latin Americans as the reserve army of labor. This so-called Great Migration of 10.6 million African Americans contributed to the growth of a multiracial urban working class in major cities, where they were employed at lower wages than the whites, segregated into urban ghettos in the US Midwest, Northeast, and on the Pacific coast, and experienced high unemployment, poverty, discrimination, and police violence.[13] Immigration reform legislation in 1965 (the Hart–Cellar Act) eliminated the national origins quota system, and the population of workers whose national origins were outside Europe expanded dramatically in the United States, primarily migrants from Mexico and Central America, the Caribbean, Asia, and in the 1990s, Africa. As the labor supply increased and immigrant workers competed with native-born laborers, particularly when the economic crisis deepened in 2007–08, nativism increased, leading to initiatives to place new restrictions on entry by government officials.

Canada, as a country of settlement, has been frequently in search of low-wage labor to fill severe labor shortages, and has persistently promoted migration, particularly from Western Europe, to facilitate the country's interest in developing corporate-dominated agriculture, natural resource extraction, and manufacturing.[14] After initial French settlement in the 18th century, Canada was occupied by the British, who dominated the political system and national economy, especially after the war of 1812. In the 19th and 20th centuries, Canada favored the immigration of Europeans over those from the Global South to expand its labor force and develop the national economy.

The Canadian government encouraged labor migration from Europe by developing and facilitating maritime transportation from Europe in the late 19th century; it also tended to be more welcoming to migrants who were excluded from the United States. Migrants formed part of the peasant and urban workforces, though during times of economic downturn, many were impoverished and had to travel westward in search of employment or land. The country's demand for European migrants was most prominent during periods of economic expansion, and declined during periods of recession and depression. When capital sought new immigrants to work in the agrarian, natural-resource extraction, transportation, and manufacturing sectors in its expansive commonwealth, the Canadian authorities were obliged to promote migration.

While anti-Chinese nativism halted migration to the United States in the early 1920s, the Canadian government also passed an Order-in-Council law in 1931 (during the Great Depression, when the country suffered from high unemployment) preventing all but British or northern European migrants from entering and working in the country. The country's preference for Western Europeans also limited the number of Jewish refugees from Germany and Eastern Europe, who were deemed ineligible to enter both Canada and the United States. Many refugees who escaped persecution in Nazi Germany fled to Russia, the United Kingdom and Latin America, until the restrictive migration acts were lifted after the Second World War. Ironically the US Immigration Act of 1952 permitted skilled immigrants from Germany and other European countries to enter and settle in the country. The United States, Argentina, and other Latin American countries even sought former Nazi scientists, academics, and intelligence officers to immigrate to work in their military-industrial complexes and to counter leftist movements in Europe.[15]

In the post-Second World War era, migration opportunities expanded for Caribbean, South Asian, and Chinese and East Asian workers, who had faced discrimination and were excluded from the country from the late 19th century to 1945. From the 1990s to 2010, Canada has relied increasingly on temporary seasonal workers from the Caribbean and Central America for its agricultural sector. Seasonal migration has grown further with the passage of the North American Free Trade Agreement (NAFTA) and other multilateral agreements.[16] Women's migrant labor programs have expanded dramatically, with the growth of demand for domestic workers, particularly from South-east Asia and the Philippines.[17]

In the 19th and 20th centuries, South America (with regional exceptions) promoted mass European immigration to encourage industrialization and economic development. In particular, Argentina, Paraguay, and Uruguay fostered European migration without interruption to expand their national populations and develop industry, agriculture, and economic production. Although the continent had been initially colonized and settled by the Portuguese and Spanish empires, Italians became a leading source of migrants. In striking contrast to the United States, Brazil, Argentina and other South American countries recruited and welcomed Italian émigrés as a developed workforce, even if they brought anarcho-syndicalist traditions to the region. Over time, Italian immigrants diversified the ethnic composition of states in the Americas.[18]

A leading destination for European migration in the Americas in the 19th and early 20th centuries, Argentina received significant foreign investment, particularly from Britain. In the 20th century, particularly in the post-Second World War era, the composition of the immigrant population from Europe diversified to include Central and Eastern European populations from Germany, Poland, Ukraine, and Russia.[19]

AFTER THE SECOND WORLD WAR: A NEW GLOBAL LABOR MIGRATION PATTERN

The end of the Second World War produced a fundamental shift in migration patterns within Europe, North America, East Asia, and Australasia. The post-Second World War era is defined by three periods of migration patterns, particularly as a consequence of labor shortages and demands:

- demand for labor to rebuild war-torn economies (1946–60)
- decolonization and postcolonial South–North immigration (1960–90)
- regulating migrant labor flows to Europe in response to demands from capital, immigration laws, and restrictions on new immigrants in response to the growing economic crisis (1990–2012).

Rebuilding War-Torn Economies

The economic devastation inflicted by the Second World War on Europe and East Asia contributed to a growing demand for labor to rebuild the infrastructure of those regions. Rebuilding Europe's industrial base necessitated internal as well as regional migration. Thus the Italian economy demanded laborers from the south of the country as more and more relocated to work in West Germany. In the ensuing years, the German economy relied on Turkish migrants as laborers throughout the country. In the United States and the United Kingdom, returning soldiers by and large replaced women, who lost their jobs in factories. Mexican workers recruited under the *bracero* program in the United States largely remained as farm laborers in the corporate farming industries.

Australia, which suffered a severe labor shortage, was a leading destination for many immigrants from Europe from 1945 to the 1960s. Following the end of the Second World War, millions of European immigrants who were identified as displaced persons were welcomed to Australia, which was in search of workers because of a severe labor shortage. Australian government authorities reached bilateral agreements with Britain and other European countries to foster European immigration, leading to more than 4 million newcomers in the four decades immediately following the end of the war. By the early 21st century immigrants constituted approximately 23 per cent of the country's total population of some 22 million. From 1945 to 1957, the government implemented a racially exclusionary migration policy, which was finally abolished in 1973. However, the initial exclusionary policies played an important factor in ensuring that Europeans retained a majority in the country.[20]

Decolonization and Postcolonial South–North Immigration

Pressure for independence in the European and US colonial empires expanded following the end of the Second World War, leading to a rapid transformation of the map of the world, as most occupied territories in the colonial world gained independence from 1946 to 2000. Labor migration within newly independent countries was influenced in the postwar era by those countries' attempts to develop their own economies through import substitution industrialization (ISI), a system that generates GDP growth by restricting external capital flows and investing at home.

The ISI model collapsed in the 1980s. Poor countries unable to develop industry internally became indebted to multilateral lending agencies and banks, and were unable to repay loans at high interest rates, leading to the imposition of onerous terms that would undercut state efforts to industrialize and reduce poverty. Investments were frequently squandered on large infrastructural and industrial projects whose benefits primarily accrued to the upper classes and government leaders. Structural adjustment policies (SAPs) were imposed by the International Monetary Fund (IMF), forcing countries to curtail and/or eliminate spending on social welfare (education, health care, housing, sanitation) and to accept neoliberal policies that opened markets to foreign trade, allowing foreign-targeted investments to be made in the most profitable sectors – frequently raw materials – with no restrictions on the extraction of capital.

The result was that in most countries widespread impoverishment was accompanied by super-profits through monopoly-capitalist development in low-wage regions. The consequence of the neoliberal commodification process was the growth in internal migration among populations who could not survive in poor regions of the country, together with the expansion of urban areas. The dramatic trend towards urbanization was predicated on internal labor migration to centers where workers could find jobs – mostly part-time and precarious, often in sectors that were highly dependent on production for foreign markets. The threat of the withdrawal of international capital by multilateral agencies such as the IMF prevented governments in the Global South from selecting alternatives to neoliberal development.[21]

By the 1990s, demand for labor, together with poverty in source countries, triggered rapid migration from rural regions to cities of the Global South, and for those with higher skills or easier passage, to the Global North. In destination regions, workers found that low wages typically provided barely enough to pay for housing, education, and health care. By 2000, 50 per cent of the entire world population lived in urban areas, in what Mike Davis called the 'Planet of Slums,' often in squatter communities afflicted with rundown and makeshift shelters, unsanitary conditions, and inadequate education.[22] Davis maintains that the pattern of urban population growth in the South is analogous to 19th-century European and North American expansion, with the distinction that most of the new residents will not live in inner-city slums, but settle in makeshift unauthorized zones on the periphery of major cities:

> The real macroeconomic trend of informal labour, in other words, is the reproduction of absolute poverty. But if the informal proletariat is not the pettiest of petty bourgeoisies, neither is it a 'labour reserve army' or a 'lumpen proletariat' in any obsolete nineteenth-century sense. Part of it, to be sure, is a stealth workforce for the formal economy, and numerous studies have exposed how the subcontracting networks of Wal-Mart and other mega-companies extend deep into the misery of the colonias and chawls. But at the end of the day, a majority of urban slum-dwellers are truly and radically homeless in the contemporary international economy. Some laborers from the Global South have been educated and trained in positions that were in high demand in North America and Europe from farm laborers to hospitality workers to high-skilled business services.[23]

Migration has also been promoted by bilateral labor agreements between the North and South facilitating the temporary migration of guest workers from South Asia, South-east Asia, and the Caribbean to advanced capitalist countries in the Arabian Peninsula, Europe, and North America. By 2004, the United Nations provided significant evidence that international migration was advantageous to capital in the Global North, where low-wage labor in situ and in the 'developed countries' was in demand (see Table 3.1).

But in its 2010 *Development Report*, the United Nations called on international NGOs to lead an effort to reduce the most harmful effects of migration:

Table 3.1 Indicators of the stock of international migrants by major area, 1960–2000

Major area	(Number millions)					Ave. ann'l growth of no. (%)				Percentage of population		Distribution by region (%)	
	1960	1970	1980	1990	2000	1960– 1970	1970– 1980	1980– 1990	1990– 2000	1960	2000	1960	2000
World	75.9	81.5	99.8	154.0	174.9	0.7	2.0	4.3	1.3	2.5	2.9	100.0	100.0
Developed countries	32.1	38.3	47.7	89.	110.3	1.8	2.2	6.3	2.1	3.4	8.7	42.3	63.1
Developed countries excluding USSR	29.1	35.2	44.5	59.	80.8	1.9	2.3	2.9	3.0	4.0	8.3	38.4	46.2
Developing countries	43.8	43.2	52.1	64.3	64.6	-0.1	1.8	2.1	0.0	2.1	1.3	57.7	6.9
Africa	9.0	9.9	14.1	16.2	16.3	0.9	3.6	1.4	0.0	3.2	2.0	11.8	9.3
Asia[1]	29.3	28.1	32.3	41.8	43.8	-0.4	1.4	2.6	0.5	1.8	1.2	38.6	25.0
Latin America and Caribbean	6.0	5.8	6.1	7.0	5.9	-0.5	0.7	1.3	-1.7	2.8	1.1	8.0	3.4
North America	12.5	13.0	18.1	27.6	40.8	0.4	3.3	4.2	3.9	6.1	12.9	16.5	23.3
Oceania	2.1	3.0	3.8	4.8	5.8	3.5	2.1	2.3	2.1	13.4	18.8	2.8	3.3
Europe[2]	14.0	18.7	22.2	26.3	32.8	2.9	1.7	1.7	2.2	3.3	6.4	18.5	18.7
USSR (former)	2.9	3.1	3.3	30.3	29.5	0.5	0.5	22.3	-0.3	1.4	10.2	3.9	16.8

Notes:

1 Excluding Armenia, Azerbaijan, Georgia, Kazakhstan, Kyrgyzstan, Tajikistan, Turkmenistan, and Uzbekistan.
2 Excluding Belarus, Estonia, Latvia, Lithuania, the Republic of Moldova, the Russian Federation, and Ukraine.

Source: Derived from Department of Economic and Social Affairs (2004) *World Economic and Social Survey 2004 International Migration* (New York: United Nations), E/2004/75/Rev.1/Add.1; ST/ESA/291/Add.1.

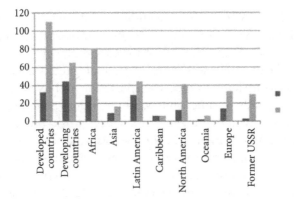

Figure 3.1 Number of international migrants, 1960–2000 (millions)

Data source: UN Department of Economic and Social Affairs, *World Economic and Social Survey 2004: International Migration* (New York: United Nations, 2004), E/2004/75/Rev.1/Add.1; ST/ESA/291/Add.1

Until a more favourable situation emerges for permanent immigration, temporary labour flows could be managed in order to enhance global welfare and protect the human rights of migrants. Given their prior work on migration, ILO and the International Organization for Migrants (IOM) might cooperate in creating a global clearing house for world labour demand and supply. Such a global labour regime could bring order to the currently chaotic situation of spontaneously arising labour flows, some of which are illegal, which impose significant costs on the migrants themselves (they sometimes pay with their lives) and often provoke the ire and resentment of the people in destination countries.[24]

GLOBAL CAPITAL, LABOR MOBILITY,
AND STATE REGULATION

Since the 1990s, the World Trade Organization (WTO) has pursued multilateral negotiations to impose a global neoliberal order to cover temporary and circular workers through the General Agreement on Trade in Services (GATS). This new 'global law' requires all members of the WTO to participate in a multilateral system that would facilitate the use of temporary labor, in most cases supplied by the Global South, in countries of the Global North.

These policies rarely serve the interests of guest workers, who are forced to contribute to their transportation and living expenses for varying periods of time while working in low-paid jobs where wage rates are typically unenforced. Guest work programs are viewed by the World Bank and the IMF as a means of economic development in countries of origin because workers theoretically send home remittances that develop local economies. However, the record of the period between 1990 and 2015 demonstrates that most guest workers are unable to earn enough money to pay their own expenses. Most do not return enough money to their countries of origin to develop new economic activity beyond paying for basic costs of education, health care and housing, giving rise to a circular migration process that reinforces and maintains poverty rates in poor countries and reduces wages in the developed world.[25]

MIGRATION, PROLETARIANIZATION, AND POVERTY

The legacy of imperialism and occupation is a significant factor in the migrations of the postcolonial period. As a consequence of economic, linguistic, social, and cultural bonds, workers in the post-colonial world have migrated in large numbers from the Global South to Europe and North America, reversing the pattern of emigration from the Global North to countries of settlement in the 18th and 19th centuries. In addition, since the end of the Second World War, labor shortages have generated demand for labor to fill crucial occupations in manufacturing and services. The aging of the European population has generated greater demand for women migrants and the growth of female labor force participation, mostly to serve in caring positions as nurses, child-care and elder-care providers, educators, and domestics, in the postwar era – a demand that accelerated in the late 20th century with the growth of sex trafficking and marriage migration from Eastern Europe and South-East Asia.

The most significant stimuli for labor migration, however, remain poverty and lack of opportunity. Without a means of sustenance, migrants have been forced to migrate to new destinations in search of work to support themselves and their families back home. Undeniably, while skilled migrants may individually decide that they may fare better in destination countries, most workers have few alternatives and are in most cases forced through market mechanisms to migrate and sell their labor power.

While economies of the Global North have recruited skilled migrants from the Global South to fill labor shortages and expand the reserve army of workers in a range of labor markets, they have also encouraged skilled migration between advanced capitalist economies.[26] While skilled immigrants tend to travel to Europe and North America from China, India, and the Philippines, migration within the Global South is primarily from poorer countries to work as day laborers in financial centers, oil states, and mineral extraction.

In the 25 years following the passage of the Immigration and Control Act of 1986, between 12 and 14 million immigrants – chiefly from Mexico and Central America – entered the United States to satisfy capitalist demand for low-wage employment. A majority of the new workers were undocumented, and they were frequently excluded from membership in traditional labor unions, which were already in a period of mass decline and erosion. Immigrants from Latin America were frequently forced to work in marginal and precarious jobs in tertiary sectors of the economy, and were paid rates below the minimum wage:

> Essential to the growth of guest work under advanced capitalism is a dialectical relationship between capital and labor. Capital almost always requests open migration to enlarge the reserve army of labor and increase competition with native-born workers as a means to lower wages and job standards.[27]

Mass migration to the United States was also stimulated by NAFTA, which eroded the living standards of Mexicans in the agricultural sectors of the economy.

As the number of immigrants expanded dramatically through the 1990s and early 2000s, unions recognized the necessity of mobilizing them into the service economy: health care, food services, cleaning and domestic services, hospitality, building services, and other key sectors of the US economy. Although more unions were eager to organize immigrant workers, even when successful their wages and working conditions remained inferior to those of US-born workers. Undocumented workers were eligible for the same wage rates as US-born workers, even if their status and positions were precarious and they were subject to deportation in many regions of the country where nativist sentiment dominated. However, gradually enforcement of wage rates reduced demand for immigrant workers, as was the case in the post-9/11 period when immigrant control policies redounded negatively on Latin American workers and other foreign laborers.

The economic and political status of immigrant laborers was further compromised by the 2008–12 economic crises which contributed to high rates of unemployment. In many instances, the expansion of enforcement continued a trend, begun in the 1990s, that militarized the US border with Mexico.[28]

According to Marxist analysis, the 'reserve army of labor' that filters through the turnstiles as the needs of capital require is a central feature of capitalism because it enables capital to create and maintain surplus value, keeping costs down and, in the process, maintaining a powerful weapon against workers. Moreover, as low-cost labor is utilized in the periphery, higher-waged workers in the center are laid off or never hired. In the current age this affects migrant workers more than any other group, since, whether internally or internationally mobile, they are not typically represented by existing trade unions and are therefore vulnerable to exploitation, in the form of low wages, substandard working conditions, violence and discrimination and poor prospects and opportunities. In the case studies that follow in Part II, we shall see how this has worked out in three key industrial disputes in three major recipients of foreign investment in the Global South – India, China, and South Africa – from 2000 to the present.

Part II

Case Studies

3

India: Neoliberal Industrialization, Class Formation, and Mobilization

For nearly 200 years the Indian subcontinent has been a source of labor serving the interests of global capitalists. As neoliberal policies are enacted by the Indian government, and multinational companies demand strict subservience and impose exploitative conditions on precarious workers, new class-struggle unions are forming and expanding in India's industrial belts. The insurgency among auto workers in India, and in particular at Maruti Suzuki manufacturing plants, discussed in this chapter, is representative of the expansion of direct struggle by workers against rapacious multinational employers and a compliant state which serves the interests of the capitalist class.

This chapter examines the rise of independent rank-and-file workers' unions at the epicenter of global manufacturing in India. While the class conflict between workers and management is expanding in manufacturing industries, weak central unions are unable to consolidate power on a national level. If the conditions of industrial workers in export-producing factories and installations in India are to be improved, they require a major workers' movement that embraces the aspirations of the young men and women (mostly rural migrants) who comprise the vast majority of the workers.[1]

The chapter reviews the creation of a marginalized urban low-wage labor force comprised of rural migrants in the two decades following the national implementation of neoliberal reforms in 1991, and their integration into the world capitalist economy dominated by the imperialist countries of the Global North. According to Marxist economist Prabhat Patnaik the decline of inter-imperial rivalry following the Second World War has unified European and

Map 4.1 India, with a focus on Haryana State

North American imperialism through the dominance of the US dollar and international financial organizations to exploit Third World economies through international finance capital.[2] I consider the interplay of multinational capital and the mobilization of new proletarian workers into labor unions and workers' organizations.

The rapid growth of foreign investment has dramatically transformed major cities into modern hubs of production for export to the Global North, and has markedly increased gross domestic product (GDP). However although India is regarded by economists as a successful model for economic development, the country's investment linkages with the imperialist economy neglect the vast majority of the population, and intensify their inequality and exploitation.

Independent rank-and-file workers' unions in India have arisen in direct response to rising foreign direct investment (FDI) aimed at eroding the power of traditional labor unions. As multinational companies demand strict subservience and impose exploitative conditions on precarious workers, new unions focused on the class struggle are forming and expanding in India's key industrial belts around New Delhi, Chennai, Pune, and Ahmedabad.

MANUFACTURING AND WORKER MILITANCY IN INDIA'S AUTO SECTOR

The rise of Maruti Suzuki illustrates the expanding significance of independent unions in India's massive manufacturing industries in the ten years to 2015. This has prompted business and government leaders to stage an offensive against unions that workers have organized in an attempt to gain improved wages, working conditions, and democratic labor representation. As private contractors for international manufacturers seek to restrict trade unions, independent unions are forming to represent worker interests in industrial belts and export processing zones (EPZs). Throughout India most workers employed in the factories in EPZs are young male and female migrants from rural areas.[3]

The rise of independent and syndicalist unions in the epicenter of global manufacturing industries demonstrates the salience of consolidating the struggles through a central rank-and-file union, along the lines of the Industrial Workers of the World (IWW). While the class conflict between workers and management is expanding in manufacturing, weak central unions are unable to consolidate power on a national level. Over the last two decades of the restructuring of labor in the Global South, India has become a significant source of low-wage industrial labor for the global capitalist economy. Traditional labor unions have lost their capacity to respond to state and monopoly capitalist policies that erode wages, laboring conditions, health and safety, and the human rights of workers – broadly defined as the ability to work and live in dignity.[4]

Since the early 1990s India has adopted neoliberal policies encouraging FDI that dramatically expanded new production in non-union factories in special economic zones (SEZs) provided with government subsidies for development, low-cost land, tax abatements, and lowering of tariffs. At the same time working conditions for the minority (about 7 percent) of workers in unionized industries have been significantly eroded. In some cases agreements with management are not enforced by government or even by the unions. The power of traditional unions, formed and controlled by mostly left political parties in India's parliament, has weakened significantly, leading to the rise of autonomous and syndicalist forms of worker organization directly in factories.[5]

This weakening of existing unions has severely eroded the power of those who could count on parliamentary agreements to defend working conditions. As new industries have grown through FDI, labor agreements have been seriously undermined, according to Satyaki Roy, professor at the Institute for Studies in Industrial Development in New Delhi. In the past, unions gained concessions through official strikes and stoppages.[6]

While Indian labor protections established at independence in 1947 permit workers to organize into unions, since the initiation of neoliberal reforms in 1991 corporations have flouted these laws with the active support of state and central labor authorities, thwarting the formation of trade unions unless they are controlled by management. Capital investment has flowed to the manufacturers and contractors who employ informal laborers earning a fraction of the wages of full-time permanent workers, with no job security. But the vast discrepancy in wages between permanent and contract workers in the rapidly expanding auto sector, rather than dividing workers, has generated solidarity and a rejection of two-tier labor forces. Independent unions are forming to represent worker interests in industrial belts and SEZs.

The Demand for Contract Labor

Chandrajit Banerjee, director general of the Confederation of Indian Industries, a leading manufacturing association, considers contract labor to be a significant factor in the foreign investments that drive Indian employment growth:

> As against a labour force of 470 million in 2009–10, only 15.6% had regular wage employment/salaried work while about one-third was casual labour and over half was self-employed. This has deprived large sections of society of the benefits of work security and emoluments, leading to social rifts. ... One must appreciate that the ability to use contract labour enables a very large part of the labour force, who would have otherwise gone without any employment or livelihood options, to be employed. One of the reasons for the preference for contract labour is that while competition and globalisation have brought in their trail severe fluctuations in market conditions, the labour law framework in India discourages flexibility and exit in the use of labour. This is why the ability to use contract labour provides a win–win situation for both sides.[7]

The absence of regulation for labor contractors prevents workers from organizing themselves into cohesive units. Ironically, regulations barring existing unions from recruiting workers in the industrial belts have established conditions that foster intensified labor militancy. Militancy and insurrections have expanded between 2007 and 2013 in new SEZs, with the auto industry being a pivotal center of protest that has spread from major production companies to parts producers throughout the country. In the six years from 2004/05 to 2010/11 annual passenger vehicle production in India increased from 1.2 million to 3 million vehicles, according to the Research Unit for Political Economy in Mumbai.[8] The rapid expansion of the auto industry for the domestic and regional markets is in no small measure a consequence of central and state government subsidies and regulatory support through widespread non-enforcement of labor and union laws by multinational manufacturers, thus containing labor costs and increasing worker productivity.

Corporate Restructuring and Labor Union Bureaucracy

As Indian labor unions lost political and social power, insecurity rose among workers. In this section I examine the efficacy of new forms of democratic worker organization, and how representation and demands shift from parliamentary bargaining to innovative organizing approaches at the firm level.[9]

Until the 1990s, labor was managed by states through a combination of repression and institutionalized bargaining, where workers' gains were conditioned by national economies in an era when large businesses benefited from import substitution and controls. Patterns of labor-management bargaining have become extensively transformed in the Global South, with corporatist, parliamentary, and social dialogue systems eliminated because they are seen as unacceptable to multinational corporations and global capital.[10] In India, precariousness proliferates with new industrialization, unlike the social democratic systems found in 20th-century Europe and North America, as 94 percent of all workers work outside of the formal sector of labor regulation.

Most literature on the decline of labor power asserts that the erosion of union effectiveness can be addressed by devoting union resources to organizing, policy interventions, and alliances with labor-friendly political parties.[11] There is little evidence to support such prescriptions over the last three decades. Irrespective of whether they claim to be on the left or right, all governments embrace the neoliberal orthodoxy. As traditional unions contract, they are on the defensive, and must conform to neoliberal economic policies rather than promoting rank-and-file unionism.[12] In contrast, vibrant new forms of worker organization have demonstrated a remarkable capacity for innovation. Matching this has been an upsurge of workers' movements, in both North and South, which are consciously inspired by democratic and rank-and-file unionism.[13]

State Support for Indian Business, and the Decline of Unions

The Indian state and central government does not compel management to recognize unions formed by contract laborers. In the growing industrial belts that rely on foreign investments, corporate hostility to unions is reinforced by government policies that prevent union organization among contract workers. In an interview with the International Commission for Labor Rights (ICLR), Anupam Malik, Joint Labour Commissioner for Haryana State, unequivocally declared, 'It is not illegal to refuse to negotiate with an outsider. It is the management's wish. It is the right of employers to refuse to negotiate.'

When permanent workers try to form unions, management at Maruti Suzuki and other firms have applied familiar union-busting techniques for converting these permanent jobs into contract labor.[14] According to Satyaki Roy, as a result of lax enforcement 50 percent of workers in traditional unions are in fact casual workers who are not covered by labor agreements and who earn a fraction of the officially negotiated rate.[15] Indian workers on the whole are under-employed and work too few hours to earn enough for food, shelter, health care, education, and other necessities.

Traditionally labor representation at state level in India has formed around parliamentary political parties. The key labor federations are affiliated with the Bharatiya Janata (BJP, the Hindu nationalist party), the Congress Party, several communist and left-influenced parties, and regional political forces. Until the neoliberal economic restructuring of 1991, parties bargained with the state and Indian capitalists for their members and supported trade union centers by voting to fund wage gains (see Table 4.1). The weakness of traditional unions has contributed to the declining power of left parties, as demonstrated by their substantial defeat in the 2011 and 2012 elections and the 2014 victory of Narendra Modi of the BJP as India's prime minister. As a result, those unionized enterprises that represent 6 to 7 percent of all workers in formal enterprises – and perhaps an even smaller proportion if casual workers are taken into account – have come under severe pressure.

Lacking a consolidated base or federation, despite democratic representation and militancy, these unions are still at a disadvantage, and are exposed to severe employer opposition and the heavy arm of the state. India's state and central governments always favor employers and are indifferent to their use of thugs and bouncers.

Table 4.1 Indian major union organizations

Body	Date founded	Party affiliation	Membership 1989	2010
All India Trade Union Congress (AITUC)	1920	CPI	923,500	2,700,000
Indian Trade Union Congress (INTUC)	1947	Congress	2,706,000	4,000,000
Hind Mazdoor Sabha Workers' Assembly of India (HMS)	1948	SP	1,477,500	3,400,000
United Trade Union Congress (UTUC)[1]	1949	RSP	539,500	383,946
Bharatiya Mazdoor Sangh India Worker Union (BMS)	1955	BJP	3,117,000	8,500,000
Centre of Indian Trade Unions (CITU)	1969	CPI(M)	1,798,000	3,200,000
United Trade Union Congress-Lenin Sarani (UTUC LS)	1969	SUCI	802,800	1,400,000
National Front of Indian Trade Unions	1969	NCP	529,800	600,000
Self-Employed Women's Association (SEWA)[2]	1972	N/A	–	950,000
National Trade Union Initiative (NTUI)[3]	2001	N/A	N/A	N/A

Notes:
1   2002 data
2   2008 data. SEWA members are self-employed and the organization is funded by NGOs and supported by the World Bank.
3   NTUI mobilizes workers in the non-organized and informal sectors and is not recognized by the Indian Government as an official trade union with national bargaining rights.
CPI: Communist Party of India. SP: Samajwadi (Socialist) Party. RSP: Revolutionary Socialist Party. BJP: Bharatiya Janata Party. CPI(M): Communist Party of India (Marxist).
SUCI: Socialist Unity Centre of India. NCP: Nationalist Congress Party.

Frequently, state governments unleash their own police and security apparatus to quell strikes and other efforts to organize democratic worker-controlled unions.

THE NEW TRADE UNION INITIATIVE – ORGANIZING INFORMAL AND CONTRACT WORKERS

While traditional trade union centers have a foothold in old industries like steel production, shipping, and food distribution, they are all but nonexistent in new sectors of the economy that are recipients of foreign capital: internet technology, business services, construction, and new auto and electronics manufacturing installations. The growth of independent unions has opened up a new front for workers seeking direct democracy at the enterprise and plant level. Most independent unions represent workers in the 'informal sector,' which has dominated the workplace since independence.[16] These precarious laborers fill temporary jobs in the main plants of foreign manufacturers and contractors in the production chain, and can be dismissed at any time.[17]

The New Trade Union Initiative (NTUI), a national federation of independent trade unions formed in 2002, is at the forefront of the struggle to end casualization of labor and the use of 'irregular' contract workers in core production processes in contravention of the Contract Labour (Regulation and Abolition) Act 1970 and the principle of equal wages for equal work. It has about 400 affiliated unions that organize company by company in new enterprises.

Mobilization of Workers in the Gurgaon Industrial Belt

New Delhi is surrounded by new industrial districts that expanded rapidly from the early 1980s to employ about 2.5 million permanent and contract laborers for multinational corporations. They work in factories, offices, and research parks for corporations that serve the Indian, South Asian, and global markets. The precipitous growth of the industrial corridor is demonstrated by the expansion of the readership of *Faridabad Majdoor Samachar* (*Faridabad Workers News*), a respected Hindi language monthly newspaper, from 1,000 in 1982 to 7,000 in 2007. According to the newspaper, in 2013 75 percent of workers in Faridabad were not listed on company records, 85 percent were employed by contractors, and 80 percent of all permanent and contractor workers earned less than the statutory minimum wage of $83.28 a month.[18]

A meeting of activists, organizers, and representatives of almost 30 workers' organizations and labor institutes in Delhi in May 2013 underlined the significance of the rapidly expanding contract labor force, both for the erosion of acceptable working conditions for permanent workers and for declining union membership. The wage differential between permanent and contract workers ranges from 4:1 to 5:1, jeopardizing a growing number of permanent jobs.

The coordinating committee connecting unions across the industrial area of Gurgaon, Dharuhera, and Manesar with solidarity organizations in the Delhi National Capital Region (NCR) in North Central India also considers contractualization as the central issue for the labor movement throughout India. In the Gurgaon Industrial Belt, for example, contract laborers comprise 80 percent of the workforce; these workers earn 25–50 percent of the standard wage and are prohibited from organizing in unions. The area is inhabited by displaced young migrants from rural areas in Haryana and north-east India who are deliberately recruited because of their lack of social ties and unfamiliarity with the region. According to a recent report on the labor market of the Gurgaon Industrial Belt, '[t]he policy of recruiting mostly migrant workers, without local roots, has been used by the bosses as a strategy to undermine the power of workers in the case of a conflict.'

Workers employed in Gurgaon's industries barely earn enough to pay the rent on small units built on agricultural land in the city. These are old farms that have been transformed into what are known as 'villages,' where they live in 'often Spartan (3m x 3m)' lodgings 'for exorbitant rents and often with deplorable sanitary conditions.'[19] In response to low wages and poor working conditions, workers have mobilized unions and initiated major work stoppages in Haryana State and throughout India. See Table 4.2 for major recent strikes in India, which are increasing under the new government of Prime Minister Narendra Modi.

Export Promotion: The Emergence and Growth of Maruti Suzuki

The Maruti Suzuki struggle is the best known among the many labor insurgencies in the EPZs established in the sprawling industrial belt of Gurgaon. Other new factories in the city produce autos, electronics, telecommunications, IT technology, textiles, food, and pharmaceuticals for foreign multinationals, with tax exemptions and logistic incentives to Japanese, European, and North American investors.[20]

Maruti is among the most prominent examples of state disinvestment and privatization. The auto company was originally established at the behest of Prime Minister Indira Gandhi, who was seeking to build an Indian version of the German Volkswagen. Under Gandhi's son Sanjay, design and production were initiated to produce a 'People's Car.' A year after Sanjay Gandhi's death while piloting a test plane in June 1980, the Indian government nationalized the firm as a 'public sector undertaking,' and in 1981, a reconstituted Maruti Udyog Ltd (MUL) began offering a 40 percent equity stake to foreign investors. Two years later, MUL established a joint venture with Suzuki Motor Company of Japan, which steadily expanded its ownership in the company to 40 percent in 1987 then 50 percent in 1992.

Suzuki subsequently gained a controlling interest, which enabled it to make all management and production decisions.[21] In 2002 the public stake in the company was entirely sold off, and in 2007 it was renamed Maruti Suzuki India Ltd (MSIL). The company was privatized as a stock company, with Suzuki increasing its controlling stake to 71.7 percent in March 2012. Through control over the commodity production chain and outsourcing to contractors Suzuki maintains an exacting control over MSIL and its workers. The assessment and analysis of the company's annual reports demonstrates that Suzuki is in effect a foreign-held manufacturer that controls all investment and management decisions, and relies on foreign parts, contributing to lower value-added production by its workers and more outsourcing than its two leading competitors in India, Mahindra & Mahindra and Tata Motors.[22] Over 30 years from 1983 to 2013, Maruti Suzuki emerged as India's largest automotive producer, reaching 1.1–1.2 million cars per year from 2010 to 2013.[23]

AUTO WORKER MOBILIZATION IN NEW
DELHI'S INDUSTRIAL BELT, 1999–2013

Maruti Udyog Employees Union, Gurgaon, 2000–01

The strikes and worker occupations of 2000–01 at Maruti Suzuki, which were the most significant sustained resistance against a foreign-owned factory since the neoliberal economic reforms of 1991, were reminiscent of the sit-down strikes at Flint in the United States in 1937. As the Peoples Union for Democratic Rights (PUDR) states:

> The history of Maruti is marked by exploitation of workers though inhuman working conditions, extraordinary work pressure, harassment by arbitrary issuing of show-cause notices and charge-sheets, transfers, suspensions, criminal intimi- dation, terminations without inquiry, forcing the workers to take voluntary retirement, etc. The history is also marked by a militant struggle waged by the workers. Needless to say, many active workers have paid heavily for their struggle against the violation of their legal and democratic rights in the company. The persistent resistance put up by the Maruti workers has few parallels in this country and therefore becomes an important component of the history of Maruti as well as the struggle of workers across the entire Gurgaon industrial belt.[24]

From 1999 to 2001, a strike wave for higher wages at the main Maruti auto plant in Gurgaon demonstrated the longstanding militant struggle of workers for higher wages and improved working conditions. From 1995 to 1999/2000 individual workers' annual productivity increased from 77 cars to 107 cars per year. The incentive scheme was replaced with a new plan that linked higher wages to domestic car sales, a shift seen by economists as a response to growing competition in the Indian market. Suzuki expected workers to maintain auto productivity – thus destroying the link between their productivity and their wages. After a negotiated settle- ment sought by the Maruti Udyog Employees Union (MUEU) was summarily rejected by management, the workers began wearing black badges, sloganeering, working to rule, and holding meetings at the factory gates.[25]

On September 17, 1999, MUEU convened a general meeting of rank-and-file members and adopted a tactical strategy of hunger strikes and impromptu two-hour work stoppages ('tool downs') on each shift. Maruti management retaliated by suspending ten workers and firing four others, and, in early October, the firm convinced the Haryana State labor authorities to designate the industrial actions illegal. Management also had the support of local police, who arrested the union president and general secretary during the hunger strike. The 'tool downs' continued from September 18 until October 12, when management locked out most workers for refusing to sign a 'good conduct undertaking' agreeing that they would cease the 'tool down' and other actions 'adversely affecting the production and discipline,' and that management had the right to take legal action against for breaching the agreement. Labor authorities viewed the workers' action as in violation of Indian labor law.

Since most Maruti workers refused to sign the undertaking, which included an attempt to buy workers' support with a flat wage incentive of R500, management declared that the workers were on strike, and called in the police to blockade the national highway alongside the plant and prevent entry into the factory. Only workers who had signed the agreement were allowed to pass in. According to PUDR, among the 4,800 unionized MUEU members only 600 signed the management terms. The Maruti lockout of union members lasted for two months, ending on January 8, 2001. As workers protested outside the factory, the plant operated with the minority of workers who had signed the good conduct understanding – a workforce scheme that would become the norm following the strike – together with contract laborers and other informal laborers.[26] (In addition, the union claimed that apprentices and contract workers were being treated as forced laborers, locked in the plant, compelled to work, and stopped from leaving the factory.)

Maruti Udyog Ltd refused to reinstate most workers it had dismissed or suspended in spite of the pleas of government officials, who negotiated with management at the urging of workers. To publicize the suppression of their union by Maruti, workers began a 26-day sit-in adjacent to Udyog Bhawan, the Office of the Indian Ministry for Heavy Industry in New Delhi, demanding that the government defend workers' rights.[27]

In early January 2001, under intense pressure, workers acceded to management's new productivity incentive plan and accepted 'good conduct' conditions. The lockout was halted by Maruti without granting workers any of their demands, and management levied harsh financial penalties on workers. In addition to deducting wages for days lost the two-month lockout, Maruti also deducted wages for hours lost during the tool down and for the days lost during the lockout from October 12 to January 8 by those who refused to sign the good conduct agreement. Some workers did not receive wages until March or April 2001. In response to the strike wave, in 2002, Suzuki management unilaterally dismantled an incentive system initiated in 1988 that had allowed workers to earn a bonus in exchange for increased annual production per worker, setting the stage for a pattern of severe repression against workers and the development of labor struggles in the next decade.

In interviews PUDR declared that workers:

came back to a factory whose management it appeared was intent on teaching them a lesson. Not only did they have to suffer severe financial distress due to almost half a year without receiving their salaries, but also the factory atmosphere was overtly hostile and abusive.[28]

The MUEU was disbanded by management and replaced by the Maruti Udyog Kamgar Union (MUKU), a company union established by Maruti to prevent the workers from establishing an independent trade union. More than ten years later, in 2013, PUDR reported that the High Courts in India 'failed in providing any relief or justice for workers' who filed unfair labor practice charges against Maruti.[29]

Some labor activists saw the struggle as a way of destroying the independent union and substantially increasing the proportion of contract s who had no labor rights. According to J. C. B. Annavajhula and Surendra Pratap the permanent workforce was retrenched by 50 percent while informal workers at the plant increased:

> [B]y February 2004 the number of permanents fell to 2,100 in contrast to a total of 4,328 workers in 1998, alongside indirect labour that numbered 1,700 which was also brought down ... the real point is that, by now, the temps in the factory exceeded the permanents and indirect labour combined. Some workers – about 10–15% – who had accepted the voluntary retirement scheme have re-entered the factory as contract workers! ... as the summer of 2004 ushered in, the company took pride in defeating the workers by discrediting and destroying the popular union and taking away the basic rights to organize and bargain collectively, which is of course the norm rather than the exception in the Indian corporate sector, in general, and in the automobile industry, in particular.[30]

What remained troubling to PUDR and observers of the struggle of 2000–01 at Maruti in Gurgaon was the state's conspicuous support for management against permanent workers whose jobs, unlike those of contract laborers, were safeguarded by labor law.[31] A decade later Maruti workers would mobilize in a new struggle to defend informal workers – now the majority of all employees at the factories, not only in the Delhi industrial belt, but throughout India. The workers in the plant recognized that they would only prevail if they mobilized a solidarity union that consisted of both permanent and informal workers.

The Employer Assault on Maruti Suzuki Workers, 2011–13

Six years after the struggle at Gurgaon, Suzuki opened a second major plant in Manesar, a municipality 24 km to the south, and began recruiting workers from the state of Haryana and regional states in the north of India. The unit at Manesar covers a sprawling area of 600 acres, with three integrated plants that are highly automated, with advanced robotics, and high-tech paint, welding, and machining infrastructure.

The business model adopted at Manesar was based on maintaining a majority of informal contract and trainee workers and ensuring that permanent workers continuously remained a minority. From 2007 to 2011, 25 percent of all workers taken on by Maruti Suzuki at its Manesar plant were apprentices and journeymen, and 75 per cent were informal precarious workers, including contract workers, trainees, and new apprentices.

Three major sit-down strikes in June, September, and October 2011 were initiated by permanent workers seeking to eliminate a flexible pay system where no worker could achieve the standard rate of pay set by the company, to moderate the breakneck pace of the assembly line, and to regularize informal workers as full-timers. The insurgency was sparked when workers applied for registration of the Maruti Suzuki Employees Union (MSEU) with the State Joint Labour Commissioner (JLC) in Chandigarh, Haryana's capital. Management immediately sought to blunt the edge of the MSEU by

Table 4.2 Strikes at vehicle manufacturing plants in India, 2009–13

Employer	Location	Dates
Mahindra	Nashik, Maharashtra	May 2009, March 2010
Sunbeam Auto	Gurgaon, Haryana	May 2009
Bosch Chassis	Pune, Maharashtra	July 2009
Honda Motorcycle	Manesar, Haryana	August 2009
Rico Auto	Gurgaon, Haryana	August 2009
Pricol	Coimbatore, Tamil Nadu	September 2009
Volvo	Hoskote, Karnataka	August 2010
MRF Tyres	Chennai, Tamil Nadu	October 2010, June 2011
General Motors	Halol, Gujarat	March 2011
Bosch	Bangalore, Karnataka	September 2011
Dunlop	Hooghly, Bengal	October 2011
Caparo	Sriperumbudur, Tamil Nadu	December 2011
Dunlop	Ambattur, Tamil Nadu	February 2012
Hyundai	Chennai, Tamil Nadu	April 2011 Dec. 2011–Jan. 2012
Bajaj Auto Workers	Pune	June–August 2013

Sources: Abhishek Shaw and Lina Mathias, 'Bajaj auto workers' agitation, withdrawal and triumph,' *Economic and Political Weekly*, Vol. 48, No. 38, September 21, 2013; *Workers Autonomy Strikes in India: Maruti Suzuki Strike at Manesar, June, September, October 2011*, Brussels: Kolektivne proti kapitálu & Mouvement Commuiste, No. 5, May 2012, p. 19.

Table 4.3 Worker grievances at Maruti Suzuki, Manesar Plant

- Physical and psychological effects associated with producing one car every 45 seconds (increased to one every 60 seconds after the October 2011 sit-down strike).
- The lack of adequate rest time, even for meals or using the toilet.
- A wage structure that allowed up to 50% of monthly pay to be based on variable (and even discretionary) components linked to attendance and productivity. Workers lost approximately 25% of this variable component just for taking a day of sick leave, or any other statutorily guaranteed leave.
- Involuntary unpaid overtime. The workers estimated that, between the overtime work required between shift changes, and for the correction of defects, they performed an average of two hours of uncompensated overtime per day, every year.

Source: People's Union for Democratic Rights (PUDR), *Driving Force*, worker interviews, 2012–13.

creating an exclusionary union comprising permanent employees, demanding that workers declare that they were already members of MUKU, the management-dominated union which had been forced on workers in the Gurgaon facility after the worker sit-in and employer lockout in 2000–01.

In addition to permanent employees, MSEU sought to mobilize workers in all classifications at the Manesar plant, including apprentices, trainees, and contract workers. The workers' demands included employer recognition of their union, elimination of tiered wages and reclassification of informal workers as permanent employees, increased wages, reduction of the speed of work that impinged on wages, and an end to management tyranny. (See Table 4.3 for a list of worker grievances at the MSIL Manesar plant.)

A Sit-down Strike and Employer Lockout

On June 5, 2011, workers began a sit-down strike for the right to form and join their own union. In response MSIL terminated the contracts of all eleven workers who had signed the registration document sent to the JLC. Police surrounded the factory, denying strikers access to food, water, and toilets, and threatened to enter the factory if those eleven workers did not end the strike and leave the plant. The sit-down strike was supported by workers in the Manesar region employed at other industrial facilities. After 13 days, MSIL consented to rehire the eleven workers who had been fired, and promised not to retaliate against those who had taken part in the sit-down strike or the registration of the independent union. But immediately after the strike ended management rescinded these terms and deducted 13 days' pay from worker paychecks, in addition to the 13 days' lost wages arising from the strike. Consequently workers lost a total of 26 days from a strike that was instigated by a management refusal to recognize workers seeking to legally register their union with the state of Haryana.

In April 2011, the MSEU Provisional Committee received notice that the Haryana Labor Department had rejected the application for union registration because the MUKU company union represented workers there, although most permanent workers were not aware of their membership in the union, which excluded informal and contract workers.

The June 2011 sit-down strike, supported by solidarity actions by India's leading unions, led to an uneasy standoff between workers and management, but for the first time in MSIL history the company had been forced to take back workers it had fired.[32] This victory energized the workers and renewed their efforts to form an independent union, but these efforts were thwarted by blatant collusion between state authorities and management. On August 21, 2011, Maruti Suzuki reopened the Manesar auto plant.

Afterwards, MSIL launched a lockout and strikebreaking campaign against the union analogous to its suppression of workers at the first Gurgaon plant in 2000–01, with the continuing support of Gurgaon police. On August 29, 2011, management locked out workers from the plant, demanding they first sign a company statement that they would engage in 'good conduct.' Only 18 workers signed the bond, and MSIL hired replacements, seeking (unsuccessfully) to meet production quotas. In an attempt to drive a wedge between workers, the company announced on a loudspeaker outside the plant that ten workers had signed the good conduct bond. Another 200 workers were transferred from the Gurgaon plant to Manesar, and 150 contractors from outside Haryana State were hired as informal workers. The lockout slowed production for more than a month, as most workers continued to refuse to return to the assembly line under the compulsory conditions imposed by management, transforming a lockout into a daily protest outside the plant.

The 33-day lockout ended on September 30, as workers grudgingly accepted the 'good conduct' bond and the MSIL-dominated MUKU union. A return-to-work agreement forbidding management to retaliate against union activists was signed with the Provisional Committee of MSEU, and this also allowed the participation of the MUKU company union, whose members were among the replacement workers hired during the lockout.

On returning to work on October 3, 2011, workers found that the casual workers who had supported the demonstration and occupations were locked out while some workers remained in the plant. Intent on breaking the fledgling independent union, management had violated the agreement by dismissing all contract workers and discontinuing bus transport to and from the plant. The workers responded by going on strike. This strike continued until October 14, when police entered the plant and shut off the water, the canteen facilities, and the toilets in an effort to evict workers who remained inside. On October 16, after Maruti attempted to restart the facility, the workers began a second occupation after negotiations between management and MSEU workers failed. Maruti Suzuki's response was to dispatch a private security force to disperse workers and community members congregating outside the factory. But workers maintained their unity, and management was compelled to hire back contract workers on October 19, the 17th day of the strike. They refused, however, to reinstate workers seeking to form an independent union.[33]

On October 21, workers returned to the assembly line when management agreed to reinstate all casual workers and 64 full-time workers, and to establish a grievance and labor welfare committee composed of workers' representatives, MSIL, and the Haryana state government. However, MSIL extracted a heavy price for this small concession, forcing the entire union leadership and all active union members to take a 'voluntary retirement settlement' and leave the company.

Labor Activists Renew the Workers Union

In March 2012, union activists in the plant formally registered a new autonomous organization, the Maruti Suzuki Workers Union (MSWU), with the State Labour Department.[34] The new union presented a Charter of Demands calling for equal rights for the contract workers, who comprised more than 75 percent of the workforce but were paid one-quarter of the permanent workers' wages, while receiving no benefits or job security. In response to these demands, MSIL began to plan a counter-offensive; low wages were critical to maintaining and expanding corporate profit-ability. A fact-finding mission organized by the ICLR in May 2013 found that 'management was particularly resistant to discussing the issue of contract workers, asserting that since contract workers were not members of the union, the MSWU could not negotiate on their behalf.'[35] Increasing tension between management and workers at Manesar led to workers refusing to engage in labor–management cooperation and 'team-building' training exercises aimed at increasing production quotas. In July workers actively resisting the assembly line speed-up were suspended.

Employer and Government Sponsored Violence against Workers

On July 18, 2012, after a small altercation between a supervisor and a worker had escalated, a labor-supply firm specializing in supplying 'bouncers' to provoke, threaten, and intimidate workers was brought into the plant. Bouncers dressed as workers moved into the facility during a shift change, and a melee ensued. More than 100 workers and staff were severely injured in the ensuing violence. Parts of the factory were set on fire. Avanish Dev, the human resources manager, who was supportive of the workers' organization, died of asphyxiation and smoke inhalation.[36] Even state police called to the plant were unable to enter the facility for several hours during the rampage. The commissioner of police told the ICLR delegation that to prevent the escalation of hostilities and avert violence the police would seek to intervene in a dispute: 'When we apprehend a breach of peace, we deploy force and take action.' However, official accounts suggest the police waited outside the factory until 7 pm to allow bouncers time to set fire to the facility and beat up workers. According to the MSWU Provisional Committee, there was 'total confusion … no one knew who was who' after most workers departed at the end of their shift without production restarting. Workers leaving the factory were arrested and detained by police.

The Haryana state police closed the plant and registered a first information report (FIR) in which more than 500 workers were named on arrest warrants. The Gurgaon police took this as authority to arrest any shop floor worker they could find who was remotely connected to MSIL, including 91 workers who had not been present in the plant when the incident occurred. MSIL then officially locked out all the workers, reopening the plant more than a month later without addressing any worker demands and concerns.

In the ensuing weeks and months, Haryana state police issued warrants to arrest hundreds of MSIL workers and family members. Many were tortured and accused of premeditated murder, and nearly 150 remained in jail without charges more than three years after the dispute. Police appear to have targeted activists and organizers of MSWU for arrest, including two of the five members of the Provisional Committee.[37] As expected, state police and the labor commissioner held workers accountable for the violence even though some of them were themselves seriously hurt in the incident. As yet the cause of and responsibility for the fire have not been determined.

After the July events, the police, supported by local businesses, significantly expanded their presence by establishing a police station inside the Manesar factory. G. P. Srivastava, a senior advisor to the Associated Chambers of Commerce and Industry of India (ASSOCHAM), acknowledged that industry leaders had been extensively involved in discussions with the state of Haryana regarding the creation of a special industrial security force. However, he insisted that the focus of the 500-strong battalion would be on industrial peace, rather than on criminality.[38]

On August 22, 2012 MSIL announced the mass firing of 546 permanent workers and the summary dismissal of more than 1,800 contract workers, together with plans to ramp up production from 150 vehicles per day to the full capacity of 1,500 vehicles.[39] The CEO, R. C. Bhargava, confirmed that MSIL would not rehire the contract workers, many of whom had sought equal status, with the support of full-timers, although he subsequently announced that these workers would be subjected to a 'test' to assess their competence and qualification to be hired as trainees or permanent workers.[40] Many of them had worked on the production lines for five or six years alongside similarly qualified permanent workers.

The plan to cease use of contract labor seems to have been a tactical ploy to placate established unions. The contract laborers who would lose their jobs had been supported by full-time workers in the effort to end casual work procedures, and in turn had repeatedly supported the full-time workers in their struggle to establish an independent union. As MSIL sought to ramp up to full capacity, it was uncertain whether any other workers at the plant would be rehired. In effect the company seemed to be planning to permanently replace the majority of all its workers, although it anticipated continued worker unrest and anger. For years, MSIL has defied Indian labor law which protects full-time workers by preventing their replacement with casual or skilled contract laborers who are paid a fraction of the prevailing wages for identical work.

As corporate and state authorities were vilifying workers, union activist Rakhi Sehgal summed up the heroic actions of workers seeking an autonomous union:

We must recognize and find the collective will to address issues at the centre of the ongoing dispute between workers and management of Maruti Suzuki – the right to form a union and the right to equal wages and benefits for equal work and an end to discriminatory wage systems and wage theft. These workers have shown the courage to stand up to a powerful corporation and the might of the State. They are not willing to give up their right to form an autonomous union that the management cannot control or dictate to *and* they are unwilling to sell out their casual and contract workers by accepting a settlement that does not apply equally to all workers doing the same work. This is the biggest threat to the extant production system. And management wonders why the backlash is so severe.[41]

MANAGEMENT–LABOR STANDOFF AND STATE REPRESSION

Maruti Suzuki workers were undoubtedly targeted in part as a result of the solidarity they maintained with members of the community. During the 13-day sit-down strike in 2011 workers gained enormous support from friends, family, and others who work in the Gurgaon industrial corridor. The trajectory of the struggle for workers' rights at Maruti Suzuki in Manesar reflects a new stage in a global pattern of employer and state intimidation and violence against workers seeking to organize and form unions to improve abysmal wages and conditions. The assault, which was distorted by MSI, Haryana state officials, and the media, was replayed almost a month later in the violence perpetrated by the South African police who shot and killed 34 miners employed by Lonmin plc, the platinum corporation, which sought to break a strike for improved wages and conditions (see Chapter 6).

India's mainstream press continues to blame workers for the violence. The police for their part acknowledged that not all 2,500 workers were engaged in the violence and that 'only' a few hundred workers participated in what they referred to as a 'riot.' Even with all the uncertainty surrounding the events, workers were hunted down in the ensuing weeks by state police, and official accounts of the recent events changed by the day.

Haryana authorities have supported MSIL efforts to restore the production line by providing a regiment of 500 state police, ostensibly for 'safety' and 'security' in the area. In addition, MSIL has organized a militia of 100 guards to prevent workers from engaging in concerted action. The Gurgaon police issued summonses to all workers served with termination notices requiring their presence in the Manesar police station, then issued threats designed to dissuade them from lodging a challenge to management's illegal dismissal and from 'preventing' their co-workers from returning to work at MSIL.

Haryana police and management representatives also visited fired workers at home, pressuring them to sign resignation letters, in case the government approval for mass terminations, required under the Industrial Disputes Act, 1947, does not come through.

Auto Worker Labor–Community Solidarity

Even after MSIL expelled the union and its supporters, the workers continued to demand their jobs back, together with the right to form an independent union. The MSWU, supported by NTUI, has demanded the release by the courts of those arrested and imprisoned workers, and an end to the torture of union activists by Haryana state prison guards. The corporate lockout and attack on Maruti Suzuki workers has galvanized public interest and become a lightning rod for a broader independent workers' movement in India, with numerous local and regional labor unions and solidarity organizations organizing sustained protests and demonstrations demanding the immediate release of the workers.

Community solidarity exemplified by the development of regional and community factory councils in defense of workers at Maruti Suzuki and other plants in the region has been crucial in opposing MSIL's hegemonic domination over the media, which aimed at fomenting divisions and eroding solidarity through retaliatory lockouts and plant closures. Ameresh Mishra, a political analyst of social movements in India, states that 'in Manesar a new form of class solidarity is emerging .... Before the July 16 assault by MSI, bouncers, and the state, workers had already formed alliances with villagers who lived in Manesar and 10 of 18 Gurgaon districts.'[42] Management called on 500 bouncers to expel workers, but the workers were supported by 5,000 other workers and community members.

Rakhi Sehgal maintained that labor conditions in the Manesar plant were particularly bad, considering that management and the state were targeting activist workers for harsh punishment. Sehgal reported on August 21 that in addition to the imprisoned workers, Haryana State police had warrants for arrest out for 162 employees in the factory. They were 'those workers who have been the backbone of the internal union movement'; workers who had been classified as 'comrades'; who were 'outspoken, unwilling to take management justice lying down' and who had challenged management. It also included 150 'coordinators' who acted as liaison between shop floor workers and the union leadership. Sehgal concluded that 'The major aim of these continuing police raids is to destroy the independent union at the MSIL-Manesar plant and then set up a management controlled union' similar to that at the first plant in Gurgaon. 'They're hoping to destroy MSWU and then rebuild it as they want in the mirror image of the Gurgaon plant union.'[43] Management indeed destroyed the workers union at Maruti, but the labor revolt in the Gurgaon industrial belt has continued as workers seek higher wages, improved conditions, and control over their independent unions.

CONCLUSION: CORPORATE CONTROL AND WORKER SOLIDARITY

The rapid expansion of industrial production on a global basis has placed Indian manufacturing workers at the center of the global labor force. In India, SEZs entice foreign capital to invest in modern installations in duty-free areas with abundant unorganized low-wage labor. The new imperialism of the 21st century depends on expanded direct exploitation of labor in cities like Gurgaon, where poverty and insecurity collide with state repression and violence against workers.

India represents a leading example of neoliberal imperialism, as foreign capital has exploited the country by enriching the upper classes at the expense of the majority of workers and peasants, who are driven increasingly into poverty and destitution. The actions of the Indian state have been decisive for multinational capital and its local agents by facilitating foreign investment in new manufacturing industries, safeguarding foreign investments, and commonly issuing legal rulings against workers and unions fighting for democratic representation at the workplace. Moreover, state police are readily available to intervene on behalf of multinational investors seeking to thwart labor organizations. In India, the state police and the criminal justice system are not impartial intermediaries but partisans in support of corporations against the working class as it seeks equity and humane conditions in the workplace. In addition, the state and capital are seeking to divide workers through the recruitment of young migrant workers, who are regarded as more docile than local workers and less likely to form unions.

Workers in foreign enterprises can only defend their material interests and the stability of their communities by resisting the expansion of production chains that contract services out to lower-waged employees who are part of the expansive reserve army of labor. Recognizing that local competition reproduces exploitation and increases profits for monopoly firms that impose harsh employment regimes, and that Indian businesses promote policies that set permanent and contract laborers against one another, these workers aim to reduce wage competition by forming solidarity unions to equalize and improve conditions for all workers in the production chain. The class struggles at Maruti reveal that newly proletarianized migrant workers gain class consciousness as quickly as veteran workers from the region, and resiliently resist employer domination and persecution.

Workers at Maruti comprehend that employer dependence on informal labor reduces wages for all workers, and recognize that local competition reproduces exploitation as firms compete to lower wages and intensify worker productivity. This also increases profits for monopoly firms that succeed in defeating workers and imposing harsh systems of employment.

4

China: State Capitalism, Foreign Investment, and Worker Insurgency

The application of neoliberal economic reform in China by the Communist Party of China (CPC) over the last 30 years has been viewed as indispensable to modernization and national economic development and growth, a generator of profits for multinational capital, and a source of inexpensive products to consumers primarily in the Global North. Foreign capital has recognized the Chinese model of labor relations, which was capable of suppressing the demands of a seemingly inexhaustible supply of workers, as exemplary for reliable and stable investment. Both supporters and dissenters have regarded the formidable and impenetrable Chinese state as a safeguard against mass strikes and worker insurgencies that could undermine predictable profit margins.

In the 1990s and 2000s foreign investment poured in to China's manufacturing base, particularly in the south-east, where the new proletarian class is composed of migrant laborers from rural areas who have gained power by means of their crucial position in the manufacturing sector that has driven the country's economic growth.[1] The children of migrant laborers, who are now coming of age and working in dense cities in key production zones, notably the Pearl River Delta, are prepared to strike to advance their collective economic rights in factories. The second generation to enter the workforce supports the social protections that free them from the burden of cross-generational economic responsibility. They also benefit greatly from the strict one-child policy in force until 2013, which has eroded the reserve army of labor and significantly increased workers' bargaining power.

This chapter examines worker insurgency since 2010 through a

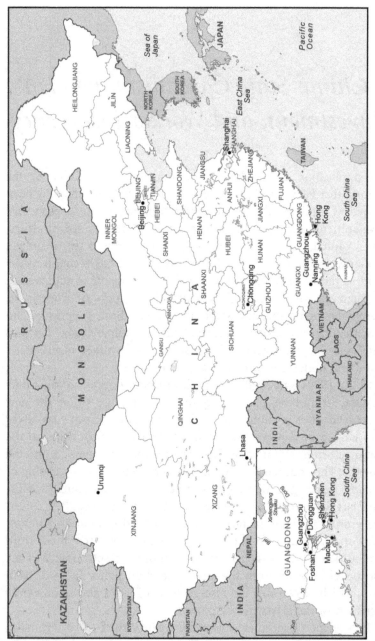

Map 5.1 China, with a focus on the Pearl River Delta

study of the political economy of the Pearl River Delta (PRD) and the massive Taiwanese shoe manufacturer Yue Yuen in Dongguan, in the context of the transforming political economy of China and the growth of rank-and-file militancy among migrant industrial workers employed by contractors for major global multinationals. The Yue Yuen strike suggests that activism among workers in the private manufacturing sector is growing dramatically as laborers expand their struggles beyond local protests that have previously circumscribed the growth of a broader movement of industrial workers.[2] Workers are defending their own rights and challenging the coercive and socially irresponsible conduct of foreign multinationals. While the development of national independent labor organizations in China is blocked by a bureaucratic state and union apparatus, the level of worker mobilization is unprecedented historically, and similar to comparable workers' movements elsewhere in the Global South.

CHINA'S MANUFACTURING EXPORTS IN THE GLOBAL ECONOMY

State-owned industries dominated the Chinese economy during the era of Mao from 1949 to 1976. The manufacturing sector at the start of this period constituted a fraction of the economy, and the vast majority of all workers were rural peasants.

In 1978, when Deng Xiaoping emerged as principal leader, the People's Republic of China was insulated from the world economy. In the 1980s and 1990s, liberalization of the economy inaugurated by Deng was initially directed at streamlining the state sector and privatizing unprofitable enterprises. In the late 1990s, privatization was expanded as the state commenced its thoroughgoing effort to draw foreign direct investment (FDI) from regional investors in Europe, North America, Japan, and the Pacific to build a massive manufacturing sector for export. Foreign multinational investors were attracted by the surplus supply of labor drawn from rural areas to work in new special economic zones (SEZs) abutting major ports in Jiangsu, Shanghai, Zhejiang, and Guangdong provinces, on China's eastern seaboard.

Exports have grown dramatically since implementation of the state owned enterprises (SOE) reform in the 1990s, especially following China's accession into the World Trade Organization (WTO). From 1990 to 1999 exports more than tripled from US$62.3 billion to US$194.9 billion. From 2000 to 2012 exports grew tenfold from US$249.2 billion to US$2,048.8 billion (see Table 5.1). In 2012, exports were dominated by production industries (Table 5.2), with machinery and electronics, textiles and clothing, metals, transportation, chemicals, stone and glass, plastics and rubber, footwear, and wood exports together accounting for US$1.714 trillion of the total (70.8 percent). Machinery and electronics accounted for an overwhelming 42.1 percent of all export products. The country is the major supplier to the world's leading automobile, computer, and diversified athletic and casual footwear brands.

For 20 years from 1995 to 2015 China was the pre-eminent exporter of consumer components and commodities for foreign markets, chiefly the United States, Japan, and Western Europe. The result of this boom in commodities is that China, alone among developing countries in the Third World, is building production and market presence in multiple sectors of the economy, and is less dependent for resources on foreign countries. Nevertheless it faces serious challenges owing to its dependence on foreign markets.

Table 5.1 China exports and imports, 1952–2012 (in US$ billion)

Year	Exports	Imports	Year	Exports	Imports
1952	0.8	1.1	2000	249.2	225.1
1957	1.6	1.5	2005	762.0	660.0
1962	1.5	1.2	2006	968.9	791.5
1970	2.3	2.3	2007	1,220.1	956.1
1975	7.3	7.5	2008	1,430.7	1,132.6
1978	9.8	10.9	2009	1,201.6	1,005.6
1980	18.1	20.0	2010	1,577.8	1,396.0
1985	27.4	42.3	2011	1,898.4	143.4
1990	62.3	53.4	2012	2,048.8	1,818.2
1995	148.8	132.1			

Sources: Derived from *China Statistical Yearbooks*, Beijing: China Statistics Press, National Bureau of Statistics of China, 2000–13; World Bank, *World Integrated Trade Solution*, Washington DC: World Bank.

Table 5.2 China exports by product category, 2012

Category	Value US$ billion	Percentage of exports
Machinery and electronics	862,367	42.09
Textiles and clothing	246,094	12.01
Metals	149,073	7.28
Transportation	108,351	5.29
Chemicals	94,351	4.61
Stone and glass	85,164	4.16
Plastics and rubber	77,605	3.79
Footwear	58,812	2.87
Wood	32,453	1.58
Hides and skins	31,739	1.55
Fuels	31,108	1.51
Food products	27,418	1.34
Vegetable	18,247	0.89
Animal	15,478	0.76
Minerals	3,815	0.19
Miscellaneous	206,766	10.09

Sources: *China Statistical Yearbook 2012*, Beijing: China Statistics Press, National Bureau of Statistics of China; World Bank, *World Integrated Trade Solution*, Washington DC: World Bank.

Political economist Sean Starrs notes that while China's economic growth is expanding dramatically, capital and wealth continues to concentrate in the United States and Western Europe and the patterns of imperial domination established in the postwar era remain, with the United States dominating the world's major economic sectors:

American companies have the leading profit-shares among the world's top 2,000 firms in eighteen of twenty-five sectors, and a dominant position in ten – especially those at the technological frontier. In a reflection of this global hegemony, two-fifths of the world's millionaire households are American.[3]

According to Starrs, to get a sense of where economic power is really concentrated it is essential to study the world's top corporations. The exception is China, which Starr maintains 'is the only country that has been described as a serious contender to join the advanced capitalist world.'[4] In this respect, overdependence on one sector of the economy presents risks to future growth. China rises above all others in its diversification:

> While some emerging markets now have a presence in the branches of the economy not linked to raw materials, none can boast China's sectoral diversity. Yet even the PRC lacks a substantial presence in a number of key areas, some of which are already dominated by foreign firms in the country itself. ... Those with diversified political economies will have the best chance of escaping this slowdown. China is by far the most likely contender, yet faces significant challenges of its own. The leading role of US capital in the global economy is thus likely to endure for some time to come.[5]

GUANGDONG PROVINCE AND THE PEARL RIVER DELTA

While manufacturing is dependent on the availability of a large supply of low-wage labor and low production costs, foreign capital has concentrated investment in plants surrounding geographic regions on China's east coast. In 2012, three of the four busiest ports in the world were in China: Shanghai, Hong Kong, and Shenzhen.[6] Shanghai, located in East Central China on the Yangtze River delta, is the busiest container port in the world, and is surrounded by Jiangsu and Zhejiang provinces. The sprawling ports of Hong Kong and Shenzhen are both strategically situated – the Hong Kong Special Administrative Region is on the south-east coast of the Pearl River estuary, and Shenzhen on the South China Sea is adjacent to Guangdong Province, the largest manufacturing center in the country (see Map 5.1).

While capital investment almost always flows to the lowest-cost producers, finance also is directed to regions with a geographic advantage which facilitates the transport of exports and imports. European trade with China has clustered in the vicinity of major deep-water ports ever since the 19th century, when the British East India Company sought to legalize and extend the opium trade to the country's interior in exchange for silver, silk, porcelain, and tea. Following the Opium Wars of the 19th century, the British colonial enterprise survived from 1841 to 1997 as a manufacturing hub and center for foreign trade, as the eastern port cities continued to retain a crucial role in the easy transportation of goods that are produced in the region. The Chinese Revolution merely interrupted the colonial system of extraction that relied on east coast port cities to ship products abroad. This pattern has returned in the 1980s, as internal migration has concentrated around the port cities rather than the interior. Thus while ports are an indisputable advantage which may safeguard production industries from disinvestment, they are also an impediment to the relocation of manufacturing to the interior.

The PRD contains China's highest concentration of manufacturing and exports. It is an economic zone situated at the geographic center of Guangdong Province on the South China Sea. Guangdong Province is the largest in China, and its gross national product (GNP) exceeds that of any other province. The zone encompasses nine major population centers surrounding Hong Kong. Together the PRD's nine major cities of Guangzhou, Shenzhen, Dongguan, Foshan, Huizhou, Jiangmen, Zhaoqing, Zhongshan, and Zhuhai form a megacity of 57.9 million people.

In 1979 Shenzhen, originally a small village just north of Hong Kong, was incorporated as a city, and a year later it was established as the region's first SEZ, where low wages and few government regulations attracted Western multinationals and billions in foreign capital investment. Steadily the Shenzhen SEZ expanded its operations from toys, plastics, and other labor-intensive consumer goods into high-technology electronic, computer, and telecommunications components. In the early 1990s, as the Hong Kong economy transitioned from manufacturing to finance and commerce, FDI further developed and expanded industrial production in the PRD.

In just 30 years Shenzhen and SEZs in Guangdong Province have become models that have been emulated in other parts of China and the developing world, a place where low wages and few restrictions on business would produce goods for the world market at the lowest price and with the highest profit margins.[7] From the late 1990s through the 2000s, low-cost production pressed forward the dramatic growth of heavy industry and high-technology goods for the export market, especially electronic equipment and machinery, chemical products, auto parts, shoes and footwear, lighting fixtures, and furniture. Hong Kong's position as a major global investment center stimulated the regional growth of manufacturing for export in the PRD. In just over a decade from 2000 to 2012 private exports in the PRD grew from $4.1 billion to $166 billion annually.[8] By 2012 the region had attracted US$21.5 trillion in FDI.

STATE CAPITALISM AND THE RISE OF THE NEW WORKING CLASS

China's rapid expansion as the world's largest commodities exporter is a consequence of the state's legacy of bureaucratic control predicated on the restriction of political and economic competitors to the CPC and its affiliated organizations. The one-party state is a vestige of a colonial history that failed to prevent imperial powers from wholesale exploitation of national wealth. Reopening the economy to foreign economic and financial penetration requires a strong state to restrain foreign control over the economy. While social control was an overriding concern, state officials retained an enduring and plausible uneasiness that domestic social unrest was advanced by foreign imperialists seeking to destabilize and undermine national sovereignty. The challenge was how to control capitalist development and modernization. The system that emerged was a form of state capitalism that combined foreign investment and state control.

By the early 2010s, even after the global financial crisis of 2008, labor shortages were emerging. Emboldened Chinese workers were escalating demands for improved wages, benefits, working conditions, and housing, since China's one-child policy had significantly reduced the labor supply without a concomitant increase in wages. By 2000 the idea of job loss was not intimidating to younger workers in possession of industrial skills, for whom the option of quitting and looking for a new job was pervasive. At the same time, older workers carrying seniority felt deserving of respect and loyalty from their managers, who represented contractors producing for multinational corporations.[9] The closure of state enterprises which triggered the growth of mass unemployment in state-sector enterprises in the late 1990s, inciting demands for worker control and self-organization within factories threatened by restructuring and closure.[10]

Three principal dynamics in China's political economy are driving the crystallization of a working class:

- a decline in the dominance of state-sector firms through restructuring and privatization
- a rise in the private-sector workforce composed of migrant laborers from rural regions
- a decline in the reserve army of labor amid growing worker demands.

According to labor activist and scholar Au Loong Yu:

[S]ince the mid-1990s, a new working class, composed of 250 million rural migrants, was formed. At the beginning, this was a large army of migrant workers with no knowledge of their rights. Local government officials deliberately kept them in the dark and shamelessly sided with the capitalists in denying their rights. Coming from rural areas, they could only passively adapt to the barrack-like factory regime, and since they did not have a high self-esteem or high expectations, the absolute majority of them adapted well to the system.[11]

Chinese working-class resistance takes the form of spontaneous single-factory struggles. Strikes and worker resistance are extensive but inchoate and dispersed, because of workers' inability to build national, regional, and community-based organizations. The protests arise typically in response to management failure to pay expected wages and benefits. From the mid-1990s to 2005 workers have filed a number of legal protests against management. A significant shift has taken place since the passage of the Labour Contract Law of 2008. The new laws have emboldened formerly timid workers to engage in direct resistance against management through strikes and public protests. From 2008 to 2014 the number of strikes has increased extensively, particularly in strategic adjuncts to the export industries.

During the transition to state capitalism, labor law protections have been largely unenforced by the Chinese government. The primary reason for this, according to sociologist Ching Kwan Lee, is the devolution of fiscal authority and welfare responsibility from the federal government to the local level, including to factory plant managers who lack the capacity to represent workers. In *Against the Law*, published in 2007, Lee argues that the Chinese government has shifted the terrain of all class conflict from the central state to restricted 'cellular' sites on the local level, with legal accountability removed from the national government and imposed on municipalities.[12] In addition organizational action is constrained by the CPC's prohibition of new independent associations.

Over the last two decades, the focus of protests has shifted from SOEs in the public sector to foreign-owned multinationals which have invested in the country's massive production industries. Conflict has shifted from rural areas to urban regions, primarily in the southeastern industrial belts. In Guangdong a new generation of Chinese workers exercising greater levels of activism has emerged, potentially expanding the scope of conflict from the workplace to opposition to the practices of foreign capital. The power of workers in Guangdong is strengthened by the formation of stronger links to their communities and also, as elsewhere in industrial China, by a labor shortage stemming from the one-child policy. Veteran workers in the region have asserted their seniority rights, and younger workers are defying employers who are unable to pressure workers by threatening layoffs.

China's local dispute-resolution system restricts the type and scope of labor protest but not necessarily their intensity. However, the positioning of factories by foreign capital in multiple regional locations also expands the magnitude of worker protests and rebellions beyond the plant and municipal level. They can disrupt production on a regional scale, as is increasingly the case in the strategic export promotion zones (EPZs) which attract foreign capital by eliminating regulations and reducing taxation. These regions in China are called SEZs.

In capitalist economies, national industrial union movements have almost always formed corporatist and neo-corporatist representational arrangements that restrict the self-activity of workers in individual factories and communities, and severely demarcate the conditions under which workers can protest and strike.[13] In China, however, because of the dominance of the All-China Federation of Trade Unions (ACFTU), other large independent unions recognized by the state and capital have not formed. Tim Pringle argues that worker self-activity and protest has increased the significance of the ACFTU as an institutional force in China, pushing the CPC to enact labor law reform from 2005 to the present.

Ironically, while most labor advocates and non-governmental organizations (NGOs) advocate and support the formation of independent unions recognized by the state, like those in the West, all the evidence demonstrates that Chinese workers may in fact have greater power through direct action without the existence of the restrictive labor laws that inevitably accompany recognition of Western-style unions. The form of labor protest emerging in China will in fact challenge the state-capitalist dominated state that tolerates worker self-organization in factories without the formation of an independent union or political party. Similarly to the Council Communists in Weimar Germany, Chinese workers' power is growing in the absence of a strong national union that determines when members may file grievances, and walk off the job.

While NGOs help educate workers about labor law and occupational safety and health, the organization of the Chinese working class will not arise through the assertion of Western concepts of what is good for them, but through their own self-activity reflecting actual experiences in their workplaces and communities.

MIGRANT LABOR, PROLETARIANIZATION, AND THE *HUKOU* SYSTEM

Modern migration in the PRC was fundamental to the expansion of a reserve army of labor in key commodity sectors, and has been the principal force in advancing export growth and national capitalist growth. In 1958, almost a decade after the Chinese Revolution, the PRC implemented the *hukou* system of migration control to regulate the movement of population from rural to urban areas. The *hukou* laws, requiring individuals and families to register, increased the burden on rural workers from 1978 onwards, as the shift to state capitalism forced millions of peasants to work as laborers in urban areas, especially the booming SEZs. At the outset, the restriction of residential rights for internal migrants allowed manufacturers to intensify labor exploitation by threatening them with deportation back to the countryside.

While urban labor migration has been crucial to China's plan to encourage foreign investment in mass production for export, the *hukou* migration laws were not immediately reformed to confer residential and equal work rights on the rural newcomers, who now comprise a majority of the national workforce. Women who were employed in the garment and the electronics sectors, for example, comprised a majority of China's new industrial workforce but had no rights to health care, housing, and education in urban areas.[14] Workers who were issued temporary permits to work for contractors in these sectors resided in overcrowded dormitories and dilapidated urban housing in the vicinity of the factories, and were expected to return to their rural homes upon completion of their work. As the economy of rural areas deteriorated, other peasants were forced to migrate to the cities without registration, and worked in the informal sector where wages were lower and working conditions were even more dangerous. However after working for more than ten years in burgeoning cities on the Eastern seaboard, the majority of migrant workers had established families and communities and, like urban migrants in other regions and eras, returning to the rural areas as peasants is no longer a feasible option.

Since the 1990s the migrant workers who have been indispensable to China's economic expansion as an industrial power have been appealing to the government to regularize their status in cities. Following growing labor unrest, the government passed a series of labor and residency laws expanding rights and protections to migrant and contract workers, and decentralizing power to the municipal level. However, as protests escalated among migrant workers in the early 2000s, the Chinese state feared that granting a semblance of permanency would stoke demands for higher wages and benefits, and create higher levels of labor protests and strikes. According to China labor researcher Tim Pringle, for China, as for most countries, migrant workers place the state and foreign capital in a predicament:

As most of these people end up working in the private sector, the numbers actually working in private or foreign-invested industry are much larger. Underpinning these transformations has been the reserve army of unemployed so familiar to capitalist economies. From both political and economic perspectives, management of the numbers was of crucial importance to the Party. One the one hand, capital required a pool of unemployed workers to maintain a downward pressure on wages. On the other hand, the state could not allow the reserve army numbers to climb too high and risk nationwide social unrest. We can see clearly here the importance of phased redundancy ... and the *hukou* regulations in terms of managing the political perils that came with economic reform.[15]

Pringle challenges dominant perspectives that the ACFTU dominates and restricts all activity among docile and passive victims of an authoritarian state. Rather, formal trade union activity 'does not equate to the absence of tactical divergence with regard to workers' rights and interests,' especially in view of the expansion of worker power at the factory and local level.[16] The evidence suggests that the expansion of rights for migrant workers, itself a response to worker militancy, has activated further militancy since 2010. According to Pringle the power of urban workers reflects the systemic labor shortage and a growing responsiveness of local government to workers' proclivity to protest in order to improve wages and conditions. Moreover the analysis of the most recent direct action and strikes suggests that workers benefit from the presence of a remote central labor union that does not control conditions on the shop floor.

MIGRANT WORKERS' PENSION SHORTFALL

In 2014, China had the world's largest urban population, of 758 million, and this is projected to expand by 292 million to 1.05 billion by 2050 (see Figure 5.1). The vast majority of this growth is a result of continued migration from rural areas, since the country's one-child policy, only recently relaxed, will limit natural population growth. From 2012 to 2013 migrant urban workers increased

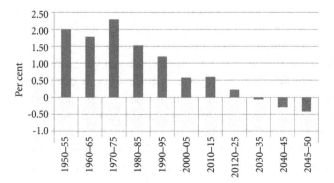

Figure 5.1 Actual and projected average annual rate of change of China's population, 1950–2015

Source: UN Department of Economic and Social Affairs, Population Division, *World Urbanization Prospects: The 2014 Revision*, CD-ROM edition (2014).

by 2.4 percent to 268.94 million.[17] As China urbanizes, the national population growth rate has contracted from 2.3 percent annually in 1970–75 to 0.61 percent in 2010–15. In the next decade the rate of population growth is projected to level off, and the population will actually decline by an annual rate of 0.42 per cent in 2045–50.

In the period 2010–15 the first generation of urban migrant laborers is approaching retirement age, and is therefore more dependent on employer–employee contributions to social security, which were made a requirement following the passage of the Labour Contract Law in 2008. Many workers who migrated to industrial zones from 1980 to 2000 were not eligible for standardized pensions equivalent to those of urban residents before the passage of the 2008 law. But since 2008, some private employers have neglected to make adequate contributions to retirement accounts in line with the new regulations, so many of their employees will not have sufficient pension plans to meet their costs when they retire. These irregularities, and the growing workers' movement, have motivated the Chinese authorities to crack down on employers who neglected to adhere to the new laws. Yue Yuen was among the largest violators of the pension law.

Despite the expansion of the labor law's requirements in 2008,

Yue Yuen, which prides itself on its corporate social responsibility record, has not paid its share of social security and housing funds to workers. According to Liu Kaiming of the Institute of Contemporary Observation in Shenzhen, 70 percent of employers do not provide social security for migrant workers. Many will not be able to survive in the city without pensions.[18] Social security payments are dependent on employers accurately reporting and making payments to local governments on the basis of the time served in each plant.[19] Workers can receive social security payments after 15 years of service. According to Rena Lau, younger workers have joined strikes in recognition of the importance of these payments in maintaining family living standards for parents and children.[20]

YOUTH WORKERS AND LABOR SHORTAGES

The underpayment of retirement benefits is generating a new wave of factory protests comparable to the worker protests following the restructuring of SOEs from the late 1990s to the early 2000s. However, for the younger generation, employment security is becoming more important. Foreign investors are especially troubled by the rise in worker militancy among young workers, as reported in the *Financial Times*:

> The potential for unrest is only increasing. Chinese employees have been emboldened by demographic trends that are creating labour shortages – especially for skilled positions – and tilting negotiating power decisively in their favour. Since peaking in 2011, the working-age population has declined by 5.9m. Although minimum wages are rising at double-digit rates, workers say that they are not keeping pace with soaring living costs.[21]

In addition to the significance of young workers to China's labor force, the population of China is urbanizing even more quickly than corresponding countries in the Global South, a trend that is expected to continue from 2015 to 2050 (Figure 5.2). From 1950 to 1955 China's urban dwellers comprised 11.8 percent of the

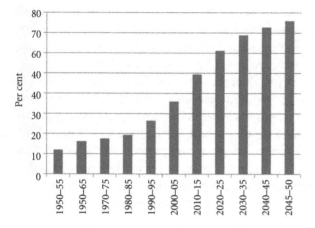

Figure 5.2 Percentage of population residing in urban areas in China, by major area, five-year averages based on mid-year figures, 1950–2050

Data source: UN Department of Economic and Social Affairs, Population Division (2014) *World Urbanization Prospects: The 2014 Revision*, CD-ROM edn.

country's population, compared with 17 percent in India. In 2015 half of China's population resides in urban areas compared with 31.1 percent of India's population. By 2050 more than 75 percent of China's population will live in urban areas compared with a projected 50.3 percent in India. This urbanization has arisen because of the enormous increase in demand for labor by private enterprises in urban areas manufacturing for global export (Figure 5.3).

At a time when younger workers are unable to obtain highly paid secure jobs, Chinese manufacturers are seeking to attract them to work in factories at lower wages than first-generation migrant workers, who are demanding higher wages and social security payments. But younger workers, who often have greater levels of training and skills than their parents' generation, are objecting to low pay in factories by showing less loyalty to contractors. According to May Wong, a labor expert with the Hong-Kong based NGO Globalization Monitor:

The younger generation of workers has no connection to the countryside as they never worked on the farm and were too

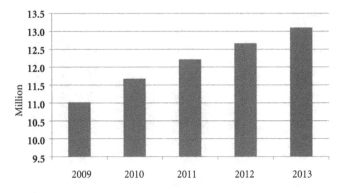

Figure 5.3 Employment growth in urban areas of China, 2009–13

Data source: Statistical Communiqué of the People's Republic of China on the 2013 National Economic and Social Development, National Bureau of Statistics of China, February 24, 2014.

young to remember their parents or grandparents migrating to the cities. They want to come to the cities and work in factories. The concept of being a worker has changed completely. On my visit to the factory I met with managers. They all complained that the younger generation doesn't give a shit about job stability. They suddenly go away. ... At one electrical factory managers say that young workers will go on leave and then resign if they are not granted the rights. If their demands are not met they will go on strike. They think they are young and don't have burdens of caring for their parents and family.[22]

ACFTU AND THE CHINESE LABOR MOVEMENT

The ACFTU, China's national labor federation (or labor center), is directly affiliated to the CPC. Founded in 1925 in Guangzhou, the ACFTU emerged as the only authorized national labor federation following the Chinese Revolution of 1949 under the People's Republic of China,[23] a function that it has held without interruption to this day.[24] In the Mao Zedong era from 1949 to 1978 its role was largely superfluous because safeguards were provided by the Communist state, but its importance has increased considerably since 1978 as

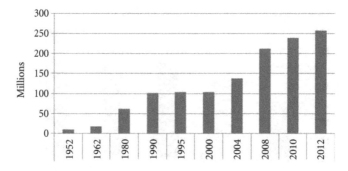

Figure 5.4 ACFTU membership 1952–2012

Data source: David Meltcalf, Jianwei Li, and Qi Dongtao, 'Progress and dilemmas of Chinese trade unions,' *East Asian Policy,* Vol. 2, No. 3 (July/Sep. 2010), pp.14–21, www.eai.nus.edu. sg/vol2no3_QiDongtau.pdf (accessed August 14, 2014).

the Chinese government has transitioned from a state-controlled to a market-dominated economy.

In the first two decades following the Chinese Revolution, ACFTU union membership was mainly limited to urban workers in state-owned enterprises. The unionized working class experienced dramatic growth in wages and improved working conditions during these years. From 1980 to 1990 ACFTU membership increased considerably, from about 60 million to more than 100 million workers. However, from the 1990s, with tens of millions of migrants moving to urban areas to work in private industry, membership leveled off and then was reduced to 100 million because of the retrenchment of SOEs, and the union's indifference and even antagonism to the organization of the industrial working class employed primarily in foreign-dominated private industries. But growing concern over the rise in working-class militancy and public protests among migrant laborers employed in these firms prompted the CPC leadership to compel the ACFTU to admit more than 150 million new members in little over one decade. From 2000 to 2012 ACFTU membership increased from just over 103 million to 258 million (Figure 5.4). By 2007, workers employed in foreign enterprises constituted 80 percent of all new union members.

The reform and liberalization of the economy in the post-Mao era introduced private ownership of the means of production, which eroded the standard of living and protections among workers employed in these firms. Chinese government officials at various levels encouraged capitalist exploitation, and many became private owners who benefited from the imposition of a market economy. Until the restructuring of SOEs, the ACFTU as the official trade union was not expected to challenge government policies, because of the legacy of the Chinese state's socialist ownership of the means of production. In the era of Mao, the working class enjoyed relatively high social status, together with a whole range of welfare provisions including free housing, free education, free medical care, and full employment, as well as very good retirement benefits, all of which meant that the ACFTU was inexperienced in addressing labor–management conflict. Since the initiation of economic reforms in 1979, the ACFTU claims to have maintained a proactive organizational and political commitment and responsibility for enforcing member rights within enterprises, and supporting legislation that defends and expands labor rights on a municipal and national level.

Between 1997 and 2002, the ACFTU was compelled to respond to the restructuring and privatization of small and medium-sized SOEs, which led to retrenchment and unemployment affecting 30 million public-sector employees, and the expansion of protests among its members. For its part, the Chinese government has become more responsive, passing labor legislation to protect contract workers and pressuring ACFTU branches to recruit new members and represent them in grievance procedures. Consequently, the institutional importance of the ACFTU as a trade union federation has vastly increased, especially through the integration into the federation of workers in export industries in south and south-east China. While tens of millions of workers have been recruited, most ACFTU local branches do not function as active local organizations, and generally only react to the mobilization of rank and file members when they disrupt production.

Workers in China view ACFTU as they do most established unions. Many existing unions formed in the West have defended capital and their own bureaucratic interests by exercising jurisdictional control over industrial sectors, which prevents competing unions from recruiting workers and prevents rank-and-file workers from forming independent unions. Thus opposition to ACFTU and other established unions in South Africa, India, and elsewhere is just as complicated (see Chapters 4 and 6). Certainly the state's support for foreign capital is at least as extensive as it is in India and South Africa, and maybe more so, depending on the sector. Some labor laws are effective, some not; their effectiveness depends on the ability of workers to ensure that existing labor laws are enforced.

In the West, unions constitute legal instruments to advance worker struggles rather than reflecting the class interests of a mobilized working class. Similarly, the ACFTU acts as an outside force that is also loyal to capital and the state. The recent wave of activism in China reveals that Chinese workers obtain concessions from management similarly to unions in the West, where there is also typically only one union in each industrial jurisdiction. But it is also true that unions in a competitive electoral arena become bureaucratic organizations that seek to exclude all forms of representation that are perceived as eroding the power and control of their leadership. The possibility of the formation of competitive workers' organizations exists, but it is a remote one given the domination of one-partyism within trade unions themselves. Most existing union models throughout the world do not want competition from independent unions, so why should the ACFTU? Labor unions in liberal democracies that fail to represent members' interests are thus a poor model for the Chinese working class.

ACFTU REPRESENTATION OF WORKERS IN THE EXPORT SECTOR

Critics charge that the ACFTU is not a genuine union federation that works in opposition to management. If the ACFTU had been a real union, they argue, foreign investors and multinationals dependent on low-wage production would have resisted the unionization of export-sector industries. An ACFTU memorandum in 2007 on the unionization of eleven Walmart department stores, for example, stipulates the importance of union–management collaboration.[25] Moreover, the unionization is based on a tripartite system including management and ACFTU officials, as well as workers in the stores. Union recognition and bargaining agreements are advanced without employer campaigns of intimidation.

The government's newfound interest in organizing and integrating migrant workers is regarded as a direct consequence of the mass migration of rural inhabitants to urban industrial areas to work in export industries that are central to national development. Migrant workers are considered by the ACFTU as a 'new type of labor force' that 'have become an important component part of the Chinese working class.' Thus the ACFTU has affirmed that the unionization of migrant workers is essential, and asserted that it has 'made every effort to absorb migrant workers as members'. According to the ACFTU, the organization of migrant workers would come about through agreements forged between trade union leaders and employers together with the negotiation of collective bargaining agreements without the participation of workers. Certainly, the Chinese application of labor relations is on the whole borrowed from the Western model of trade union representation, whereby union officials negotiate as third parties with employers without the active involvement of members.[26]

The ACFTU claims to have institutionalized practices to serve the immediate and long-term interests of migrant workers working in foreign-owned enterprises in all facets of their work and lives, including:

- collective bargaining in enterprises and industries
- establishing a grievance system to recoup unpaid wages
- rules of employer conduct: paying workers on time and in full, including social insurance
- social insurance and emergency financial support
- improving working conditions and health and safety
- worker training programs and employment agencies for jobless workers
- 'good study and entertainment environment to accommodate their spiritual and cultural needs'
- granting migrant worker legal rights and assistance in their communities ('democratic and political rights').

From the early 2000s to the present the ACFTU has reached recognition and collective bargaining agreements with the vast majority of foreign-dominated firms and contractors to absorb these new urban workers into the union. The ACFTU today is a national organization composed of 31 regional federations of labor and 10 industrial unions that set policies across major sectors of the private and state economy. The federation's day-to-day representation of workers is carried out at a local level through provincial, city, county, district, and workplace-based committees and unions, which set policy, negotiate, and file grievances on behalf of members.

The administrative structure of the modern ACFTU channels worker organization and confines worker mobilization to the plant and community level. Thus, potentially far-reaching national and industrial disputes that could challenge national legitimacy are continuously transferred for resolution to the shop floor on the local level, where conflicts are resolved superficially in a way that does not apply to workers in other locations. By implication local forms of worker representation are thus able to circumvent the likelihood of national and industry-level worker militancy. However, the local dispute-resolution system also intensifies the number of discrete conflicts through the multiplication of isolated worker protests and strikes across disconnected firms, shop floors, and communities. While the ACFTU's system of conflict resolution may deflect national conflict, it also contributes to greater inventiveness by workers in trying to defend their rights. Workers are permitted to form grassroots unions (or rank and file committees) on an individual-firm basis as long as they do not form committees or organizations that are separate from or autonomous of the ACFTU and the CPC. In most cases grassroots unions are controlled by the ACFTU. However during periods of protest and unrest, rank and file workers mobilize on a case-by-case basis.

The standard critique of the ACFTU is that it does not allow independent unions and thus does not represent workers. The International Trade Union Confederation (ITUC), the major global federation of workers, does not accord the ACFTU any standing as an independent trade union, since the ACFTU operates as an appendage of the CPC and blocks the formation of independent unions.[27] Yet the structure and operation of the ACFTU is not too different from bureaucratic trade unions that are detached from their members and that represent the vast majority of workers throughout the world. In each case the formation of competing or independent workers' organizations on a national, regional, and shop-floor level is relentlessly thwarted by existing unions.

Some scholars have viewed the ACFTU as an impediment to advancing worker rights, as it serves as a facade suggesting the presence of a functioning trade unionism, and thus diverts condemnation of the government and foreign multinationals. ACFTU allowed the state and foreign capital to maintain an appearance of worker rights primarily to reassure foreigners and as a means to counter critics of foreign capital investors. Thus the period from 2000 to 2007 is crucial because Chinese working-class militancy expanded dramatically at that time. As Metcalf and Li maintain:

> In reality although Chinese unions do have many members they are virtually impotent when it comes to representing workers. Because the Party-state recognises that such frailty may lead to instability it has passed new laws promoting collective contracts and established new tripartite institutions to mediate and arbitrate disputes. While such laws are welcome they are largely hollow: collective contracts are very different from collective bargaining and the incidence of cases dealt with by the tripartite institutions is tiny.[28]

In their study of the SEZ in Hainan Province during 2004 and 2005, Metcalf and Li were told that 'the union is only for show ... irrelevant,' and that collective contracts with employers were imposed by management and the ACFTU without negotiation, and served to advance profits rather than substantially protecting workers. To defend worker rights, the authors argued that independent unions would have to emerge in these EPZs, that accepted the conflicting interests between labor and capital, and permitted workers to engage in collective action and the right to strike to defend their interests.

The CPC's prohibition of independent organizations inhibits the capacity of workers to convert the waves of self-activity and militancy into enduring and disciplined unions even on a plant level. Conversely, the lack of interest shown by the ACFTU in representing its members in disputes with employers allows workers to engage in unique repertoires of struggle through recurring rank-and-file action, and at least the potential for maintaining a lasting parallel union structure.

As export industries have expanded, labor disputes over wages and benefits have proliferated throughout new manufacturing industries in the export production centers around the SEZs. From 1995 to 2006 official labor disputes increased 12-fold from 33,030 to 447,000 per year.[29] The expansion of worker militancy in the SEZs has prompted the ACFTU to recruit workers into unions in foreign enterprises. In the five years from 2003 to 2008 the proportion of foreign enterprises employing ACFTU members increased from 33 percent to 80 percent. In an effort to circumvent mass worker unrest, the CPC and ACFTU have drafted national provincial laws and regulations protecting workers employed in multinational firms, culminating in the Labour Contract Law of 2008, which among other provisions gave official rights to workers employed by private and foreign contractors on behalf of multinational corporations. The union also formed legal service centers to represent workers in disputes with management, which won 85 percent of cases filed in 2008–09.[30]

THE FIRST WAVE OF LABOR PROTESTS, 1997–2002

From 1997 to 2002, the first wave of worker activism against Chinese state capitalism appeared, primarily in the form of spontaneous wildcat strikes in opposition to the industrial restructuring of the SOEs and growing demands among migrant industrial workers to expand their rights as contract laborers in EPZs.[31] In response the ACFTU rapidly recruited millions of members into the federation, even if it did not have the capacity or will to represent and defend worker rights on the local level.

The most prominent worker protests in the SOE sector occurred in response to factory closures in the PRC's production hub in the north-east. In March 2002, spontaneous street demonstrations broke out among several thousand Ferro Alloy workers in Liaoning Province against the bankruptcy of the factory. Over a period of several weeks the numbers taking part in street demonstrations swelled to 30,000 workers. Police arrested the organizers of the protests in April 2002.[32] Simultaneously, 50,000 petroleum workers protested against the wave of layoffs and retrenchment by the Daqing Petroleum Administration, where between 1999 and 2002, 86,000 out of a total of 260,000 workers were dismissed as a result of government cutbacks.[33] While the protests were viewed as isolated and spontaneous, they formed a pattern of mass unrest in response to government cutbacks in China's older basic industries. The ACFTU was caught off guard, conspicuously absent from both protests organized by rank-and-file workers and those organized by community activists. Following the wave of protests by workers, the ACFTU initiated efforts to provide a patina of legitimacy to the market reforms, as the state was actively pursuing privatization and promoting foreign direct trade in new industries in the east and south-east.

The challenge for the CPC and ACFTU was to manage and control the unavoidable grievances and protests arising from liberalization, which presented serious challenges to the government among retrenched workers with established rights who were accustomed to stable jobs in SOEs, as well as among migrant workers from rural areas with few rights who were making new demands for living wages and improved working conditions. In 2002, ACFTU chairman Wei Jianxing publicly recognized the challenge:

The problems at the moment are: on the one hand, following the structural adjustments and the restructuring of SOEs and collectively-owned enterprises (COEs), a considerable number of trade union organisations [and branches] have collapsed and their members washed away. On the other hand, the organisation of trade unions in newly-established enterprises has simply not happened. ... When there is not even a trade union, what is the point of talking about trade unions upholding the legal rights of workers? Or trade unions being the transmission belt between the party and the masses?[34]

This realization quickly led the state to initiate a process of codifying trade union laws that enumerated the rights of workers, and also to assert the uncontested domination of the ACFTU. In 2001 the Trade Union Law had affirmed the ACFTU as the only mandated legal trade union representative of workers across industries, and its position as an arm of the government capable of advancing the interests of the working class. Fear of the formation of an independent radical labor movement stirred the CPC and ACFTU to take pre-emptive action to recruit migrant workers employed in the burgeoning EPZs. In the late 1990s the ACFTU had already embarked on a sweeping policy to formally represent workers in the only national union recognized by the government.[35] But even as the ACFTU conveyed trepidation about foreign influence, the union also sought recognition and approval from these same labor bodies. Yet in 2001 the ACFTU also openly disparaged what it called the endless meddling and hypocritical criticism of the 'international trade union movement.'[36]

THE 2008 LABOUR CONTRACT LAW

The Labour Contract Law of 2008 was heralded by the CPC and foreign observers as a major step in expanding labour rights, achieved by codifying employer obligations and stipulating the rights and protections of the workers.[37] The culmination of direct engagement with contract labour workers, it was amended three times in response to public comments and suggestions solicited through a government website before its passage at the National People's Congress in June 2007 and implementation on January 1, 2008.[38]

The 2008 law was primarily directed at formalizing the rights of contract workers employed by foreign multinationals, standardizing wages and benefits, and abolishing arbitrary management practices. To address the lack of rights for migrant workers it introduced the following provisions:

- written labor contracts
- limits on the use of temporary and short-term contracts and rights for long-term workers employed for a minimum of ten years
- rights for workers approaching retirement age
- support for collective bargaining rights governing wages, occupa-

tional safety and hygiene, and protection of the rights of women workers
• limits on part-time work, including outsourcing, and overtime.

The passage of the law noticeably expanded the awareness of worker rights among employees in the export production sectors, and activated direct action against contractors, primarily through grievances directed at municipal government authorities. The ACFTU was organizationally unprepared for the scale and intensity of these direct worker actions, and since it is slow to respond, workers are able to organize larger and more costly mass walkouts and strikes. In this way, without recourse to a union, workers in China's export production industry are successfully defending and advancing their rights more effectively than their counterparts in traditional trade unions. Where management does not respond to demands promptly, independent rank-and-file workers have mobilized on the shop floor and in their communities through strikes and public protest.

The Labour Contract Law increased scrutiny among urban migrant workers of wages, benefits, and working conditions, increasing rank-and-file claims against employers in strategic export industries. From 2010 to 2014 protests and strikes expanded at the premises of Chinese contractors involved in the production of clothing, electronics, and automotive brands. In 2010, 14 workers committed suicide at Foxconn, a leading Taiwanese components producer in China for the global IT industry. The suicides were accompanied by protests and strikes by workers in response to low pay, abusive treatment, poor working conditions, the housing of migrant workers in decrepit dormitories, and inadequate wages for mandatory overtime.[39] Foxconn is among the leading electronics firms in China, employing about one million workers. In response to the negative publicity surrounding the suicides and the threat of strikes, the company agreed to settlements which increased wages. At the same time the global contractor also accelerated its relocation to new plants in China's rural areas, and beyond to lower-cost producers throughout the world.

The growth of migrant worker defiance also affected the automotive industry. In February 2010, migrant workers at Honda Auto

Parts Manufacturing Ltd in Foshan, Guangdong, downed tools for 19 days, compelling the government and the company to increase wages and recognize an independent plant-level trade union. The strike showed that workers no longer felt hopeless and were entering a new period of militant mobilization. While the ACFTU has sought to re-exert control over independent union leaders, rank-and-file workers have remained active in defending their gains.[40] The 2010 Foxconn and Honda strikes were emblematic of hundreds of strikes that followed on the shop floors of contractors for foreign brands and producers, and have expanded to challenge unions and the control of the CPC and ACFTU.

The growing organizational power of Chinese workers expressed through the intensity of worker mobilizations in 2013 and 2014 is of critical significance to global investors, as summarized in the *Financial Times*:

> Factories find it increasingly hard both to find skilled workers as China's labour force shrinks and to manage them. Workers have been empowered by their ability to tap social media with cheap smartphones, allowing them to compare employment conditions more easily and mobilise support for strikes. ... Local governments, especially in export centres in southern Guangdong province, worry that routine double-digit annual wage rises will prompt manufacturers to move their operations to other regions or countries. Many multinationals operating in China have been taken aback by the surge in labour unrest, especially in situations where workers did not previously flex their muscle.[41]

The vast FDI investments in China during the 1990s and 2000s reflected the recognition by major multinational brands that China would ensure the lowest production costs to foreign contractors who would take responsibility for all labor practices while upholding rigorous quality control standards. The billions in FDI facilitated huge investments in productive capacity and logistics, while the demanding Chinese state ensured that foreign multinationals would have no financial connection with or administrative responsibility towards workers in the modern plants, even though they depended on low-wage labor to maintain high levels of surplus value. The systematic use of contractors allowed multinationals to exclude workers from any wage effects and preclude any potential labor–management disputes.

Yue Yuen Industrial Holdings Ltd, headquartered in Hong Kong, a subsidiary of the Taiwanese conglomerate Pou Chen Corporation, is the world's largest manufacturer of athletic shoes. It accounts for 20 percent of the global wholesale trade in the market, and is the principal manufacturer of shoes for Adidas, Asics, Nike, Reebok, Salomon, Timberland, and other brands at its factories in China, Vietnam, and Indonesia.[42] Yue Yuen was among the first manufacturers to commence production in the PRD, opening its first factory on the port city of Zhuhai in 1988 and one year later expanding to Dongguan to take advantage of the rapid increase in the number of rural migrant workers and the relative absence of labor regulations. In 2005, Yue Yuen invested in new shoe production factories in Jiangxi Province to take advantage of its rural location and lower labor costs, with further investment in the province following in 2007. Although Yue Yuen's shoe sales continued to rise through the 2000s, hitting 96 million pairs in 2006, growing labor costs and crude oil prices caused the company's profits to decline from US$495.8 million in 2010 to $429 million in 2013.[43]

In 1992, the average monthly salary for Yue Yuen workers was only 400 yuan, about 13 percent of the monthly wage level when the Dongguan strikes broke out in 2014. In 2004, following worker complaints about rising costs for housing and living expenses, Dongguan City municipal authorities increased the legal minimum monthly wage from 450 to 574 yuan. By 2010, the minimum wage had increased to 930 yuan. In response, the company began to develop major factory operations in Indonesia and Vietnam, where at $6 and $3 respectively, the average export price per pair was far lower than in China ($20). In 2011, Yue Yuen's management sought to contain labor costs through pay cuts and layoffs of workers with seniority, and by transferring production capacity from the PRD plants to its factories in Jiangxi Province. Between 2010 and 2013, the Yue Yuen workforce in Dongguan fell by more than 50 percent from over 100,000 to 46,000, as the minimum wage in the city increased, reaching 1,310 yuan in 2014.[44]

According to Yue Yuen chairman Lu Chin Chu, rising labor costs in the Chinese footwear industry have been a primary cause of the declining profitability that has compelled the company to relocate production to new locations in Vietnam, Indonesia, and beyond. Just days before the mass strike of workers in April 2014, he reported:

> The operating environment for footwear manufacturing was difficult. Minimum wages across the different Asia regions continued to increase in accordance with government regulations. Costs were also up on account of efficiency issues with respect to newly opened factories and production lines, allocation of production capacity, and high staff turnover in certain factories. Furthermore, rising government mandated social benefit costs in the PRC, as well as general inflation pressures across the Asia region, meant that input costs on the whole continue to move upward. Notwithstanding, the management team of footwear manufacturing operations continued to enhance factory productivity and supply chain efficiency to offset the rising input costs.[45]

The 2014 strike at Yue Yuen was the largest in Southern China since the economic reforms that advanced the widespread maturation and growth of private industry dominated by FDI. It has been called the biggest strike ever seen at a private enterprise in China.[46] At the peak of the strike (April 14–25, 2014) production was shut down for 11 days by workers in Yue Yuen's major factories in Dongguan and Guangdong.

The strike was sparked when workers discovered that Yue Yuen had underpaid social security payments for their pensions, medical insurance, housing allowance, and injury compensation, and given them fraudulent contracts.[47] Instead of contributing to social security accounts on the basis of workers' real monthly income, Yue Yuen paid them on the basis of entry-level wages. This meant that on average Yue Yuen employees were owed 238 yuan (approximately US$37) per month in social security payments that had gone unpaid since 2006.[48] The 'theft' of social security payments heightened worker bitterness about well-documented practices at Yue Yuen aimed at intensifying production while ignoring occupational and health violations and failing to provide adequate services. The company pays a basic wage to all employees of 1,810 yuan a month (US$295), which does not cover their living expenses. To earn the average monthly salary of 3,000 yuan ($490) they must work overtime and meet production quotas.

Globalization Monitor, which monitors foreign firms in mainland China and conducts labor research and advocacy primarily in the PRD region, released a report in April 2014 identifying major abuses of workers at the three plants at Dongguan:[49]

> Major safety, health, wage, and worker rights violations at three plants included: (1) neglect of occupational safety and health of workers; (2) poor dormitory and food conditions in Yue Yuen dormitories; (3) wage disparity and underpayment of social insurance premiums in violation to law; and (4) management suppression of basic legal rights of workers. The report concluded that no Chinese law prevents workers from striking and Yue Yuen has no right to organize and implement a strike conduct penalty, which is an abuse of power against the interests of the workers.[50]

The role of the rank-and-file workers on the shop floors of factories was central to the organization of the strike, with gang-leaders in particular – long-term employees who lead crews as supervisors or foremen on the assembly line – playing a crucial role, according to activists in the PRD. Li Shing Hong, China labor law and social security specialist for the Asia Monitor Resource Center, met with workers in Dongguan and identified line supervisors as crucial to the strike:

Middle-level managers played an important role in the strike. These middle-level managers have an awareness of the worker consciousness and encouraged them to strike at a time when the grievances were growing and the network of workers was becoming stronger. In the past few years before the large strike in April, workers held previous work stoppages in different Yue Yuen buildings in Dongguan over living conditions in dormitories, food, and factory occupational safety issues.[51]

Workers with seniority have the most at stake and the greatest knowledge about the operations of the factory.[52] Gang-leaders who learn about corporate decisions to restructure operations and explain the consequences to workers are the eyes and ears of the assembly line. Gang-leaders as rank-and-file activists are in effect the parallel union on the shop floor. Recognizing that Yue Yuen had commenced closures and relocated production to a new location, gang-leaders mobilized members around their rights and served as in-house agitators.[53] When they discovered that even their social insurance had not been paid, they encouraged all the workers to strike, and initiated street protests outside the factories. An internal report obtained by Reuters from Yue Yuen Holdings cynically concludes that while supervisors have the most to lose in the underpayment of social security, given that those workers with most seniority would benefit most from full contributions to benefits, supervisors were also decisively responsible for mobilizing younger workers to demand improvement in dormitory conditions and higher monthly wages. Indeed at the outset of the unrest, senior management sought to divide younger from senior workers by offering to initiate social security payments but refusing to contribute to the accounts for past work.

The Labour Contract Law of 2008 conferred new labor rights on migrant workers. Rather than being discarded after several years, workers at Yue Yuen's Dongguan plants were able to work at the plants for longer than ten years. About 50 to 60 percent have seniority of more than ten years and are over 35 years of age. They are also migrant workers who do not want to return to the rural areas and prefer to remain in the city, where the cost of living is higher, when they retire. It is they who have argued most strongly for the payment of social security insurance, which covers health care, pensions, unemployment insurance, workplace injuries, and housing allowance.

The growing power of migrant workers with seniority reflects the maturation of class consciousness among Chinese manufacturing workers toward direct action, rather than the typical US model where young workers abandon jobs after a few months. Thus, while younger workers are more apt to leave their jobs because of the labor shortage, middle-aged workers recognize their long-term stake in their communities, and serve as shop-floor organizers. They seek to improve wages and conditions so as to encourage stability in plants and encourage younger workers to stay, according to May Wong.[54]

While workers do not have official unions, they are organized by leaders, whose names are never disclosed. Indeed, the absence of an active ACFTU union branch at Yue Yuen was a major cause for the strength of the worker mobilization and the durability of the strike. Lacking a labor policy and collective bargaining standards, Yue Yuen management and the Chinese state were unprepared for the organized direct action, and were forced to respond piecemeal to the demands and worker mobilizations in the factory, in the dormitories, and in the streets of Dongguan.

In March 2014, Liu Hai, a recently retired worker with 18 years of on-the-job experience, was told by management when she reported the shortfall in social security payments that they would not credit her social security account with the missing payments. She returned from retirement to the dormitory to mobilize fellow workers. According to May Wong:

> The workers organized all the factories and walked off the job three times. It impressed us that for the first time they demanded that the company pay social security according to the law when many companies do not pay these funds. This is not a side issue like wage increases but the most important issue to workers in their 30s.[55]

The workers self-organized at the plant, at their dormitories, and interactively via social media, especially through a Tencent QQ chatroom group that was launched in early April, and which thousands joined to gain information about the dispute.[56] Workers in China, perhaps more than anywhere else in the world, are using internet technology to make contacts and exchange ideas. The Yue Yuen struggle was covered extensively by Reuters news agency, which uncovered Yue Yuen internal reports seeking to undermine the central role of shop floor organizers before and after the strike.

The work stoppage began before the end of the working day on Saturday April 5, 2014, when hundreds of rank and file workers organized by gang-leaders downed tools to demand payment of back wages, wage increases of 30 percent monthly, and improvement of conditions at the housing facilities. The workers claimed that Yue Yuen determined social security payments on the basis of workers' basic monthly salary rather than on their actual monthly pay, which included overtime and bonuses for meeting production quotas.[57] Further demands addressed the grievances of younger workers, mainly calling on the company to provide housing and meals free of charge, and improve the dormitory quarters and quality of food.

After work, hundreds of workers staged public protests and blocked a bridge. The city sent riot police to intimidate workers and disrupt the demonstration by charging workers, and arresting and beating those it considered organizers, resulting in several reports of injuries. The police response and Yue Yuen's obstinacy in refusing to contribute back payments to workers' social security retirement accounts encouraged more workers to mobilize across the three plants. The collective demands were reflected in the placards that workers held outside their dormitories, such as 'Pay back the social security and public housing fund' and 'Shame on Yue Yuen's illegal activities!'

After the upsurge in worker unrest, Yue Yuen offered an initial concession to mollify recent recruits and set them against older workers. Continuing to reject back payments to workers, the company offered to pay social security and public housing contributions in the future for new contracts, an offer which was rejected by the workers, and which intensified the insurgency among

employees at all three factories. By April 14 about 30,000 workers
– 80 percent of the 43,000 workers at all of Yue Yuen's Dongguan's
factories – had joined the strike. According to numerous corrobo-
rating witnesses and reports, more than 10,000 workers joined the
street protests and demonstrations, and thereafter all the factories
were closed and shuttered. Since the strike was initiated by gang-
leaders, the walkouts were sanctioned and workers did not have to
worry about penalties. Thousands who joined the strike benefited
from government law specifying that workers can only be fired for
unauthorized absences of more than three days.

In the days following April 5, workers went to work, clocked
in, and returned to their housing in on-site dormitories or in the
surrounding area, where they planned the demonstration and
protest that took place on April 14, when according to estimates
up to 500 police guarded the road and demonstrating workers were
attacked.[58] According to Rina Lau, on April 17, when Yue Yuen sent
in a new factory manager from Taiwan to control the strike, he was
thrown into the river by the workers.[59]

Yue Yuen aggressively opposed the social security payments
throughout April. Most of the workers returned only after April 25,
when the Chinese Ministry of Human Resources and Social Security
issued a public statement finding Yue Yuen had failed to 'truthfully
report' benefit payments to its employees. The Ministry ordered the
company to rectify the discrepancy and catch up with its payments
through contributions to the workers' social security accounts, and
Yue Yuen finally agreed to bring the accounts up to date by June
2014.[60] The company has made contradictory statements about the
social security contributions, at first refusing to pay, then offering to
only pay new hires, and finally conceding to government demands.
In August 2014, it reported a decline in profits which it claimed
was a result of the April strikes in Dongguan and the extension of
the social security settlement to all its other factories in mainland
China, and that the cost to its bottom line was projected to be
$194 million for the year. Company officials stated:

> The main reasons for making the employee benefit contri-
> butions are to assist the company in staff retention and

recruitment under the increasingly competitive labour market conditions in China to ensure the company's normal business operation in the other factories.[61]

The rising worker militancy in April 2014 at Yue Yuen Dongguan's plants resulted in increasing producer and multinational uneasiness about the ability of Chinese manufacturers to continue to maintain a global competitive advantage. During the strike Nike, Timberland, and Adidas were under heavy pressure from activists and students to support the workers. Protesters from the PRD mobilized to oppose Yue Yuen and the multinational brands that profited from the underpayment of workers. Panicking at the scale of the strikes, Adidas and other global brands distanced themselves from responsibility for contractor policies leading to the industrial action, and said they were considering relocating production. Yet in the face of negative publicity for relocating after the strikes, Adidas said it would retain Yue Yuen as a contractor.[62]

In interviews during the strike, rank-and-file activists clearly viewed the municipal branch of the ACFTU as having been entirely unhelpful to the striking workers and largely supportive of management. As the official representative of the workers, the ACFTU weakened the ability of the workers to make legitimate demands against management. In the absence of an independent union the workers complained they could only rely on their self-organization, reducing the effectiveness of their strike. The workers were also wary of foreign NGOs.[63]

Kevin Slaten, program coordinator of China Labor Watch, a New York-based NGO that is typically critical of the government, contends that the Chinese authorities recognized the intensity of the workers' insurrection and the justifiable demands of the strikers to make their social security accounts whole, and responded with restraint to the workers' mobilizations:

The first days of the Yue Yuen strike seemed to follow a similar script when riot police violently dispersed workers during a march toward the Dongguan city government building. Two labor activists were detained for aiding the striking workers.

One is still in custody. But security forces seemed less intent on ending the massive labor action than containing it within the factory premises, allowing it to continue for 14 days. Moreover, the government did not emphasize the criminality of the strike.[64]

The magnitude of the Yue Yuen strikes requires a reconsideration of the dominant perspective among labor scholars that Chinese workers are locked into local cellular-level protests and job actions. The Dongguan strike covered three major plants in the city and gained support among workers in Jiangxi Province during the walkout, and it forced Yue Yuen to update social security payments for all its employees in mainland China.[65] Two months later, in July 2014, workers at Yue Yuen's factory in Zhuhai went on strike to protest about the company's delays in processing social security applications.[66]

The implications of the mass mobilizations were not confined to Yue Yuen. Dongguan became a nucleus of worker protests and strikes that extended from manufacturing to the service sector. For example, the government crackdown, in February 2014, on the sex work industry concentrated on Dongguan. It contributed to a decline in wages for taxi drivers, who went on strike in April and May 2014.[67] Unrest spread in the ensuing months to workers in factories owned by other contractors for major foreign multinational brands.

On September 9 and 10, 2014, industrial action involved more than 10,000 employees at Masstop Liquid Display, a subsidiary of Wintek Technology, a Taiwanese manufacturer that supplies touch screens to Apple (although Apple does not recognize the Dongguan subsidiary plant as an official supplier). Nearly all the 10,000 workers at the Dongguan plant went on strike to protest at the company's cut in the holiday pay for the mid-autumn festival. Workers received cash bonuses of 100 yuan rather than the expected 700 yuan, and considered this cut in holiday pay as a cut in salary. The next day the strike spread to a second Wintek Technology subsidiary in Guangdong – Songshan Lake High-tech Industrial Development Zone in Guangdong Province – as 1,000 workers went on strike. The workers were persuaded to return to work by management, which claimed that it was facing significant losses, of more than US$300 million in 2013 and $100 million in the first half of 2014.

The Masstop strike challenges the dominant perspective that older workers seeking pensions are more prone to strike. According to the report, most employees at the plant were young workers in their early 20s. For Zhong Li, a 20-year-old worker at the Songshan plant:

> It's a covert act of cutting our pay. …The factories promised workers a cash bonus of about 3,000 yuan each year for the three main lunar festivals. Now they have refused to keep their promise. … Many young workers know Wintek is an Apple supplier. It's very unfair and mean when they sell an iPhone for more than 6,000 yuan but cut our pay. If the company cuts our cash bonus, we will think of additional strikes for a better base pay.[68]

Stoppages and strikes across China in the spring of 2014 indicate that the manufacturing sector is a major flashpoint for industrial action that will move to other sectors as the capacity of workers to engage in direct action becomes much greater, with or without ACFTU sponsorship.[69] The ability to disrupt production for extended periods has taken a toll on profits, and demonstrates the centrality of manufacturing sector workers to private investors and the Chinese government. Mobilization and organization of manu-facturing workers in the Global South demonstrates a capability and willingness to exert power through protests and strikes in the decades to come, which will have important connotations for the world economy.

CONCLUSION: CAN WORKERS ORGANIZE INDEPENDENT TRADE UNIONS IN CHINA, AND SHOULD THEY?

The main controlling force over the workers' movement used to be the organizational monopoly of the ACFTU. Organizational domination thwarted the development of a legally consti-tuted counter-hegemonic representative body but did not preclude formation of a parallel rank-and-file movement. This movement may have lacked official legitimacy but the actions and understanding of worker power were recognized widely.

The two-week work stoppage among more than 40,000 workers at Yue Yuen plants in Dongguan was the most prominent among a growing wave of strikes in China, revealing the rising trend of militancy among middle-aged workers who are striving to protect their living standards on retirement. As the labor market contracts, second-generation migrant workers in their 20s who see older workers demand their rights are also mobilizing for higher wages and improved conditions. More than 25 years after the Tiananmen Square protests, the contemporary workers' movement has become the foundation of activism that is challenging bureaucratic state institutions and foreign capital.

The Yue Yuen strike demonstrates that as long as the ACFTU restricts the formation of independent labor organizations within workplaces and foreign multinationals, workers will continue to pose a threat to management dominance by striking to improve immediate wage conditions, a pattern that will disrupt production without workers facing major reprisals. In addition, the wildcat strike is emerging as a standard model of collective bargaining to improve the conditions of the new urban working class in opposition to a powerful constellation of foreign capitalists.

The prevailing perspective among most advocates promoting the formation of trade unions globally has always been rooted in how workers can organize power within the confines of the liberal democratic capitalist state. Trade union formation has generally occurred within the context of a political party or parliamentary system. Hence, during the 20th century, labor-based parties often mobilized within multiparty states. These parties were typically aligned with trade union federations that developed out of industrial labor mobilization (as in Brazil, South Africa, South Korea, and India). However, the historical dependency of trade unions on traditional political parties to protect and advance worker rights and wages has largely faded in the neoliberalist era of global capitalism. Increasingly, center-left parties are advancing policies advocating minimal social protection without the electoral support of formerly robust labor movements. Accordingly moral exhortations from international human rights organizations and NGOs about the importance of civil society organizations and the promotion of party and labor competition ring hollow. The deterioration and ineffectiveness of responsible competitive political parties over 30 years of neoliberal policies has reduced the tangible institutional power of workers to a relic of the past. Even the most devoted trade unionists in the West recognize the futility of rebuilding a workers' movement in the neoliberal capitalist era using the customary institutional means of the capitalist state. The failure of Syriza in Greece to challenge multinational capital is but one of many examples of the impotence of left and labor-based political parties which seek to challenge the neoliberal diktat.

Thus, what are we to make of the condition of the working class in China? How do we assess the one-party state and union?

As noted in Chapter 2, multinational capital has a direct interest in maintaining low wages in order to extract higher levels of surplus, thus exercising direct control over workers. Certainly building a mass workers' organization requires a discipline that extends widely and deeply among workers. The Chinese model prohibits both electoral and independent organizations, but almost always maintains third-party relationships as intermediaries between the rank-and-file working class and the employer. However, under neoliberalism, notwithstanding the continued domination of the CPC and the ACFTU over official electoral and trade union policies, we have seen the appearance and expansion of extensive rank-and-file protest and strikes, in what Beverly Silver and Lu Zhang call the 'epicenter of world labor unrest.'[70]

The rapid expansion of foreign capital and private employment has contributed to a unique form of class-struggle unionism, since the ACFTU does not serve as the intermediary between labor and management. Although the Chinese state is dominant and engages in autocratic activity that severely restricts workers, it is important to understand how this process works. The fact that no union may compete with the ACFTU for membership cuts two ways. On the one hand workers do not have the right to form recognized independent unions, but on the other a single union can regulate the conditions of all workers across public- and private-sector industries. The Western model of unions allows private capital to select and recognize those unions that are most docile. In contrast, a national union offers the possibility of uniform and standardized conditions for all workers irrespective of industry or region, and workers may retain the possibility of shaping labor conditions in their local areas.

In this analysis of contemporary Chinese labor struggles, we have found workers resisting in the context of a bureaucratic central state and union federation that is relatively remote from the daily struggles of workers in foreign-dominated industries with strategic importance for economic growth and expansion. The evidence shows that in the absence of independent trade unions, disciplined rank-and-file workers can achieve tangible and sometimes extensive economic progress through direct opposition to contractors who must provide products under tight budgetary requirements. The 2010s strike wave demonstrates that Chinese workers do not necessarily require an independent trade union to gain higher wages, health and medical benefits, and pensions, or to form local enterprise committees in factories. A future Chinese labor movement, shaped by local independent activist leaders, is emerging out of the major battles by mobilized workers against capital and the state.

5

South Africa: Post-Apartheid Labor Militancy in the Mining Sector

Since 2009, South Africa's Platinum Belt has seen a dramatic expansion of worker demands for living wages, an end to the contract system, and improved conditions, with several hundred thousand mine workers involved in strikes sit-ins and mine takeovers. These developments have been met with violence by police and security forces, and it is clear that the political establishment in South Africa, in collusion with capital, is acting as a repressive agent to stifle dissent and create a docile labor force. In response, rank-and-file activists supported by AMCU (the Association of Mineworkers and Construction Union) and other independent unions have established defense committees.

The state's embrace of neoliberal capitalism in the post-apartheid era has been accompanied by an unequivocal decline in organized trade union power under an ANC (African National Congress) government that has sought to channel spontaneous worker agitation and dissent against corporate management into a formal system of labor relations directed at regulating and containing strikes and rank-and-file militancy. The failure of the state and organized labor to address the rise of precarious employment and declining wages has stimulated informal and migrant worker self-activity, and unsanctioned mass action that is challenging the credibility of the government and trade union leaders.

THE RISE OF MINING AND MANUFACTURING IN NEOLIBERAL CAPITALISM

The importance of mining to multinational capital has increased in the early 21st century, with an expansion in global production and in

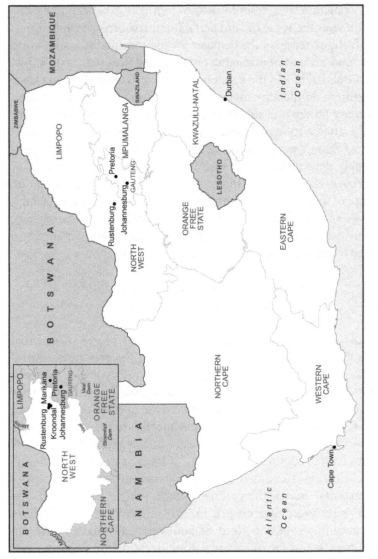

Map 6.1 South Africa, with a focus on the North West

149

the requirement for minerals and energy to service technology across industrial sectors. Multinational mining conglomerates have sought, with mixed success, to gain greater control over strategic mining sectors through capitalist investment and direct ownership. The dramatic growth in direct ownership of land and minerals by food, mining, and energy conglomerates, from Monsanto to Anglo-American to Exxon-Mobil, reveals the value of land and natural resources to capitalism.

Profitability relies on the demand for the commodity in the world market and the cost of extracting or producing it, as well as on industrial consolidation and the development of cartels that eliminate labor competition, dominating markets and fixing prices.[1] The production of primary products is almost always dependent on the cost of labor and the ability to exploit and plunder ecosystems without consequences.[2] Silver's temporal-spatial approach confirms that labor costs are highly dependent on the organization of labor in a country or region over time and space. In mining industries with militant unions, the price of the commodity will tend to increase, especially if demand is extensive and the mineral is scarce. Mining conglomerates throughout the world have constantly sought to restrict union organization through technology, repression, and use of migrant labor.

SOUTHERN AFRICAN PLATINUM AND THE GLOBAL ECONOMY

The African continent has served as a leading source of essential metals for export from the colonial period to the present neoliberal era. The presence of massive deposits of minerals in the Kaapvaal Craton and Zimbabwe Craton geological regions of Southern Africa are a source of military contestation, and are of historic significance to the regional and global economy. Minerals are the most substantial source of exports for South Africa, which is the largest economy in the entire continent. In 2011, mining extraction, refining, and fabrication accounted for over 30 percent of South Africa's total exports, nearly three times motor vehicle production, the country's second major export. In 2013, chromium and platinum alone accounted for 8 percent of South Africa's total exports. An additional 21 percent of earnings were derived from iron ore and coal, and 8 percent from gold.[3] Already recognized as a leading exporter of gold, diamonds, and other precious metals, South Africa's reliance on mineral exports has expanded in the post-apartheid era due to sustained and growing demand for minerals that are essential to production industries from Germany and Japan, and increasingly from China and India.

Over 100 years since Southern African platinum was first mined in the 1910s, more than 75 percent of the world's known reserves are found in the Bushveld Complex, a mineral-rich geological formation located in the Merensky Reef, which extends from North West province in South Africa into southern Zimbabwe. The Russian Federation and Canada are the only other countries with substantial platinum reserves. However in South Africa the mineral is more highly concentrated in the ore than elsewhere in the world. Government efforts to reduce pollution deriving from vehicle emissions have led to platinum becoming essential to the production of catalytic converters in most modern automobile exhaust systems. Platinum is also essential for producing electrical equipment that must withstand exceptionally high temperatures, such as electrodes, dental equipment, and thermometers. In the 2010s South Africa's platinum exports account for more than 80 percent of world production.

Platinum is a scarce mineral, requiring specialized technology and labor for the time-consuming and complex processes of extraction and refining. According to Amplats, which claims to produce 40 percent of the world's platinum, the length of the production process may reach six months from mining to refining. The company claims that 'on average seven to 12 tonnes ore yields one ounce of high grade platinum.'[4] The costs are reflected in the high price of platinum, which closed on January 10, 2014, for example, at $1,437 per troy ounce, about $190 more than the $1,246.90 quoted for an ounce of gold.[5]

MINING, CAPITAL, AND CONTRACT LABOR IN
POST-APARTHEID SOUTH AFRICA, 1994–2015

As the demand for platinum has grown, multinational capital has flowed into the South African industry to construct technologically advanced mining installations. In the two decades since the institution of majority Black rule in 1994, South Africa has vigorously instituted neoliberal reforms that opened the economy to fiercely competitive foreign capital investment. This has been directed at labor-saving technology that has led to flexible production, but also to higher levels of unemployment, contract work, and the recruitment of migrant workers from outside the Bushveld Complex.

In the mining sector, migrants have comprised a large share of the workers since the discovery of minerals. The multinational conglomerates controlling the mining industry and the state have long asserted that locals reject jobs in the platinum industry, and migrants are the only workers willing to work under the arduous and dangerous conditions. However this questionable assertion fails to recognize the economic benefit of recruiting migrant workers, who are strangers in the region and disconnected from social ties when they come to work in the remote rural regions of the North West province. In the post-apartheid era migrant laborers have worked as rock drill operators (RDOs) and at other skilled and dangerous jobs. As contract laborers from outside the region, skilled workers often do not even have job security equivalent to that of unskilled local workers.

A fundamental feature of South Africa's mining economy both pre- and post-apartheid has been the isolation of mineworker communities in dilapidated housing near the mines. The removal of the exclusionary pass system has expanded mobility and legalized the migration of workers with their families. But the basic conditions have often remained the same, as hostels have merely been converted into run-down dwellings, often without electricity and clean water, in informal communities that are lacking in basic services and amenities.

Maintaining a system of migrant labor by recruiting far and wide to expand the reserve army of labor is essential to the expansion of mining profits. The reduction of the number of migrant laborers directly employed in the mining sector has been accompanied by the expansion of recruitment through private contractors who pay and supervise miners employed on short-term contracts. This system circumvents the laws that require the mining giants to hire local workers and improve conditions in exchange for obtaining mining licences. The definition of 'local' can extend from laborers living in a nearby village to workers who live in the same province but 250 miles from the mine. Labor researcher Kally Forrest's study of the Rustenburg Platinum community points out that new laws reducing migration have reduced labor competition, but have also increased unemployment in traditional regions of South Africa that had been dependent on remittances:

> [T]he focus on local recruitment threatens jobs for workers from elsewhere. Parts of the Transkei have been devastated and the economies of labour-sending countries have suffered. Labour broking also reproduces the low-wage migrant system, with which it merges. The overt coercion of apartheid mine capital has morphed into a more hidden form, which still puts workers under enormous pressure.[6]

A United Nations report in 2012 on minerals and African development recognized the deleterious influence of neoliberal economic reforms on labor conditions throughout the continent:

> In Africa's mineral dependent economies the most significant job losses occasioned by the global financial and economic crisis of 2008 were experienced in the mining sector with the Southern African Development Community region being the worst hit .... But the job-creating impact of the new mines has been limited because capital-intensive 'large-scale mineral extraction generally offers limited employment opportunities'. According to the United Nations Economic Commission for Africa, data from foreign affiliates of US firms in Africa show that manufacturing foreign investment is 17.5 times more labour-intensive than mining foreign investment.[7]

In addition to reducing labor costs, the contractors impede the formation of labor unions in the mines. According to Forrest:

> Mines use brokers to circumvent unions ... brokers can keep

wages low, offer competitive rates to mines and make their own profit. Permanent labour employed directly by mines is extensively unionised, so it appears that mines are adhering to labour laws, whereas in fact a large part of their workforce is weakly organised or unorganised, brokered workers.[8]

In South Africa's mineral-rich North West, the mobilization of workers from 2009 to 2014 has forced multinational mining companies to directly retain more permanent workers and negotiate with trade unions, resulting in higher labor costs and lower profits. It also forces them to take financial responsibility for compensating permanent employees for workplace injuries or cancellation of contracts, which are more often evaded by labor brokers.

LABOR UNIONS IN MODERN SOUTH AFRICA

The formation and consolidation of the South African labor movement from the 1860s to the present is inflected by the legacies of European imperialism, the marginalization of the Black working-class majority, and the liberation struggle to end racial oppression and to shape trade unions as the societal instrument for working-class and racial justice and equality. Historians Nicole Ulrich and Lucien van der Walt sum this up:

> The union movement in twentieth-century South Africa operated in a context in which capitalist relations were built upon relations of colonial domination. The persistent use of state power against labor movements, heavy-handed intervention in the supply and control of labor, and close linkages between the state apparatus and private business help explain the persistent tendency of the labor movement to break out of the bounds of bread-and-butter issues, and fight battles around civil and political rights.[9]

From the 1880s to 1902 the conflict for political control over South Africa set British colonialists against descendants of Dutch settlers, culminating in the two Anglo-Boer Wars. The second Anglo-Boer War, ending in 1902, led to the formation of the autonomous Union of South Africa in 1910 as a British dominion, where European ethnic differences were set aside to ensure white domination over a segregated Black majority.

As the South African economy expanded, white workers formed racially exclusive but militant trade unions throughout the Cape. In South Africa, as in North America and elsewhere, the revolutionary-syndicalist Industrial Workers of the World (IWW) was the only union to welcome African and Asian workers, but by the early 1920s the union dissolved in the wake of the Rand Revolt, the Afrikaner and immigrant mine workers' general strike and labor insurgency of 1922, as a result of state-armed repression. The Rand Revolt was induced in part by a palpable fear among white mine workers of replacement by low-waged Black laborers, a fear fomented by mining companies which was to contribute to racial tensions and divisions between white and Black workers.

From the 1920s to the end of the Second World War in 1945, the Communist Party of South Africa (CPSA) was committed to expanding inter-racial trade unions, and as in the United States, it privileged support for the Soviet Union and Allied war effort over establishing militant unions in the mining and manufacturing sectors.[10]

In the May 1948 elections, the National Party emerged victorious on a platform of racial separation (apartheid) and white domination, the exclusion and subservience of Africans, and fierce antagonism to foreign economic interference. The consolidation of the National Party in South Africa during the 1950s was synchronized with a concerted government policy outlawing the expression of African power throughout the white-dominated apartheid system. Apartheid was extended through all forms of civil society, as separate institutions were established to administer labor and industrial relations on the basis of race. The passage of the Native Labor Act of 1953 banned strikes by African workers, and in 1956 the national Industrial Conciliation Act labor law was revised to bar the registration of new multiracial unions. These new laws had the effect of dividing and isolating workers' organizations on the basis of race, thereby also diminishing the power of the organized South African working class.[11]

The South African Congress of Trade Unions (SACTU) was formed in 1955 out of left-leaning unions as the leading labor opponent to the apartheid system, along with the ANC and the South African Communist Party (SACP), which was established after the banning of the CPSA. Despite the banning of strikes among African workers, the SACTU supported national strikes and demonstrations commemorating massacres of Africans, political opposition to the pass system that turned Black Africans into foreigners in their own country, and other forms of organized political action against the repressive state. In 1961 the SACTU aligned with the ANC and the SACP to form Umkhoto we Sizwe (the Spear of the Nation), an activist organization aimed at destabilizing the infrastructure of the apartheid state through acts of sabotage against installations. In 1964, the union's activists were arrested, charged with participating in a campaign of sabotage, and sentenced to life imprisonment along with key ANC and SACP leaders. SACTU developed into labor's political wing of the anti-apartheid movement, but as it went into exile it was outflanked by two national trade union federations in South Africa: the Trade Union Advisory Coordinating Council (TUACC), formed in 1974, and the Federation of South African Trade Unions (FOSATU), formed in 1979.

Over the next decade, as manufacturing exports expanded, the growth of Black African industrial labor activated a militant workers' movement in the auto and mining sectors, strengthening the South African trade union movement, which in 1983 jointly formed the United Democratic Front (UDF) in opposition to the apartheid system. Two years later the Congress of South African Trade Unions (COSATU) was formed, a 500,000-member federation that included the National Union of Mineworkers (NUM), the formidable union representing workers in the country's most strategic industry. COSATU allied with the ANC in political opposition to the apartheid state. As John Saul maintains, by the late 1980s, COSATU was viewed by most observers as a linchpin in mobilizing and channeling the revolutionary sentiment of South Africa's Black working class at a critical historical moment:

COSATU was to remain a visible and active force of real prominence throughout the 1980s. Indeed, when ... [the UDF] was temporarily banned by the government in 1988, it was COSATU that sprang forward to take up the political slack, anchoring the freshly minted 'Mass Democratic Movement' that, for a period, took the UDF's place in coordinating the vast internal popular movement that fought back against the negation of resistance intended by the state's especially brutal response to the near revolution of the mid-1980s.[12]

In 1990, as the apartheid system was collapsing, the ANC and SACP formed the Tripartite Alliance with COSATU to demonstrate an authentic partnership with workers and the masses. The transition to non-racial majority rule in the elections that brought Nelson Mandela to power committed the state to political and economic democratization,[13] and a new constitution that protected white economic privilege even while it granted formal democratic rights for the Black majority. In 1995, the Tripartite Alliance overturned the system of racial segregation that had denied Africans civil rights as citizens in their own country through the pass system, which disallowed freedom of movement and association.

The apartheid system, however, had also become unworkable as a result of the global economy itself transitioning to neoliberal capitalism through the opening-up of production and consumer markets throughout the world. Anti-apartheid sanctions had closed much of South Africa's economy to foreign capital investment in the burgeoning automotive and mining industries. Would the post-apartheid South Africa government address racial and class inequality, or advance the interests of international capital?

For COSATU and the South African labor movement, the tangible outcome of the 1994 ANC election victory and the transition to majority rule was revisionist, rather than a form of revolutionary transformation. The major plank of the ANC's policy in 1995 was amending the Labor Relations Act to extend legal labor rights for African workers within a state that divided the working class on the basis of racial privilege. The amendments conferred collective bargaining rights on the African majority through allowing public sector employees, domestic workers, and farm laborers to unionize. However, the Act retained restrictive and time-consuming constraints on the right to strike. Meanwhile the state adhered to International Monetary Fund (IMF) guidelines to minimize public welfare for economic sustenance, as exchange controls were removed, a move that allowed foreign capital and banks to invest in the South African economy.[14]

THE TRIPARTITE ALLIANCE AND
POST-APARTHEID TRADE UNIONS

In the transition period leading up to the new constitution, COSATU was the organizational representative of Black working people. In the late 1980s, it could not check the wave of mass strikes and worker insurrections in the manufacturing and mining sectors. Political economist John Saul maintains that the constitutional changes gave formal electoral and representative politics precedence over egalitarian goals. COSATU, having served a legitimization function, was summarily marginalized in the coalition, and the promise of an egalitarian post-apartheid era was disregarded as the ANC adopted neoliberal capitalist reforms coveted by the IMF and multinational capitalist investors:

> True, there is little doubt that many within the COSATU camp failed to appreciate the fact that, even as the ANC and COSATU first met, the ANC was already in the process of refusing to countenance any counterhegemonic perspectives whatsoever towards capitalism. For if COSATU was just too strong to be, like the UDF, merely removed from the scene, ultimately it was, in the 1990s, only to be permitted member- ship within a new ANC-SACP-COSATU alliance as a distinctly junior partner.[15]

The absorption of COSATU into the South African government kept alive the promise of improved wages and working conditions for the insurrectionary working class in the immediate post-apartheid era, but 15 years on, disheartened by the government's neoliberal

Table 6.1 South African trade unions

Organization	Date founded	Membership 2010–14*
Federation of Unions of South Africa (Federation)	1997	560,000
Confederation of South African Trade Unions (Federation) (COSASTU)	1985	1,800,000
NUM members of COSATU	1982	250,000
NUMSA members of COSATU	1876	350,000
National Council of Trade Unions (Federation)	1986	400,000
AMCU members of NACTU	2001	75,000
Confederation of South African Workers' Unions (Federation)	2003	290,000
Including Solidariteit/Solidarity (White Union)	1902	130,000

• estimated total members in union or federation.

reforms, they were again demanding higher wages and increased rights for contract workers employed in the informal sectors of the economy. These demands were abruptly put on hold and forgotten in the name of political equality for Blacks. Indeed, Franco Barchiesi argues that the post-apartheid state has welcomed the transition to neoliberal capitalism, which has created higher levels of poverty and inequality, and has failed to provide economic security for the Black majority. This has reduced the significance of the citizenship and voting rights that were conferred in the post-apartheid era.[16]

See Table 6.1 for details of the leading trade unions in post-apartheid South Africa and the status of the rival mineworkers unions, the NUM and the AMCU.

Mine-worker militancy did not decline in the aftermath of the post-apartheid revision of the South African Labor Relations Act in 1995, which restricted the right of workers to strike. Confining the parameters of politics to electoral and legislative action, the ANC-SACP-COSATU tripartite partnership limited the capacity of trade unions to formally challenge multinational conglomerates, relinquishing the terrain of class struggle to the autonomous action of workers employed directly in the mines. Accordingly workers came to be disillusioned with COSATU and its blatant pretense that its theoretically left and socialist ideology corresponded with a commitment to the workers. It is also significant that COSATU General Secretary Zwelinzima Vavi did not publicly respond to the growth of violent repression against insurrectionary mine workers in the platinum and gold fields of North West South Africa from 2009.[17]

By 2014, while still asserting itself as one of the fastest-growing labor federations in the world since the 2009 global crisis, COSATU had lost credibility among key members and non-members of affiliates in the formal and informal sectors of the economy, with fundamental contradictions within its ranks. The viability of the federation itself is now in jeopardy: affiliated unions are withdrawing and workers are forming new national unions and local assemblies to represent workers in key sectors, most notably mineral extraction.[18]

An upsurge of unauthorized strikes occurred in the late 1990s, when dissent broke out among coal-mining workers seeking improved wages and conditions. Notably in September 1999 some 3,000 coal miners went out on a two-week wildcat strike protesting about dangerous working conditions at the Douglas Colliery in Mpumalanga Province, west of Pretoria, following the dismissal of NUM branch chair Joseph Mathunjwa. The workers only returned to the mine after Mathunjwa was reinstated, but he was then expelled from the NUM as part of a union disciplinary action. Two years later, in 2001, the AMCU was registered as an official trade union by the South African government and Mathunjwa was elected president. The new union gained popularity among migrant coal, gold, and platinum mining workers. These formed the majority of the informal and contract workers who had felt neglected by the NUM.

While the NUM has supported management in dismissing mine workers who have participated in the increasing number of wildcat strikes since 2009, the AMCU has grown in strength. In view of the NUM's partnership with multinational mining conglomerates, workers who have been dismissed have increasingly joined the AMCU after management rehires them, adding to the union's growth in membership to 50,000 workers in 2013.[19] The future of the union is thus largely defined by decisions of local assemblies of rank-and-file workers who call local strikes. In contrast, irrespective of its left ideology, the NUM's centralization of bureaucratic control and management collaboration only leads to the further erosion of its membership, as members strike and are then fired.

Informalization and Union Complicity

The growth of informalization and casual labor in the South African mining sector is supported by multinational conglomerates. It also benefits COSATU and the NUM by clearing the way for them to dominate industries without the support of the majority of workers. As John Saul observes, the proliferation of informal labor that does not form part of the permanent labor force has allowed COSATU and other traditional unions to repel membership competition:

> [T]he new ANC government's macroeconomic policies after 1994 saw both a decline in the number of stable jobs in industry and the emergence of an economy that would become ever more reliant on a part-time casual and insecure labour force. Moreover, there was to be a growing number of workers in very precarious jobs (seasonal, temporary, casual or fixed-term contract work) – up to as many as 30 per cent of the active labour force. This latter group of workers also largely remains without trade union representation, with COSATU itself having as yet shown little vocation for organizing the unorganized.[20]

South African Regional Migration and Mine Worker Insurgency

The NUM, the largest trade union in COSATU with 300,000 members, has benefited concretely from labor contracting and the informalization of the mining industry by defending a unionization system based on representing just 20 per cent of all workers in a mining installation, excluding the vast majority of all workers from democratic representation. (The AMCU, meanwhile, has campaigned to increase the level of representation to 35 percent of all workers.[21]) NUM union officers have consistently urged workers to accept agreements offered by management that were almost always less generous than workers demanded. During the height of the insurgency, from 2009 to 2014, the union typically reserved especial disdain for the migrant rock-drillers, whose wages declined for over a decade from 1997, and who were often employed by labor contractors.

Worker insurgency across the platinum belt originated at the Crocodile River Mine in North West Province in June 2009, as mine workers employed by JIC and Sendele, two labor brokers subcontracting work for Eastplats (Eastern Platinum), went on strike to improve wages, halting production through a two-day sit-down strike at the Zandfontein section of the facility, where they also held hostage several supervisors. The failure by the labor brokers to prevent labor militancy forced Eastplats to its fallback position, which involved terminating the arrangement with the contractors and supervising workers directly employed by the company. The NUM was brought in to approve the dismissal and punishment of the contract workers, to broker a labor peace by sanctioning the firing of striking workers, and to negotiate a contract covering 1,500 unionized workers and new recruits hired to replace the striking workers.[22]

From August to November 2009, militancy among platinum miners expanded throughout the Bushveld Complex, as mine operators reinforced a campaign of targeting predominantly migrant contract workers, who had spearheaded the agitation and sit-down strikes for improved wages and conditions. Beginning in August 2009, 3,900 contract laborers employed by Murray & Roberts Cementation went on three wildcat strikes at the Krundal and Marikana mines, which halted production. Workers were initially rehired through the mediation of the NUM. In November 2009, a sit-down strike by platinum miners in the Rustenburg region shut down production at the Kroondal Platinum operations owned by Aquarius Platinum and Anglo-American Platinum, multinational operators in a formal partnership agreement to extract and process platinum ore and share profits until all reserves from the mine are exhausted in 2023.[23]

The November 20 sit-down strike at the Kroondal location was suppressed when 34 strikers were forcibly removed, arrested for trespass, and summarily fired, with the active support of the NUM. In a press release on November 23, 2009, Lesiba Seshoka, an NUM head spokesperson, noted the union's agreement with Murray & Roberts that the workers were engaged in 'illegal strikes at Aquarius Platinum in Kroondal.' He went on:

> The NUM has repeatedly encouraged those workers to return to work prior to their unprotected strike action. They however vowed to continue with the action even though a settlement agreement was reached and the majority had accepted it. Murray & Roberts then dismissed them and as a union we intervened on their behalf to be reinstated of which the company agreed. On reinstatement, they went on another illegal strike action. The NUM further renegotiated with the employer after their second dismissal and got a reinstatement [after] which they later went on another illegal strike and were then finally dismissed.[24]

Platinum Miners' Insurgency in the Bushveld, January–April 2012

The strikes that began in 2009 set in motion a wave of unrest. By 2011 rank-and-file workers in the mines were experiencing and comprehending the disempowering consequences of labor–management cooperation that maintained a system of low wages and dangerous working conditions. In January 2012, the workers' insurgency commenced at the Impala Platinum Holdings Limited (Implats), one of South Africa's three largest platinum-mining firms. The company boasts that low-cost production is a major factor in its profitability. This has been sustained by subcontracting migrant workers from across Southern Africa. Two years after the mass strike at the largest facility in Rustenburg, Implats claimed that contract workers comprised nearly 30 percent of the 57,000 workers at all its facilities.[25]

On January 12, 2012 Implats announced an 18 percent monthly wage increase for local workers employed at Rustenburg, excluding

5,000 RDOs. The RDOs are chiefly migrant laborers recruited from rural regions in the Eastern Cape and Lesotho. They labor under oppressive and dangerous working conditions, as depicted by Greg Marinovich of the *Daily Maverick*:

> These are the men who work right down at the rock face, who have to work with a 25kg drill that vibrates wildly for the duration of an eight-hour shift. When there is a rock fall, it is generally the drillers who are the victims, who lose fingers or lives. It is the most dangerous job in the business.[26]

At once, RDOs at Rustenburg 14 shaft began a six-week strike, which expanded dramatically to include all the Implats mines, and later extended throughout the platinum belt in the Bushveld Complex. This action challenged the hegemony of the multinationals and called into question the legitimacy of the NUM, which claimed to represent 70 percent of the 18,000 mine workers at the company.

Striking workers rejected Implats' and the NUM's demand that they return to their posts, after which the strike continued to expand. On January 24, the mining company obtained a court order deeming the walkout by 5,000 RDOs 'illegal' and 'unprotected,' and summarily terminated all the workers, with the condition that they return to work by January 27 as new hires, losing their accrued pension benefits. On January 30, the strike spread to a majority of all workers (around 17,000 of them) at Implats in support of the dismissed RDOs, and two days later the company terminated the contracts of all the workers who had joined the strike.

The dismissal of nearly all workers at Implats Rustenburg instigated a violent conflict, extending from the mines to the community, and setting private security guards and the South African Police Service (SAPS) against the striking workers. This led to deadly skirmishes through the month of February, in which workers and security guards were killed, as the workers gradually returned to work under pressure from management and the NUM.

In February, the NUM and COSATU declared the strike illegal and called on Implats to reinstate the workers without the previously announced 18 percent wage increase,[27] but in April Implats

agreed to restore the wage increase. Meanwhile, the autonomous RDO strike committee directed the AMCU to negotiate on
its behalf, requesting and obtaining a wage increase from about
R4,000 to R9,000 (US$400 to 900) a month.[28] Labor analyst Shawn
Hattingh observes, 'It was, however, clear that AMCU was not
involved in organizing the strike, which was self-organized by the
workers directly. In the end, and due to the militancy of the strike,
the workers won their full demand.'[29]

For the duration of the strike, the rank-and-file workers formed
assemblies that held regular meetings and collectively deliberated a
tactical strategy that challenged the NUM's resolutions imposed by
its central bureaucracy. As Tito Mzamo reports:

> Workers have learned the tradition of organizing meetings
> for mass action from their Unions; this was evident when
> the media, particularly SABC [South African Broadcasting
> Corporation, the state-owned broadcaster], showed workers
> addressing their assemblies without any leadership in a disci-
> plined manner. This, and the impact the militancy had on
> the Congress of South African Trade Unions (COSATU), put
> pressure on the NUM leadership, and forced the leaders to
> shift from their initial 'moderate' stance of not recognising the
> strike, a position which had only served to play into the hands
> of the employers. The bosses had no qualms about taking a
> hard line position and after two weeks the initial workers who
> had come out on strike had been dismissed. The NUM leaders
> had in fact been portraying their own members as being
> victims to immature unions seeking relevance by organizing
> an 'illegal strike'.[30]

On March 15, just two weeks following the end of Implats strike,
3,000 workers at the Modikwa Platinum Mine walked out after
NUM officials failed to reach agreement over a wage increase with
mine owners African Rainbow Minerals and Anglo Platinum. The
strike ended after four weeks, and workers returned on April 11
with a new agreement providing for pay increases ranging from
8.5 to 10 percent.[31]

The unauthorized wildcat strike at Implats Rustenburg placed the NUM in the awkward position of opposing wage increases and calling workers back to work who were at risk of losing their jobs, at a time when workers' assemblies were forming throughout the platinum industry. The union also failed to support skilled temporary and migrant workers employed by labor contractors. NUM recognized the significance of the worker-directed insurgency too late to restore its own authority in the platinum mines, and beyond in the gold mines as well.

The Marikana Workers' Mobilization and Government Massacre of August 16, 2012

Events at Marikana would represent the defining moment in the mineworker struggle for autonomy and dignity, in what was to be the most violent government massacre of Africans since the Soweto Uprising of June 16, 1976.

Following a wave of wildcat strikes, rank-and-file workers, organizing independently, sought to improve conditions at the Lonmin Western Platinum mine near Marikana. Kwanele Sosibo of the *Guardian and Mail* reported that the workers were seeking to triple minimum monthly wages from about US$400 to US$1,150:

> While the violent strike has been blamed on clashes between NUM and AMCU, the striking workers said they were a united force currently with no allegiances to a particular union. [and on August 15] ... taking to spirited song and reiterating their demands of R12,500 minimum salary and request to speak to Lonmin CEO Ian Farmer.[32]

The formation of an independent union at Marikana suggests that mine workers viewed the NUM suspiciously as aligned with management. The AMCU's appeal owed more to a profound suspicion of the NUM than to an authentic loyalty to the new and largely inexperienced union. Corporate management and NUM leadership mistrusted and feared militant striking mine workers equally. The NUM's distrust of local rank-and-file participation is at the root of

Marikana, as it was time and again at other mines. Seeking a bureau-cratic and disciplined union, on every occasion the NUM opposed local self-directed unions that questioned the central leadership. This fierce suspicion was confirmed in late May 2011, when the NUM suspended the union branch chairperson Khululekile Steve, who had the support of workers at Marikana's Karee mine. The Marikana Commission later found that this action had been decisive in undermining the confidence of the mine workers in the union:

> When asked by Lonmin legal representative Mr Schalk Burger, Mr Gcilitshana explained that the strike action in Karee mine started in May 2011 after Mr Khululekile Steve, NUM branch chairperson was suspended. Mr Gcilitshana said that the intimidation and violence that ensued was caused by some people who were close to the branch leadership.[33]

Following the suspension of Khululekile Steve, the mine workers requested the support and representation of the AMCU in place of NUM officials. At Karee, one of the three mines at Marikana, most rank-and-file workers backed the AMCU. While some miners continued to support the NUM, the vast majority had already turned to the AMCU for support. According to the Marikana Commission of Inquiry, by May and June 2011 the NUM was anxiously seeking to retain rank-and-file workers at Karee who had disavowed member-ship in the union, and was resolute in preventing 'unauthorized' strikes, which were often called by its own members.[34]

Following Steve's suspension from the NUM, workers' anger escalated, as 9,000 Marikana workers protested through an 'unpro-tected' strike against the union's decision to discipline their branch chairperson, who had been seeking to access a trust fund to assist mine workers. Lonmin's dismissal of the workers paved the way for the massive growth of the parallel rank-and-file workers' organiza-tion among rank-and-filers who simultaneously left the NUM for the AMCU:

> Because they were 're-hired' rather than 're-instated', workers

had to join the union anew. Understandably, few requested membership of NUM, so significantly (and ironically), the union lost its base at Karee. ... Even though NUM had been discredited, some workers considered bringing it back, believing that any union would be better than none. However the majority were opposed to this scenario, and it was at this point that most of the Karee workers went over to ... AMCU .... AMCU's presence at Marikana is, then, a recent phenomenon, and, as with the union's formulation back in 2001, the catalyst was NUM's suspension of a popular leader. By July 2012 there was widespread dissatisfaction over pay.[35]

Identification with the AMCU did not demonstrate workers' unqualified support for the emergent Marikana workers' organization. It was rather a tactical alliance with a recognized union that was willing to advance rank-and-file objectives designed to achieve dignity on the job.

South African labor historian Peter Alexander maintains that the conditions under which Lonmin workers, especially RDOs, labor are even more arduous and dangerous than analogous mine working conditions in the 1920s:

Poverty ... at Lonmin, and fear of losing their jobs means [workers] tolerate some of the most arduous and dangerous working conditions imaginable. ... [U]nderground workers ... perform heavy manual work, often doubled up, under the threat of rock falls and machinery accidents. Making matters worse, the air underground is 'artificial' and full of dust and chemicals. TB is widespread and illness is common. ... In South Africa, a typical working day lasts eight hours, but Lonmin workers we spoke to said they could not 'knock off' until they had reached their target, which often meant working 12 hours, sometimes more .... Lonmin workers often slave more hours a week than the 1920s workers I studied, and they probably work harder. What does a worker get paid for such hazardous and strenuous work? With few exceptions those we spoke to said they received between R4000 and R5000 per month.[36]

From July 2011 to August 2012 Marikana workers held meetings of a rank-and-file general assembly to formulate their demands, culminating in an August 9 collective memorandum that specified raising wages from an average of R4,500 to R12,500 for all workers at each of Marikana's three mines: Eastern, Western, and Karee. On the same day the general assembly elected a workers' committee to negotiate with Lonmin management, and called for a work stoppage. The workers continued to meet in mass assemblies, and confronted a unified opposition of Lonmin management, the NUM mine workers, and state police, which set into motion a week of violent struggle. This culminated in the massacre of 34 mine workers on Thursday August 16, 2012.[37]

On August 10, Lonmin management was granted a court order proclaiming the work stoppage 'unauthorized,' and in the early hours of August 11 the NUM dispatched a vehicle through the surrounding settlements publicly declaring the union's non-endorsement of the strike, an action that provoked outrage and anger among the workers against the union. On August 11, some 2–3,000 workers who were members of both the AMCU and the NUM began a peaceful protest march from their hostels to the NUM office in the town of Wonderkop. They were blocked by armed NUM officials and company security personnel. Witnesses reported that nearly 20 armed men in red t-shirts opened fire, severely wounding two of the workers. This action which began an escalating series of violent incidents in which both workers and union officials were murdered.

Following the initial confrontation, two protesting workers were shot dead at the Karee mineshaft by NUM snipers, according to witnesses to the Marikana Commission. After the shooting workers armed themselves for self-defense with walking sticks known as knobkerries, crude weapons carved from tree limbs that were used widely in the apartheid-era protests. They established a protest camp at the nearby Wonderkop Koppie hillock, which is close to Nkanini, their informal settlement near the Karee shaft. Here they established an open-air workers' assembly. Lonmin management called in police to disarm the striking workers. The strikers refused to surrender their arms, claiming the police force had been infiltrated by NUM operatives. Lonmin management then threatened to force them back to work by appealing to the South African Labor Board to declare the strike illegal.

On August 12 and August 13, strikers, security guards and strike breakers were killed in armed skirmishes set off by the armed assault against workers by NUM and Lonmin guards. All through the strike Lonmin officials unyieldingly refused to meet with the elected workers' committee. On August 14 and 15, as striking mine workers formed a workers' assembly on the Marikana koppie, they were urged by both Senzeni Zokwana, president of NUM, and Joseph Mathunjwa of the AMCU to withdraw and return to work.

On August 15, vociferous workers at the redoubt on the koppie outcrop stopped NUM president Senzni Zokwana from continuing a speech urging their return to work, which he had been making from inside an armored police vehicle. Mathunjwa, who was granted permission to address the workers, assured them that he would apply his skills in negotiating wage gains and improved working conditions in the South African platinum belt.[38]

The next morning mine workers returned to the hill to protest about their wages and conditions to the Lonmin management. They were encircled by heavily armed state police ready to unleash force. In the afternoon Mathunjwa returned to the assembly and appealed to the 3,000 workers gathered there to leave. But, as became clear in subsequent testimony before the Marikana Commission of Inquiry, the strikers consisted of both NUM and AMCU members, and their loyalty was not to either union but to their nameless rank-and-file parallel workers' organization. They were determined to remain on the koppie come what may until management consented to their wage demand.

At 4 pm the same day armed SAPS officers fired live ammunition on strikers without warning. Sixteen workers were killed in cold blood as television cameras were recording, while 18 others were executed off-camera in a paramilitary-style operation on a small ridge to which they fled to escape the initial onslaught. This was in addition to 78 workers who were injured at the two sites.

Greg Marinovich described the stark nature of the standoff between Marikana workers and the state in the days after the massacre:

Several thousand men cover the orange outcrop of igneous rock like a single organism, spilling onto the dry thorn-veld below .... They are wrapped in blankets; their spears and fighting sticks protruding menacingly as they chant songs of war. ... The hill is encircled by riot police in more than a dozen armoured Nyalas .... Further down the rutted road, more than a hundred policemen from the tactical unit and a private security firm eat their supper from plastic containers. They are dressed in bulletproof vests and are armed to the teeth.[39]

While the South African media held the striking workers responsible, President Jacob Zuma set up an official investigation through the Marikana Commission of Inquiry, under the direction of Judge Ian Farlam, to ascertain the facts that had led to the massacre. Of decisive importance was the Commission's finding that the South African Police Service anticipated the killings in the hours before the assault against the encampment.[40] On the morning of August 16, more than eight hours in advance of the police shootings, aware that dozens of workers might be killed in a police assault, Colonels Klassen and Madoda of the SAPS ordered four mortuary vehicles to the scene from the health department, each with a capacity to carry eight bodies.[41]

The report also implicated senior government officials, including ANC official and former NUM general secretary Cyril Ramaphosa, a shareholder and director of Lonmin. The Marikana Commission released an email from Ramaphosa to Albert Jamieson, Lonmin's chief commercial officer, written one day before the massacre: 'The terrible events that have unfolded cannot be described as a labour dispute. They are plainly dastardly criminal and must be characterised as such. There needs to be concomitant action to address this situation.'[42] In June 2014, incumbent president Jacob Zuma was reelected and Ramaphosa was appointed deputy president, and the presumptive ANC candidate to be the next president of South Africa.

As for the official unions, rather than risk the NUM's withdrawal from the federation, COSATU General Secretary Vavi chose to close ranks with the union, even though it was unmistakably implicated in the use of force that led to the assassination of the 34 mine workers at Marikana. Patrick Bond explains that the Marikana wildcat strike and sit-in that culminated in the massacre threatened post-apartheid labor relations and substantially improved bargaining leverage, as the platinum and gold conglomerates sought to moderate labor costs with the support of the NUM:

> [W]hat these wildcat strikers were doing might, unionists reckoned, even throw the institutions of centralised bargaining into chaos. The demand for higher wages was both extreme, and thus opposed by NUM, and ultimately successful in the case of Marikana's courageous workers. The 22 percent raise – at a time inflation is around 6 percent – they won after a month of striking was remarkable, and inspired the country's labour force to look at their own pay packets askance. ... Indeed Vavi's most conspicuous moves throughout the mining belt in subsequent weeks were out of character: hand-in-hand with NUM's leadership, using his enormous prestige to throw cold water on the workers.[43]

In the aftermath of the Marikana massacre workers maintained their strike and held to their demands. Lonmin eventually agreed to meet with the workers and granted them wage increases. The RDOs received a wage settlement of 22 per cent and a R2,000 bonus for returning to work.[44] Beyond the wage increase, the expansion of AMCU influence reflects growing disaffection with the Tripartite Alliance, as Sam Ashman and Nicolas Pons-Vignon explain:

> The majority of the platinum strikers are members of the Association of Mineworkers and Construction Union (AMCU) which has grown rapidly as the previously dominant National Union of Mineworkers (NUM) – whose leaders are central to the ANC – has degenerated as an effective union force. Although it may not necessarily be articulated in this way by workers and strike leaders, the AMCU action was an expression of workers' independence from the Alliance.[45]

More than this, the platinum workers' strike and Marikana massacre revealed the deep-seated economic divisions in South African society. These had been disregarded for too long by the post-apartheid government, and had contributed to high poverty and inequality for the growing Black population, which is mostly still segregated in townships and rural areas. Over the ensuing 18 months demands from low-wage workers for raises were extending into the auto and other export industries.

THE SOUTH AFRICAN STRIKE WAVE OF 2014

In the aftermath of the Marikana massacre South African workers entered an extended period of nationwide strikes for higher wages, across a range of industries. The strike wave peaked in January 2014 with strikers against South Africa's three leading platinum producers, Amplats, Implats, and Lonmin, seeking a 'living wage' that would raise wages by R5,000 to R12,500 (US$1,200) a month.[46] This time the mine workers unified behind the AMCU, repudiating the NUM as a representative of their interests. Unwavering in their commitment to continue the strike, many survived on charitable donations or returned to live in their rural communities. The three producers, despite losing an estimated US$2.25 billion in revenue, resolutely refused the wage demands, and even threatened to permanently close the platinum mines.[47] The South African economy contracted by 0.6 per cent during the first quarter of 2014.

After 21 weeks a general settlement was reached between the AMCU and the three mining companies. Falling short of the demands to nearly double wages across the platinum industry, the agreement signified the strikers' enduring commitment to 'a living wage' and underlined the importance of lifting the pay of the lowest-paid entry-level workers. The final three-year settlement called for raises that would lift the minimum wage to R8,000 a month. Even after the agreement was reached and workers returned to the mines, the AMCU declared its intention to pursue the goal of raising entry-level wages to R12,500. One month after the settlement Amplats announced its intention to sell its mines to local operators.[48]

The 2014 platinum strike was a defining moment for the South

African labor movement, symbolizing the power of rank-and-file workers to define demands rather than leaving it up to distant and inaccessible leaders in the Tripartite Alliance. The AMCU improved its standing among mine workers as an independent trade union that could represent their interests. The NUM and ANC, which expressed opposition to the strike, scorned the AMCU for its inexperience in running the strike and negotiating with management, but lost further credibility among the South African working class. Emerging as a representative of South African mine workers, the AMCU will have to remain accountable in order to keep their loyalty, or risk the same fate as the NUM.

The neglect of workers by the ruling alliance has also stirred dissent in the metal workers' union NUMSA, South Africa's largest union, which represents workers in the country's automobile, metal, and mining industries. In the aftermath of the Marikana massacre NUMSA has been the most militant affiliate of COSATU, conducting strikes in each of its major sectors and espousing the implementation of a socialist Marxist-Leninist politics developed in the apartheid era.[49] Irwin Jim, NUMSA's executive secretary, understands both the NUM's and COSATU's crisis of legitimacy and the uprising among rank-and-file workers in South Africa's mining and production industries, who have seen their living conditions erode over the past 20 years. Jim has openly opposed ANC's concessionary policies, and has reaffirmed support and advocacy for the nationalization of South African industry:

NUMSA maintains a policy of nationalization of major industries in South Africa. 1. ... [w]e believe in the centrality of the working class in the ownership of the means of production. Nationalisation must be based on a state that is really of the whole people. It involves a political struggle. 2. Our resolution on nationalisation, without compensation, of the leading heights of the economy has been and remains a correct position. 3. Our immediate perspective is the nationalisation of the major means of production and centralisation of the major means of communication and transport in the hands of the state.[50]

Following the ANC's re-election in May 2014, NUMSA was placed in the difficult position of steering an independent course from the ANC and COSATU while acknowledging the perseverance of platinum strikers weeks before its own planned work stoppage. Still, as it was desperately seeking support from COSATU and allies, Jim expressed solidarity for the platinum workers in their strike: 'We salute those workers in Rustenburg who are on strike for four months .... For now there is no alignment with AMCU. We're supporting the platinum strike. But why not? Workers must unite.'[51]

A week after the settlement of the platinum strike, 220,000 members of NUMSA walked out, seeking a 15 percent wage increase for entry-level workers in the metal and engineering industry. The union said that the wage demand constituted a 'living wage' for low-wage workers employed by suppliers and contractors to the auto, rubber and tire, and power sectors. Notably, NUMSA also called on the banning of labor brokers and intermediaries who circumvent wage standards. In its third week, the strike against metals and engineering contractors forced Toyota, General Motors, and Ford assembly plants in South Africa to suspend production.[52] The strike was settled a month later when the metal sector agreed to a settlement that would raise wages for the lowest-paid entry-level workers by 10 percent per year over the three years of the contract. While the union did not achieve its goal to prohibit labor brokers, NUMSA succeeded in tightening enforcement to monitor non-compliance and abuse of the wage system.[53]

CONCLUSION

Since the early 20th century, successive white-dominated colonial and nationalist regimes have deferred the demands of popular working-class movements through political maneuvers subordinating equality and welfare goals to social control and capitalist profitability. The events at Marikana were a predictable consequence of the corporate drive to profit at any cost, together with the failures of union bureaucracy and grave errors by the South African government. The tragedy represents the conclusion of the first phase of the post-apartheid era under the ANC, the Tripartite Alliance, and Nelson Mandela and his successors. But it is also a turning point for the South African labor movement, which historically has been sidestepped by electoral and political calculations, forcing militant working classes to resort to directly expressed rank-and-file struggles. Marikana was at once a massacre and a workers' uprising against an opaque state that ignored the conditions that had given rise to the growth of poverty and inequality among the African majority.

The dynamics of the South African trade union movement reveal that suppressing worker insurgency may have short-term success but always imperils the union leadership, if expectations for improved wages and conditions are frustrated and rank-and-file members are excluded from participation. The Marikana massacre demonstrated that any pretense that the ANC Tripartite Alliance only required time to implement policies favorable to the majority had been illusory. In October 2012, political economist Patrick Bond asserted that the mine workers' resistance to the post-apartheid state's keen embrace of neoliberal capitalism through violent state repression had brought to a conclusion the government's grace period in which to establish a new order:

> What is definitive ... is the waning of any remaining illusions that the forces of 'liberation' led by the ANC will take South Africa to genuine freedom and a new society. Marikana will have that effect, permanently, I suspect, so long as protesters keep dodging police bullets and moving the socio-economic and political-ecological questions to centre stage, from where ANC neoliberal nationalism could either arrange a properly fascist backlash, or more likely under Zuma's ongoing misrule, continue shrinking in confusion and regular doses of necessary humility.[54]

Arrayed in opposition to the insurgent working-class movement that has emerged in the mining industry in South Africa are not only multinational capital and compliant bureaucratic trade unions closely aligned to the South African state, but also a violent well-armed state system of repression. The repressive apparatus is institutionalized in the labor laws that criminalize workers who dare to challenge a legal system organized to defend capital against labor. Marikana has shown that when an insurgent workers' movement effectively mobilizes to defy the validity of hegemonic laws that contest the power of capital, the post-apartheid South African government will readily unleash its state security forces to destroy and obliterate all dissent. But it also demonstrates that South African workers who are deprived of legitimate labor representation will resist the state-capitalist system in order to advance their collective rights.

The emergence of an autonomous workers' movement a decade after the formation of the post-apartheid government was a categorical rejection of labor–management collaboration schemes. Not only have rank-and-file workers in the platinum mines challenged the legitimacy and future of COSATU as a national labor federation, they have also effectively replaced the powerful NUM with the AMCU, a union that its critics considered amateur and unsophisticated in collective bargaining. Under the Tripartite Alliance COSATU sanctioned the ANC government's implementation of neoliberal policies that caused low wages, severe pay disparities, subcontracting to labor brokers, and the erosion of wage standards for the Black majority employed in production industries. Staunchly opposed to the workers' movement, the NUM was outflanked by the AMCU, a new rival independent union that was formed by ostracized dissidents who were reviled by the government and the multinational mining companies.[55] As the credibility of the NUM and COSATU declined, the AMCU's integrity as an independent union has spread among mine workers.

NUMSA, the leading manufacturing union, has become increasingly disillusioned with the ruling alliance, charging the ANC with abandoning the working class in favor of neoliberal policies that have undermined South Africa's masses. At a special congress, delegates unanimously voted for a resolution calling on COSATU to break with the ANC, stating the union's intention to lead a struggle to establish a 'new United Front to coordinate struggles in the workplace and in communities.'

The split in the South African labor movement intensified in early November 2014 when the COSATU constituent unions suspended NUMSA from the federation by a vote of 33 to 24 of its central executive committee. The expulsion, condemned by NUMSA as arbitrary and a 'factional responsible action,' was a major blow to the trade union movement, which is cutting itself off from the major workers' movement in South Africa. The fissure in the South African labor movement augurs further labor strife that could further increase wages as unions compete for members.[56] The expulsion also sets the stage for the possible merger of NUMSA and the AMCU, and the growth of a militant workers' movement to challenge the dominance of COSATU, the governing ANC, and the Tripartite Alliance.

While the future configuration of the unions remains to be determined, it is clear is that rank-and-file workers are helping to build oppositional unions that are shaping a struggle against the economic imperialism, insisting on ending the system of exploitation and inequality that remains a fixture in the post-apartheid era, and that has engaged in ridicule and repression in order to suppress labor dissent.

Conclusion

Since the 1970s a consensus has emerged on both the right and left that the working class has disappeared and we must abandon the customary Marxist understanding of labor. It is true that, in the West, the industrial working class that for long towered over the economy is a thing of the past. The pervasive view is that new technology has mostly rendered manual work redundant, and we must now visualize a new future of labor, or perhaps even reconceive the very idea of work.

The majority of accounts lament the end of the bygone industrial era and the commencement of a period of wage stagnation, joblessness, economic inequality, and the decline of unions. This narrative assumes that work is done in the global North, and advocates Keynesian growth strategies to surmount unemployment, low wages, and job instability. As the working class vanishes in Europe and North America, however, industrial production is expanding at breakneck speed in the Third World, and the global working class of the 2010s is larger than at any time in history.[1]

This book demonstrates that work has not disappeared but has been relocated to the Global South, where we must comprehend the presence of a global working class. Moreover the majority viewpoint fails to consider the fact that the production and manufacture of inexpensive commodities in the South, undergirded by devaluation of the labor of Third World workers, supports comfortable lifestyles in the North. (In sharp contrast to the working class of Europe and North America, the state and capital in the Global South do not view the members of their emergent working class as future consumers of commodities.)

From the 1980s, the economies that dominated the world in the post-Second World War era entered a period of far-reaching transition away from state participation to private-sector dominance. The conversion process was not uniform: in some cases the shift to market control occurred gradually through the withdrawal of state subsidies for social welfare, and in other instances a radical shift away from public welfare was imposed all at once, in what came to be known as shock therapy. In the South, where most states had limited social welfare nets, economic liberalization converged on privatization of state production and market integration into the global capitalist economy. While 20th-century industrialization in the capitalist and socialist economies of the North typically took place in the context of social welfare states, in the South, massive industrialization was carried out without provision for health care, adequate food, child care, housing, education, unemployment insurance, and old age pensions for workers and their families.

PROMOTING FOREIGN INVESTMENT
FOR EXPORT PRODUCTION

In manufacturing, foreign direct investment (FDI) is concentrated in special zones such as special enterprise zones (SEZs) and export processing zones (EPZs) where workers have few rights. Finance capital has become dominant over production decisions, on the basis of criteria that have largely regulated wages and working conditions. How has it done this? Through investing in contractors that pay workers the lowest wages (in other words, super-exploitation). Industrial contractors are subservient to foreign multinational investors: if they fail to meet profit expectations financiers withdraw support and shift to lower-cost producers. Even in the mining and petroleum industries, capital reinvests in new forms of extraction when labor costs rise and threaten profits. The threat of disinvestment compels producers to restructure their operations to lower costs and restore high levels of profitability.

Developing countries seek to attract foreign capital by establishing separate governmental regions and enclaves such as EPZs, following a model developed in Mexico and China in the 1980s, as a way of generating investment in manufacturing. In addition to private local producers, labor contractors and real estate firms, the primary beneficiaries of EPZs are multinational brands that provide specifications on production standards and designs for contractors. Profits are guaranteed by the lower production costs achieved

Conclusion

through the great disparity between wages available in EPZs in the South, and those prevalent in the North. By setting the price of goods, in most cases multinational brands can in effect set low wage rates. Foreign brands typically maintain agreements with contractors in several countries and regions, which provide multiple production options in the event of labor disputes between contractors and workers.

EPZs provide a government partnership to ensure the abundant availability of compliant low-wage labor to foreign export production firms. To achieve this objective EPZs must:

- draw in an oversupply of low-wage workers
- support the capacity of producers to exploit workers through the removal of labor regulations governing wages and working conditions
- promote a union-free environment to warrant continuity in low-wage labor and prevent the possibility of worker stoppages and strikes that potentially interrupt production.

Thus the EPZs extract a high price from the working class of developing countries in exchange for the foreign currency revenues that flow from manufacturing for export.

EPZs are managed by government and corporate-appointed authorities to regulate the operation of the entire region. A primary characteristic of the EPZ is to establish an environment which promotes the development of infrastructure that facilitates foreign investment in logistics, including regional and international transportation networks, energy and power grids, and supports the development of social services and accommodation for a compliant labor force to work in the manufacturing industries. Police and security forces employed to guard against crime in EPZs are also, more importantly, used to prevent and impede worker mobilization and organizing against foreign firms in the Global South. The security apparatus in SEZs and in foreign firms includes surveillance and CCTV systems to monitor worker organizing and identify rank-and-file leaders.

RELIANCE ON A MIGRANT WORKFORCE

The industrialization of Europe and North America in the 19th and 20th centuries depended heavily on the availability of migrant labor. European immigrant workers were employed in the American garment, steel, auto, and electronic manufacturing industries, which largely excluded and marginalized Black, Mexican, Asian and unfree workers. In a similar manner, but to a far greater extent, today's industrialization in the Global South depends on laborers who migrate from rural regions into industrial zones where they are often marginalized.

Hiring migrant workers is a corporate strategy to increase the size of the reserve army of labor and reduce wage rates. Migrant workers are preferred because as newcomers they are not organized into traditional trade unions, allowing employers to maintain authoritarian control over the workplace. The vast majority of workers in new industrial zones are young people from rural areas who are unfamiliar with their rights and typically isolated from other workers. As the dominant force in the workplace, employers can entirely control wage rates and the labor process: they can discipline workers with impunity by avoiding collective bargaining, seniority systems, and formal grievance procedures; and they can relinquish social responsibility to workers while continuing to rely on the abundant reserve army that is unable to survive in rural areas, and so is desperate for any paid work.

In India's industrial zones, the career of an industrial worker may not last more than five or six years, and by the age of 25 workers are considered old and replaceable. As a consequence of the over-supply of labor and the relatively short working lives of these migrant laborers, capital depends on informalization and job insecurity to rotate workers out of the system and guarantee surplus profits under contemporary capitalism. Those workers who do have permanent positions are forced into precarious jobs, and in some cases encouraged to return to the countryside. However, as Jan Breman shows, urban informal work is becoming the norm in South Asia, and industrial workers cannot return to survive in rural areas because the commodification of land has destroyed their former way of life.[2]

Conclusion

In the early 21st century industrial workers in the Global South frequently live in dormitories managed by contractors or regional commissions established to deliver basic services to migrant laborers. Arriving as newcomers in transient municipalities, most laborers have few social bonds with long-term residents, and more often are reliant on fellow workers from rural areas and family members who have accompanied them. As new residential zones, SEZs are typically isolated from the political and social arena, and provide workers with few social contacts outside the work-places and living quarters. Although social isolation may preclude migrant worker contact with trade unions and community allies, it frequently creates stronger links with fellow factory workers, who are also exposed to continuous danger on the job and under threat from replacement by new workers. Marx's depiction of an alienated and estranged workforce in the 19th century can be applied to the condition of workers in the Global South today:

> We have seen how this absolute contradiction between the technical necessities of modern industry, and the social character inherent in its capitalistic form, dispels all fixity and security in the situation of the labourer; how it constantly threatens, by taking away the instruments of labour, to snatch from his hands his means of subsistence, and, by suppressing his detail-function, to make him superfluous, We have seen, too, how this antagonism vents its rage in the creation of that monstrosity, an industrial reserve army, kept in misery in order to be always at the disposal of capital; in the incessant human sacrifices from among the working-class, in the most reckless squandering of labour-power and in the devastation caused by a social anarchy which turns every economic progress into a social calamity.[3]

Living in new communities on the margins of major cities, migrant workers in each of the case studies presented in this book often lack the citizenship rights and residency privileges enjoyed by those living in the region who are officially documented and entitled to government services. Spouses and families are prohibited from joining workers; no formal education is provided for children; few rights to health care services exist outside the factory; casualization of the workforce allows employers to dismiss workers at will for any reason, and set permanent workers against an informal and temporary workforce; and young women are often subject to the highest level of exploitation as informal and temporary workers.[4]

IMPERIALISM AND THE GLOBAL WORKING CLASS, NORTH AND SOUTH

The central issue confronting the development of a socialist movement today is to recognize and surmount the inequities arising out of the hierarchical system of international value transfer that inflects the global capitalist order, which relies on super-exploitation of the working class in the Global South.[5]

The modern global system of production and accumulation is shaped by the historical dependence of capitalism on global imperialism to expand profitability, and by more than 250 years of class struggles. A distinct feature of contemporary capitalism is the emergence of foreign capital investment in firms that directly exploit not only land, resources, technology, and markets,[6] but also low-waged labor employed in the export-production industries of the Global South. In the mines and mills of the Global South, the disruptive and isolating labor and working conditions that produce alienation and estrangement also activate militancy comparable to that which has developed among low-wage undocumented migrant workers employed in major cities of the Global North.

TRADE UNIONS AND WORKERS MOVEMENTS IN THE GLOBAL SOUTH

Trade unions emerged in the 20th century to represent a Northern working class that has not survived into the present era. In the South most established trade unions are an inheritance from labor movements immersed in anti-colonial struggles, and have few connections to the contemporary working class. Even ACFTU, the

Chinese labor federation, is a legacy from the past. An array of unions was formed, and these continued into the period of formal independence, and have in various ways defended the rights of workers. Like those in Western Europe, unions in the South were formed in periods of struggle and labor exploitation, often acting to oppose colonialism and pave the way for independence.

In the 2000s, across the Global South most existing labor configurations are descended from earlier worker mobilizations, and have formed within party systems that have defined the scope of trade activity and power in the post-Second World War era. These regimes delineate the limits of official trade unions, and reveal the boundaries for the expression and development of unauthorized working-class militancy. It is always an open question whether existing labor unions can contain the concrete development of independent working-class organizations. The examples of China, India, and South Africa studied here reveal that industrial workers are engaged in direct action against institutionalized exploitation in various arenas, and are making demands that are reshaping traditional unions.

India

Since independence in 1947, trade union federations affiliated with political parties have represented public and private sector workers primarily through parliament in a system that confers standing and provides legitimacy. In the post-independence era, trade unions have been unable to end the system of contract labor which allowed industrialists to employ contract laborers alongside permanent workers, and to use the caste system to maintain employment segregation, and thereby divide the workforce. Following the introduction of free market reforms in the 1990s, Indian employers and the state have sought to diminish the influence of trade unions in the industrial sector as a means to attract foreign capital. With foreign investment flowing into the non-union private sector, the government withdrew economic support for the unionized state-owned sector, decreasing membership and the influence of trade unions in electoral politics. Independent unions established on a plant-by-plant basis are unable to negotiate national agreements and rely primarily on strikes and direct action to improve wages and workplace conditions. The wave of sit-down strikes in India from 2012 to 2014 has been met with harsh violence by corporate security and state police, but the strikes are nevertheless becoming ubiquitous in the EPZs.

By rejecting the contract system and demanding equal status for all employees, the Maruti-Suzuki Workers Union in Gurgaon has challenged the Indian model of production that rests on accentuating worker divisions. Solidarity served the interests of all the workers: full-timers would not be threatened by a subservient workforce and informal workers would gain equal rights and wages through a union that did not distinguish between workers on the basis of their status. The state responded with mass repression, violence, and imprisonment.

On the whole the nature of established unions remains unchanged. Trade unions are not integrated into the state structures, and the lack of a dominant union contributes to their weakness. As a consequence unions are losing membership, and since workers are typically not mobilized in these unions, the formation of independent unions is one of the only alternatives available. Thus far, established unions have not challenged the contracting system in India. Worker organizing continues to involve only the full-timers, which exposes it to challenges from independent labor organizations. These will become the center of struggle in the years to come.

China

The Chinese model of industrialization which began in the late 1980s is founded on the ability to produce quality products for export at the lowest possible cost. A large reserve army of labor was achieved by establishing industries in strategic geographic port regions and forcing the rural peasantry off the land, creating inequality in urban areas. Extensive industrialization and modernization has significant ramifications for class relations and the evolving class conflict. To promote FDI the public sector was reorganized and free markets established, causing major protests in older urban industries of the Chinese north-east.

The Communist Party of China (CPC) and the ACFTU dominate the landscape, and prohibit the formation of all independent organizations; workers were typically seen as subservient and incapable of organizing independently. However, the expansion of legal protection covering migrant workers in new export promotion industries has ignited a militant workers' movement that has witnessed a wave of strikes in the foreign-dominated export sector between 2010 and 2015. Without official unions and intermediaries, and without laws defining the precise terms of work stoppages, workers are free to strike over a range of grievances on a local level and increasingly these have been articulated in public protests and mass strikes that extend beyond local factories. In new export industries, women workers who have recently migrated are emerging as important participants in resistance against contractors.

While ruling out the formation of organizations that may be controlled by foreign non-governmental organizations (NGOs), the CPC and ACFTU have expanded labor law to protect migrant workers and their families, and have urged local governments to respond to worker demands for higher wages, benefits, and living conditions. Chinese rank-and-file activists recognize that militancy can be successful without establishing a competing party or union, but through direct struggle on the job and within communities.

South Africa

In the late 1980s the pivotal factor motivating the South African government to end the apartheid system was the need to join the global capitalist economy. Trade sanctions were restraining economic growth in its major industries, minerals and auto manufacturing. By 1990, however, the South African economy was shifting toward export promotion and becoming increasingly interdependent with the world economy. The post-apartheid government conferred political rights on South Africa's Black majority without granting them equivalent economic rights. Moreover, the government put off significant wage increases to the industrial working class in the very mining and manufacturing industries that were crucial to the South African economy. Poverty, unemployment, and inequality have increased.

In South Africa the corporatist system has failed to represent the interests of the working class, especially workers in the mining and manufacturing sectors. COSATU, South Africa's leading trade union federation, is controlled by the Tripartite Alliance which has dominated the political sphere in the post-apartheid era. The Alliance has supported the neoliberal policies which permitted labor contracting arrangements to create multi-tier wage systems.

RANK-AND-FILE WORKERS AND THE FUTURE OF TRADE UNIONS

Today trade unions are at a historic crossroad that will determine their future viability. We are deafened by the mantra that all unions need to do is grow larger so they can advance worker interests. In fact, however, capitalist globalization constrains the capacity of unions to adapt to changing conditions in the contemporary era. Trade unions are becoming outmoded under neoliberal capitalist industrialization in the South. While unions are under attack by the state and capital, they are also losing their credibility with workers. Given the origin of unions within the political and legal frameworks of independence and anti-capitalist struggles, it remains an open question whether specific unions will survive and even perhaps thrive in the future.

As in previous eras, poverty and inequality are related to gender, race, ethnicity, caste, religion, and other social divisions.[7] Wage inequality and job insecurity have increased in the North since the 1970s, but poverty and inequality are far higher among workers in the modern manufacturing industries of Asia, Africa, and Latin America. In the South, newly proletarianized workers labor in factories, mines and plantations, typically with little or no job security, and in many cases are represented by unions which are unable to negotiate for contract or temporary labor.

Meanwhile traditional trade unions, an inheritance of 20th-century European and North American models, contribute to the marginalization of workers in the Global South, by supporting their incorporation into dominant bureaucratic state structures where at best union leaders are relegated to a subordinate and consultative position, and more typically they are ignored. Furthermore, traditional unions are committed to preserving and improving the wages and conditions covered by past agreements for a privileged few members, while ignoring the majority of workers who are not core members.

This book asserts that workers can no longer rely on bureaucratic union leaders to defend them. Authentic worker struggles proceed from industrial workers themselves, who are both building independent unions and, where the workers' organizations they build are not officially unrecognized, challenging existing labor unions to represent their interests. It is the development of worker radicalism that will shape the form and survival of decaying traditional unions. In the absence of recognized unions the results of these rank-and-file struggles are mixed, but the evidence in this book demonstrates that these movements are gaining traction, and achieving real wage gains and improvement in conditions.

The evidence drawn from the South is that a profound movement is emerging among workers demanding action on grievances outside the system of established unions. Workers' movements are operating within the interstices of existing trade union structures, with or without the sanction of the unions. Rank-and-file workers in industries are forming independent associations and compelling existing unions to represent their interests:

- In India the dominant unions are unable to solve crucial issues facing workers for a number of reasons: unfamiliarity with the conditions of workers in EPZs; the perpetuation of a contract system dividing permanent and contract employees, often on the basis of caste, gender, and age; and fierce opposition to unionization by capital and the state. In response to the obstacles to joining existing unions, workers are forming independent unions to represent their interests.
- In China, compulsory membership in the ACFTU gives workers the capacity to push the federation and the state to represent and enforce their interests. Industrial workers in export industries are expanding the scope of strikes, and are benefiting from the initia-

tion of labor laws that place the migrant workers who have domi-nated the industrial working class in the same position as other members of the union. In a growing number of cases, rank-and-file committees have been effective in advancing worker interests when local unions fail to represent their members.

• South Africa has witnessed the emergence of the AMCU, a wholly new union in the mining sector that has arisen in response to the unwillingness of the NUM to represent mine workers against multinational mining companies, and that opposes government cooperation with management. Worker self-organizing expanded across South Africa's mining sector from 2009 to 2014, culminat-ing in a five-month nationwide strike of platinum miners against mining conglomerates. The insurgency spread to the auto and electronics industries, where the main union, NUMSA, recog-nized the need to represent the interests of excluded workers or risk the same fate as the NUM. In November 2014, NUMSA distanced itself from the position of the ruling African National Congress in support of multinational capital, and mobilized workers in key industries. The union was expelled from the COSATU labor federation.

Each case demonstrates that organizational representation is subor-dinate to the workers' movements themselves. To build on these struggles workers will need a disciplined and strong class-based orga-nization. It is in the interest of capital to undermine trade unions of any form. Eventually the worker mobilization that is taking place both inside and outside established structures will cohere into disci-plined organizations. But each of the struggles demonstrates that the time when workers can be taken for granted or ignored is over. Workers' movements are emerging, and will expand to contest the legitimacy of capital, the state, and existing unions.

Notes

1 The New International Working Class

1 Daniel Bell, *The Coming of Post-Industrial Society: A Venture in Social Forecasting* (New York: Basic Books, 1999 [1973]), 1999 foreword, p. lxv.

2 André Gorz, *Farewell to the Working Class: An Essay on Post-Industrial Socialism* (originally published in 1980 in French, trans. into English by Michael Sonenscher) (London: Pluto Press, 1982), pp. 67–8. See Vivek Chibber, *Postmodernism and the Specre of Capital* (New York: Verso 2013) for a broad-ranging critique of the lack of material basis within postcolonial theory and the abiding significance of class.

3 Labor–management disputes in the Global South are reported on frequently by the *Financial Times* and *Bloomberg News* among other publications intended for the investment community.

4 On the development of the informal economy among low-wage workers in major cities of the Global North, see Saskia Sassen, *The Global City: New York, London, Tokyo* (Princeton, N.J.: Princeton University Press, 2001); on non-waged household work see Eileen Boris and Jennifer Klein, *Caring for America: Home Health Workers in the Shadow of the Welfare State* (New York: Oxford University Press, 2012); Kathi Weeks, *The Problem with Work: Feminism, Marxism, Anti-Work Politics and Postwork Imaginaries* (Durham, N.C.: Duke University Press, 2011); Silvia Federici, *Revolution at Point Zero: Housework, Reproduction, and Feminist Struggle* (Oakland, Calif.: PM Press, 2012); on sex work, see Melissa Gira Grant, *Playing the Whore: The Work of Sex Work* (London: Verso, 2014). Carisa R. Showden and Samantha Majic, *Negotiating Sex Work: Unintended Consequences of Policy and Activism* (Minneapolis, Minn.: University of Minnesota Press, 2014). On the contemporary struggles around precarious labor see Guy Standing, *The Precariat: The New Dangerous Class* (London: Bloomsbury Academic, 2011), Ruth Milkman and Ed Ott, *New Labor in New York: Precarious Workers and the Future of the Labor Movement* (Ithaca, N.Y.: Cornell University Press, 2014); Vinit Mukhija and Anastasia Loukaitou-Sideris, *The Informal American City: Beyond Taco Trucks and Day Labor*, Cambridge, Mass.: MIT Press, 2014).

5 Maybe this implies that successful organizing campaigns in the contemporary era can only be conducted through challenging the state rather than authentic struggles by workers in their workplaces. But if that is so, then why do Walmart workers organize directly in the workplace in China but not in the United States?

6 Gary Gereffi and Joonkoo Lee, 'Why the world suddenly cares about global supply chains,' *Journal of Supply Chain Management*, Vol. 48, No. 3 (July 2012), pp. 24–32.

Notes

7   John Bellamy Foster and Robert W. McChesney, *The Endless Crisis: How Monopoly-Finance Capital Produces Stagnation and Upheaval from the USA to China*, New York: Monthly Review Press, 2012, p. 130. In this book Foster and McChesney analyze the contemporary global restructuring of monopoly capital through financialization, which creates the conditions for expanded class struggle on a global basis.

8   For Foster and McChesney, industrial employment consists of mining, manufacturing, utilities, and construction, or infrastructure.

9   Friedrich Engels, *The Condition of the Working-Class in England in 1844* (London: George Allen & Unwin, 1943), English Preface 1892, pp. 3–4.

10   Ronaldo P. Munck, 'Globalization and the labour movement: challenges and responses,' *Global Labour Journal*, Vol. 1, No. 2 (May 2010), p. 222.

11   Michael Yates, 'Poverty and inequality in the global economy,' *Monthly Review*, Vol. 55, No. 9, pp. 41–2.

12   Richard H. Chilcote, 'Globalization or imperialism?' *Latin American Perspectives*, Vol. 29 (2002), pp. 80–4. See also Paul Mason, *Live Working or Die Fighting: How the Working Class Went Global* (London: Vintage, 2007).

13   Jeffrey D. Sachs, *The End of Poverty: Economic Possibilities for Our Time* (New York: Penguin, 2006).

14   An exception to this rule in the early 21st century is the nationalization of natural resources in South America, notably in Venezuela and Bolivia. However, given the dominance of international finance capital, privatization efforts are also widespread, for example the Mexican President Enrique Peña Nieto's plan to privatize PEMEX, the state oil company in 2013.

15   Chilcote, 'Globalization or imperialism?'; Martin Hart-Landsberg, *Capitalist Globalization: Consequences, Resistance, and Alternatives* (New York: Monthly Review Press, 2013); William I. Robinson, *Promoting Polyarchy: Globalization, U.S. Intervention, and Hegemony* (Cambridge: Cambridge University Press, 1996).

16   See Samir Amin, *Capitalism in the Age of Globalization: The Management of Contemporary Society* (London: Zed, 1997), p. 75.

17   Vladimir Il'ich Lenin, *Imperialism, the Highest Stage of Capitalism* (Sydney, NSW: Resistance Marxist Library, 1999 [1917]), p. 45.

18   Harry Magdoff, *The Age of Imperialism: The Economics of U.S. Foreign Policy* (New York: Monthly Review Press, 1969), p.15.

19   More than ever, by the early 2000s, global imperialism and monopoly capitalism in the contemporary era have become dependent on the availability and ready application of foreign military power and domestic police forces to control and restrain working class unrest. The United States, the United Kingdom, other European countries, and Japan have all supported the international repressive system through the direct or indirect use of violence to crush and erode local opposition to neoliberal capitalism in regions with abundant oil wealth, natural resources, and land crucial for global monopoly capitalism.

Accordingly, resource-rich countries in the Americas, the Middle East, and increasingly in Africa, are sites of foreign invasion and police violence. As global manufacturing has shifted to China, India, Indonesia, and Brazil, among others, nation states in industrial regions of the Global South have more and more resorted to the use of police force to crush worker strikes and peasant insurrections.

20   See Magdoff, *The Age of Imperialism*, p. 40.

21   Magdoff, *The Age of Imperialism*, p. 167.

22   Ironically, if World Bank economist Branko Milanovic were to apply his plan for reducing inequities in the global economy through modest foreign aid with the greatest precision, those countries most eligible for foreign assistance in the Global South would ironically be those undermined by Western countries in the post-independence era, which sought to pursue policies to redistribute wealth and income. These include Indonesia under Sukharno, Ghana under Kwame Nkrumah, contemporary Cuba, and Venezuela, where, despite significant obstacles, governments have continued attempts to reduce inequality.

23   Magdoff, *The Age of Imperialism*.

24   Samir Amin, *The Implosion of Capitalism* (London: Pluto Press, 2014), p. 150.

25   Tom Brass, *Labour Regime Change in the Twenty-First Century: Unfreedom, Capitalism and Primitive Accumulation* (Leiden, Neths: Brill, 2011), p. 4.

2 The Industrial Proletariat of the Global South

1   World Bank, World Development Indicators 2013, last updated September 23, 2013. Note the data includes European workers in the former Soviet Bloc. See also John Bellamy Forster and Robert W. McChesney, *The Endless Crisis: How Monopoly-Finance Capital Produces Stagnation and Upheaval from the USA to China* (New York: Monthly Review Press, 2012, pp.127–8).

2   Beverley Silver, *Forces of Labor: Workers' Movements and Globalization since 1870*. Cambridge, UK: Cambridge University Press, 2003

3   Silver, *Forces of Labor*, p. 20.

4   Silver, *Forces of Labor*, pp. 20–1.

5   Silver, *Forces of Labor*, p. 9.

6   Silver, *Forces of Labor*, p. 170.

7   See John Smith, 'The GDP illusion: value added versus value capture,' *Monthly Review*, Vol. 44, No. 3 (July–Aug. 2012), for a criticism of GDP as a means of measuring value creation; see Zak Cope, *Divided World Divided Class: Global Political Economy and the Stratification of Labour under Capitalism* (Montreal, Quebec: Kersplebedeb, 2012) for a critique of FDI figures as a means of measuring the contribution of developing countries workers to the global economy. A huge proportion of the value in the capitalist world economy is generated by developing country labor. Note that the discrepancy between inflows and outflows on a world scale is considerable. UNCTAD compiles FDI

statistics based on national international sources. There is an apparent lack of comparability of FDI data reported by different countries. The methodology for compiling these data varies between countries. For a given transaction, host country and home country often do not register it in exactly the same way. For example, country A might include reinvested earnings in its outflow statistics while country B receiving this FDI might not include the earnings in its inflow statistics. Furthermore, corporate accounting practices and valuation methods differ between countries. These two factors lead to discrepancies in FDI data. See UNCTAD's explanation for the discrepancy: http://unctad.org/en/Pages/DIAE/Frequently%20Asked%20Questions/Why-dont-data-on-global-FDI-inflows-and-outflows-match-with-each-other.aspx (accessed August 8, 2014).

8   For a discussion of the rise of the global reserve army of labor and economic imperialism from 1975 to 2010 see Foster and McChesney, *The Endless Crisis*, pp. 125–54. Ellen Meiskins Wood, *Empire of Capital* (London: Verso, 2005, pp. 9–25) emphasizes the abiding significance of the 'territorial state' as the political and legal power that allows global capital to expand through 'the detachment of economic power'.

9   For an examination of the global growth of megacities concentrated in the global South, see Mike Davis, *Planet of Slums* (London: Verso, 2006). For detailed research of the lack of essential services in the South, in his study of Ahmedabad, India, see Jan Breman, 'The myth of the social safety net,' *New Left Review*, Vol. 59 (Sept.–Oct. 2009), pp. 29–36.

10   John Smith, 'Southern labour – "peripheral" no longer: a reply to Jane Hardy,' *International Socialism*, No. 140 (2013), www.isj.org.uk/index.php4?id=922&issue=140 (accessed October 21, 2014).

11   Smith, 'Southern labour'.

12   Stephen Roach, 'How global labour arbitrage will shape the world economy,' http://ecocritique.free.fr/roachglo.pdf (accessed October 21, 2014).

13   UNCTAD, *World Investment Report 2011* (Geneva: United Nations, 2011), p. 10.

14   Patricia Hoffman, *The Impact of International Trade and FDI on Economic Growth and Technological Change* (Heidelberg: Springer, 2013), p. 25.

15   Andrew Glyn, *Capitalism Unleashed: Finance Globalization and Welfare* (Oxford: Oxford University Press, 2006), p. 101.

16   World Bank, *Global Development Horizons 2011: Multipolarity – The New Global Economy* (Washington, DC: World Bank, 2011), p. 5.

17   Gérard Duménil and Dominique Lévy, *The Crisis of Neoliberalism* (Cambridge, Mass.: Harvard University Press, 2011), esp. ch. 1.

18   Duménil and Lévy, *The Crisis of Neoliberalism*, p. 9.

19   Prabhat Patnaik, 'Notes on contemporary imperialism', Networkideas.org, December 20, 2010. http://networkideas.org/featart/dec2010/Notes.pdf (accessed July 14, 2014). Patnaik argues that the contemporary era of impe-

rialism, dominated by finance capital, severely undermines the ability of states in the South to determine economic policy as they are threatened by the withdrawal of investments and expulsion from the international capitalist economy: 'The process of globalization of finance therefore has the effect of undermining the autonomy of the nation-State. The State cannot do what it wishes to do, or what its elected government has been elected to do, since it must do what finance wishes it to do.'

20 Sarah Mosoetsa and Michelle Williams (eds), *Labour in the Global South: Challenges and Alternatives for Workers* (Geneva: International Labour Organization, 2012), p. 6. www.ilo.org/wcmsp5/groups/public/---dgreports/---dcomm/---publ/documents/publication/wcms_187420.pdf (accessed June 5, 2014).

21 Sam Moyo, Paris Yeros, and Praveen Jha, 'Imperialism and primitive accumulation: notes on the new scramble for Africa,' *Agrarian South*, Vol. 1, No. 2, pp.181–203. Quotation is from p. 186.

22 For an analysis of the composition and condition of the new working class in South Asia see Jan Breman, *At Work in the Informal Economy of India: A Perspective from the Bottom Up* (New Delhi: Oxford University Press, 2013).

23 In Brazil, the CUT (Central Única dos Trabalhadores) was formed in 1983 in alliance with the Workers Party and Landless Workers Movement, which went on to form the governing party in 2003; in South Africa, COSATU (Congress of South African Trade Unions) joined in 1994 with the African National Congress and the South African Communist Party in the Tripartite Alliance; and in 1995 the KCTU (Korean Confederation of Trade Unions) was formed as an independent force in opposition to the government-dominated FKTU (Federation of Korean Trade Unions) and often remains an oppositional force to neoliberal government policies. Among the three trade federations, the KCTU is the most representative of an independent union force.

24 See Gay Seidman, *Manufacturing Militance: Workers' Movements in Brazil and South Africa, 1970–1985* (Berkeley, Calif.: University of California Press, 1994).

25 Jeremy Waddington, 'Trade union membership in Europe: the extent of the problem and the range of trade union responses', paper for ETUC/ETUI-REHS top-level summer school, Florence, July 1–2, 2005, http://library.fes.de/pdf-files/gurn/00287.pdf (accessed November 25, 2014).

26 European Industrial Relations Observatory (EIRO), 'Trade union membership 1993–2003', 2004, www.eiro.eurofound.eu.int

27 Tom Bramble and Neal Follett, 'Corporatism as a process of working class containment and roll back: the recent experiences of South Africa and South Korea.' *Journal of Industrial Relations*, Vol. 49, No. 4 (2007), pp.569–89.

28 See Kevin Gray, 'The global uprising of labour? The Korean labour movement and neoliberal social corporatism,' *Globalizations*, Vol. 5, No. 3 (Sept. 2008), pp. 483–99; Bramble and Follett, 'Corporatism.'

29 E. A. Wilkens, 'In defense of the new working class? Labor union embeddedness, labor migration and immigrant integration.' *Political Science* –

Dissertations, Paper 95 (2010), http://surface.syr.edu/psc_etd/95 (accessed July 16, 2014).

30 See Gray, 'The global uprising of labour?'

31 Anna Zalik, 'Oil sovereignties in the Mexican Gulf and Niger Delta,' in Kenneth Omeje (ed.), *Extractive Economies and Conflicts in the Global South: Multi-Regional Perspectives* (Aldershot, UK: Ashgate, 2008), pp.181–9/

32 Andy Cumbers, Corinne Nativel, and Paul Routledge, 'Labour agency and union positionalities in global production networks.' *Journal of Economic Geography*, Vol. 8, No. 3 (2008), pp. 369–87.

33 Martin Lynch, *Mining in World History* (London: Reaktion, 2009), pp. 322–3.

34 Stuart Kirsch documents the deliberate environmental devastation and the associated catastrophic health and social consequences brought about by unregulated copper and gold mining conglomerates from 1970 to the 2010s in Papua New Guinea, in *Mining Capitalism* (Berkeley, Calif.: University of California Press, 2014).

3 Migration and the Reserve Army of Labor

1 Frederick Engels, *The Condition of the Working Class in England in 1844*, with intro. by David McLellan (Oxford/New York: Oxford University Press, 2009). See ch. 3 on competition and the reserve army of labor, and ch. 4 on Irish immigration and conditions.

2 Karl Polanyi, *The Great Transformation: The Political and Economic Origins of Our Time* (Boston, Mass.; Beacon, 2nd edn 2002).

3 Frederick Engels, *The Condition of the Working Class in England* (London: Oxford University Press, 2009).

4 Michael P. Todaro, *Economic Development in the Third World: An Introduction to Problems and Policies in a Global Perspective* (London: Longman, 1977).

5 George J. Borjas, *Economic Research on the Determinants of Immigration: Lessons for the European Union* (Washington, DC: World Bank, 1999), p. 8.

6 Costas Lapavitsas, *Profiting without Producing: How Finance Exploits Us All* (London: Verso, 2014).

7 Raúl Delgado Wise, 'The migration and labor question today: imperialism, unequal development, and forced migration,' *Monthly Review*, Vol. 64, No. 9 (Feb. 2013), pp. 25–38 (quote p. 30). http://estudiosdeldesarrollo.net/administracion/docentes/documentos_personales/15015RDW%20MR%20 2013.pdf (accessed June 18, 2015).

8 Delgado Wise, 'The migration and labor question today', p. 31.

9 Ronaldo Munck, *Globalization and Social Exclusion: A Transformationalist Perspective* (Bloomfield, Conn.: Kumarian Press), chs 2–7, p. 101. See also Ronaldo Munck, 'Globalization, governance and migration: an introduction,' *Third World Quarterly*, No. 297 (2008), pp. 1227–46.

10 David Oliviere, Barbara Monroe, and Sheila Payne (eds), *Death, Dying*

and Social Differences (Oxford: Oxford University Press, 2011); see also Thomas W. M. Pogge, *Politics as Usual: What Lies behind the Pro-Poor Rhetoric* (Cambridge, UK: Polity, 2010), for an examination of the ethical motivations for improving conditions for the world's population living in abject poverty.

11   Michael J. Piore, *Birds of Passage: Migrant Labor and Industrial Societies* (Cambridge: Cambridge University Press, 1979); D. S. Massey, J. Arango, G. Hugo, A. Kouaouci, A. Pellegrino, and E. Taylor, 'Theories of international migration: a review and appraisal,' *Population and Development Review*, Vol. 19, No. 3 (Sept. 1993), pp.431–66.

12   Nina Glick Schiller, 'A global perspective on transnational migration: theorising migration without methodological nationalism,' in Rainer Bauböck and Thomas Faist (eds), *Diaspora and Transnationalism: Concepts, Theories and Methods* (Amsterdam: Amsterdam University Press, 2010), pp. 114–15.

13   James N. Gregory, *The Southern Diaspora: How the Great Migrations of Black and White Southerners Transformed America* (Chapel Hill, N.C.: University of North Carolina Press, 2005); Thomas J. Sugrue, *The Origins of the Urban Crisis: Race and Inequality in Postwar Detroit* (Princeton, N.J.: Princeton University Press, 2005); Joe W. Trotter (ed.), *The Great Migration in Historical Perspective: New Dimensions of Race, Class, and Gender* (Bloomington, Ind.: Indiana University Press, 1991).

14   Sandra Mantu, *Constructing and Imagining Labour Migration: Perspectives of Control from Five Continents* (Farnham, UK: Ashgate, 2011); H. Clare Pentland, *Labour and Capital in Canada 1650–1860* (Toronto, Ont.: Lorimer, 1981), pp. 61–95.

15   William C. Davis, *Warnings from the Far South: Democracy versus Dictatorship in Uruguay, Argentina, and Chile* (Westport, Conn.: Praeger, 1995); Linda Hunt, 'U.S. coverup of Nazi scientists,' *Bulletin of Atomic Scientists*, Vol. 41, No. 4 (April 1985), pp.16–27; Fred Jerome, T*he Einstein File: J. Edgar Hoover's Secret War against the World's Most Famous Scientist* (New York: St Martin's Press, 2003).

16   Vic Satzewich, *Racism and the Incorporation of Foreign Labour: Farm Labour Migration to Canada since 1945* (London and New York: Routledge, 1991).

17   J. H. Momsen, *Gender, Migration, and Domestic Service* (London: Routledge, 1999), pp. 65–91; Habiba Zaman, *Breaking the Iron Wall: Decommodification and Immigrant Women's Labor in Canada* (Lanham, Md.: Lexington, 2006).

18   Donna R. Gabaccia and Fraser M. Ottanelli, *Italian Workers of the World: Labor Migration and the Formation of Multiethnic States* (Urbana, Ill.: University of Illinois Press, 2001).

19   Peter Stalker, *The Work of Strangers: A Survey of International Labour Migration* (Geneva: International Labour Office, 1994).

20   Jean-Christophe Dumont and Gilles Spielvogel, *A Profile of Immigrant Populations in the 21st Century: Data from OECD Countries* (Paris: OECD,

2008); Georges Lemaître and Thomas Liebig, *Jobs for Immigrants* (Paris: OECD, 2007–08).

21   Delgado Wise, 'The migration and labor question today', pp. 25–38.

22   Mike Davis, 'Planet of slums: urban involution and the informal proletariat,' *New Left Review*, Vol. 26 (March–April 2004), pp. 5–34.

23   Davis, 'Planet of slums,' p. 26.

24   United Nations Development Programme (UNDP), *World Economic and Social Survey 2010: Retooling Global Development* (New York: UNDP, 2010), E/2010/50/Rev. 1, ST/ESA/330, pp. 144–5, ww.un.org/en/development/desa/policy/wess/wess_archive/2010wess.pdf (accessed December 14, 2013).

25   See David Bacon, *The Right to Stay Home: How US Policy Drives Mexican Migration* (Boston, Mass.: Beacon Press, 2013), chs 7 and 8; and Joseph Nevins, *Operation Gatekeeper: The Rise of the 'Illegal Alien' and the Making of the US-Mexico Boundary* (New York and London: Routledge, 2002) for analysis of human rights abuses, poverty wages, and other coercive policies confronted by Mexican migrant workers to the United States.

26   In particular, workers employed in temporary labor migration programs in the United States and the Arab Gulf States tend to experience higher levels of repression than even undocumented laborers, who can evade for a time government control. See Immanuel Ness, *Guest Workers and Resistance to US Corporate Despotism* (Urbana, Ill.: University of Illinois Press, 2011), for examination of Caribbean and South Asian migration; Adam Hanieh, *Capitalism and Class in the Gulf Arab States* (Basingstoke: Palgrave Macmillan, 2011) for migration to the Gulf states.

27   Ness, *Guest Workers and Resistance*, p. 14.

28   David Bacon, *Illegal People: How Globalization Creates Migration and Criminalizes Immigrants* (Boston, Mass.: Beacon Press, 2009); Aviva Chomsky, *Undocumented: How Immigration Became Illegal* (Boston, Mass.: Beacon Press, 2014); Nevins, *Operation Gatekeeper*.

4   India: Neoliberal Industrialization, Class Formation and Mobilization

1   The industrial workers' struggles in India are dynamic, mercurial, and ever-changing. This chapter manly covers the mobilization of auto workers at Maruti Suzuki where unionization was crushed in July 2012, after which all workers were fired and permanently replaced. A key feature of the new production industries is the informalization of production, as a large share of production is carried out by contractors for multinational firms seeking to significantly reduce labor costs and avoid regulations in EPZs. In EPZs employers often rely on temporary and informal workers who lack job security. Women tend to form a larger share of informal workers, who have few rights and are less disposed to form unions. See Rohini Hensman, *Workers, Unions,*

and Global Capitalism: Lessons from India (New York: Columbia University Press, 2011).

2   See Prabhat Patnaik, 'Capitalism in Asia at the end of the millennium,' *Monthly Review*, Vol. 51, No. 3 (Jul.–Aug. 1999), pp. 53–70.

3   In June 2011, after six years of organizing, 4,000 permanent workers, mostly women, formed an independent employees' union at a Nokia processing plant in the Sriperumbadur EPZ near Chennai. See Madhumita Dutta, 'Unionizing in special economic zone: a case study of a shop floor employees' union in an electronics SEZ in Sriperumbadur, Kancheepuram District, Tamil Nadu,' unpublished essay, June 2014; and Madhumita Dutta, 'Nokia SEZ: public price of success,' *Economic and Political Weekly*, Vol. 40, No. 44 (October 3–9, 2009).

4   The workers' struggle at MSIL that began in 2000 is representative of the rising independent union movement in India and throughout the Global South, as traditional workers lose their power and state governments obsequiously support the interests and demands of capital. The worker insurgencies reveal the unremitting resilience of the working class to employer oppression and their belief that their interests should be defended by state authorities, even while they are incessantly disappointed. The workers are in constant struggle to end informal work arrangements, which comprise more than 75 percent of all jobs in India. In the Gurgaon Industrial Belt south of New Delhi, manufacturing is divided among permanent workers and contract laborers who comprise 80 percent of all workers; these workers earn 25–50 percent of the standard wage and are prohibited from organizing unions.

5   For a survey on the declining influence of traditional unions in the automobile sector and the erosion of stable working conditions in the Chennai manufacturing center, see Ramapriya Golpalakrishnan and Jeanne Mirer, *Shiny Cars, Shattered Dreams, A Report on Precarious Workers in the Chennai Automobile Hub* (New York: International Commission for Labor Rights, 2014), www.laborcommission.org/files/uploads/2Shattered_Dreams_FINAL_website.pdf (accessed September 1, 2014).

6   Satyaki Roy, interview with the author, August 4, 2014.

7   Chandrajit Banerjee, 'Is contract labour the problem or the solution?' *Financial Express*, July 27, 2012, www.financialexpress.com/news/is-contract-labour-the-problem-or-the-solution-/980064/1 (accessed December 24, 2013).

8   Research Unit for Political Economy, 'Behind the present wave of unrest in the auto sector,' *Aspects of India's Economy*, Vol. 52 (June 2012), www.rupe-india.org/52/auto.html#note (accessed December 27, 2013).

9   In the West, a consensus has emerged that market fundamentalism has eroded working class political and economic influence through the decline of labor-based electoral parties and industry-based unions. For an examination of the decline and declining relevance of labor-based parties in the United Kingdom, see Leo Panitch and Colin Leys, *The End of Parliamentary Socialism: From New Left to New Labour* (London: Verso, 2001).

Notes

10 On restructuring under neoliberal capitalism, see Gérard Duménil and Dominique Lévy, *Capital Insurgent: Roots of the Neoliberal Revolution* (Cambridge, Mass.: Harvard University Press, 2004).

11 The numerous works on strengthening unions in the United States and the Global North include Dan Clawson, *The Next Upsurge: Labor and the New Social Movements* (Ithaca, N.Y.: Cornell University Press, 2003); Bill Fletcher, Jr. and Fernando Gapasin, *Solidarity Divided: The Crisis in Organized Labor and a New Path Toward Social Justice* (Berkeley, Calif.: University of California Press, 2008); Ruth Milkman and Kim Voss (eds), *Rebuilding Labor: Organizing and Organizers in the New Union Movement* (Ithaca, N.Y.: Cornell University Press, 2004). For transnational strategies, see Andreas Bieler, Ingemar Lindberg, and Devan Pillay, *Labour and the Challenges of Globalization: What Prospects for Transnational Solidarity?* (London: Pluto Press, 2008).

12 See Taylor Dark, *The Unions and the Democrats: An Enduring Alliance* (Ithaca, N.Y.: Cornell University Press, 1999); and Peter Francia, *The Future of Organized Labor in American Politics* (New York: Columbia University Press, 2006). Few scholars recognize the imperative of promoting labor-based social movements.

13 See Staughton Lynd and Andrej Grubačič, *Wobblies and Zapatistas: Conversations on Anarchism, Marxism and Radical History* (Oakland, Calif.: PM Press, 2008); Gay Seidman, *Beyond the Boycott: Labor Rights, Human Rights, and Transnational Activism* (New York: Russell Sage Foundation, 2007).

14 International Commission for Labor Rights meeting with Anupam Malik, Joint Labour Commissioner, Chandigarh, Haryana, India, May 30, 2013.

15 Satyaki Roy, interview, August 4, 2014.

16 Jan Breman, 'A dualistic labour system? A critique of the 'informal sector' concept. I: The informal sector,' *Economic and Political Weekly*, Vol. 11, No. 48 (Nov. 27, 1976), pp. 1870–6.

17 Rohini Hensman, *Workers, Unions, and Global Capitalism: Lessons from India* (New York: Columbia University Press, 2011)

18 See Faridabad Majoor Samchar, at http://faridabadmajdoorsamachar.blogspot.com/p/about-fms.html (accessed December 31, 2013).

19 *Workers Autonomy Strikes in India: Maruti Suzuki Strike at Manesar (June, September, October 2011)* (Brussels, Belgium: Kolektivn proti kapitálu & Mouvement Communiste), No. 5, May 2012, pp. 1–5.

20 See Government of India, *Special Economic Zones in India, Facilities and Incentives*, www.sezindia.nic.in/about-fi.asp (accessed December 26, 2013).

21 Peoples Union for Democratic Rights (PUDR), *Hard Drive: Working Conditions and Workers Struggles at Maruti* (Delhi, India: PUDR, 2001), p. 3.

22 The Centre for Workers Management, a Delhi-based labor research organization, issued a 'Maruti Suzuki background dossier,' in 2013. The report finds: 'Worker interest is ill served by decline in value added, as outsourc-

ing is accompanied by decline of regulation of rights of the worker' and leads to 'a policy that perpetuates dependence on imported technology' (pp. 5–8).

23   People's Union for Democratic Rights, Driving Force: Labour Struggles and Violation of Rights in Maruti Suzuki India Limited (New Delhi: PUDR, 2013), p. 3. The Peoples Union for Democratic Rights is a workers' rights research organization based in New Delhi, India

24   PUDR, *Driving Force: Labour Struggles and Violation of Rights in Maruti Suzuki India Limited* (New Delhi: PUDR, 2013), p. 3.

25   J. C. B. Annavajhula and Surendra Pratap, 'Worker voices in an auto produc- tion chain: notes from the pits of a low road-II,' *Economic and Political Weekly*, Vol. 57, No. 34 (Aug. 25, 2012), p. 50.

26   Annavajhula and Pratap, 'Worker voices,' p. 50.

27   Annavajhula and Pratap, 'Worker voices,' p. 50. Workers demanded that the Indian government make Maruti honor its obligations by restoring the production incentive scheme, fulfilling the wage settlement of 1998 to initiate a pension plan, regularizing contract workers, and ending subcontracting outside the plant.

28   PUDR, *Driving Force*, pp. 8–17.

29   PUDR, *Driving Force*, p. 4.

30   Annavajhula and Pratap, 'Worker voices,' pp. 50–1.

31   PUDR, *Driving Force*, p. 4.

32   The Maruti Suzuki Employees Union sit-down strike was supported primar- ily by India's left-led unions, including the All-India Trade Union Congress (AITUC), Centre for Indian Trade Unions (CITU), Hind Mazdoor Sabha/ Workers Assembly of India (HMS), All India Trade Union Congress (AITUC), and United Trade Union Congress (UTUC).

33   Agreement under Section 12(3) of the Industrial Disputes Act, 1947 between Company Messrs. Maruti Suzuki India Ltd., Plot No. 1, Phase 3 A, Sector 8, IMT Manesar (Gurgaon) and its permanent striking workers, October 19, 2011 (informal translation from Hindi). According to the ICLR Report, on October 21, 13 members of the Maruti Suzuki Provisional Committee were detained by management, Haryana labor officials, and the police, and, under threat of torture and imprisonment, were coerced to sign letters of resignation and promise never to return to the company in return for large severance payments. See ILPC, *Merchants of Menace: The Repression of Workers in India's New Industrial Belt* (New York: ICLR, 2013), pp. 6–7.

34   Stunned by the registration of a new union, management found itself presented by MSWU with a new Charter of Demands on April 18, 2012 that underscored a demand for equality for the contract workers who comprised more than 75 percent of all employees in the plant and who were paid one-quarter of the wages earned by permanent workers, while receiving no benefits or job security. In response to these demands, MSIL put off serious

negotiations while planning a counter-offensive against the independent workers' union.

35 *Merchants of Menace*, pp. 11–13.

36 *Merchants of Menace*, pp. 11–17.

37 Of those arrested in July and August 2012, 147 workers remained in jail until March 2015. In bail hearings in 2014, the Punjab and Haryana High Court rejected the release of the workers, stating: 'the incident is a most unfortunate occurrence which has lowered the reputation of India in the estimation of the world. Foreign investors are not likely to invest money in India out of fear of labour unrest': http://economictimes.indiatimes.com/industry/auto/news/passenger-vehicle/cars/jailed-maruti-suzuki-workers-granted-bail-by-supreme-court/articleshow/46346464.cms (accessed February 10, 2014). At the time of writing, in July 2015, more than 30 worker activists remain in prison.See Joel Joseph, 'Bail to 77 Maruti staff,' *Times of India*, March 18, 2015. http://timesofindia.indiatimes.com/city/gurgaon/bail-to-77-maruti-staff/articleshow/46603297.cms. *Merchants of Menace*, pp. 16–17 (accessed June 20, 2015). See also *Economic Times*, 'Jailed Maruti Suzuki workers granted bail by Supreme Court,' February 23, 2015, http://economictimes.indiatimes.com/industry/auto/news/passenger-vehicle/cars/jailed-maruti-suzuki-workers-granted-bail-by-supreme-court/articleshow/46346464.cms (accessed June 20, 2015).

38 *Merchants of Menace*, pp. 16–17; Mamta Sharma, 'Corporate groups in Gurgaon pushing growth of surveillance business,' *Economic Times*, March 7, 2013, http://articles.economictimes.indiatimes.com/2013-03-07/news/37531894_1_cctv-cameras-indian-cctv-cctv-market (accessed December 24, 2013).

39 'Update: India's Maruti to restart riot-hit plant on Aug. 21,' *Asahi Shimbun*, August 16, 2012, http://ajw.asahi.com/article/business/AJ201208160094 (accessed August 15, 2013).

40 'Update,' *Asahi Shimbun*.

41 Rakhi Sehgal, '"Manesar workers are the villains": truth or prejudice,' *Economic and Political Weekly*, Vol. 47, No. 31 (August, 4, 2014), www.epw.in/ejournal/show/1/_/2172?quicktabs_issues_tab=0&quicktabs_most_commented_read=0 (accessed October 30, 2014).

42 Amaresh Mishra, interview, August 18, 2012.

43 Rakhi Sehgal, interview with the author, August 21, 2012.

5 China: State Capitalism, Foreign Investment, and Worker Insurgency

1 Research on China's labor militancy includes identified and anonymous author interviews with labor activists and NGO investigators in the Pearl River Delta. Yue Yuen strike interviews included Rena Lau, August 28–29, 2014; May Wong, August 28, 2014; and Apo Leung, of the Asia Monitor Research Centre.

Notes

2   See for instance Au Loong Yu, *China's Rise: Strength and Fragility* (Pontypool, Wales: Merlin Press, 2012); Ching Kwan Lee, *Against the Law: Labor Protests in China's Rustbelt and Sunbelt* (Berkeley, Calif.: University of California Press, 2007); Eli Friedman, *Insurgency Trap: Labor Politics in Postsocialist China* (Ithaca, N.Y.: Cornell ILR Press, 2014); Tim Pringle, *Trade Unions in China: The Challenge of Labour Unrest* (New York: Routledge, 2011); Lu Zhang, *Inside China's Automobile Factories: The Politics of Labor and Worker Resistance* (New York: Cambridge University Press, 2014).

3   See Sean Starrs, 'Chimera of global convergence,' *New Left Review*, May–June 2014, pp. 81–96 (direct quote p. 95).

4   Starrs, 'Chimera of global convergence,' p. 93.

5   Starrs, 'Chimera of global convergence,' p. 96.

6   In 2012, seven of the ten busiest container port cities in the world were located in China: 1) Shanghai, China, 2) Singapore, 3) Hong Kong, China, 4) Shenzhen, China, 5) Busan, South Korea, 6) Ningbo-Zhoushan, China, 7) Guangzhou Harbor, China, 8) Qingdao, China, 9) Jebel Ali, Dubai, United Arab Emirates, 10) Tianjin, China. World Shipping Council 2014. www.worldshipping.org/about-the-industry/global-trade/top-50-world-containerports (accessed Nov. 1, 2014).

7   See Patrick Neveling, 'Export processing zones and global class formation,' in James G. Carrier and Don Kalb (eds), *Anthropologies of Class: Power, Practice, Inequality* (Cambridge, UK: Cambridge University Press, 2015).

8   PRD Economic Profile (HKTDC) Hong Kong Trade Development Council, March 25, 2014, http://china-trade-research.hktdc.com/business-news/article/Fast-Facts/PRD-Economic-Profile/ff/en/1/1X000000/1X06BW84.htm (accessed September 30, 2014); *Guangdong Statistical Yearbook 2013* (Beijing: China Statistics Press, October 2013).

9   Interviews with May Wong, Globalization Monitor; Fung Pikki, Labor Education and Service Network, Hong Kong, August 2014.

10 See Stephen E. Philion, *Workers' Democracy in China's Transition from State Socialism* (New York: Routledge, 2009), pp. 73–109.

11 Au Loong Yu, *China's Rise*, p.33

12 Lee, *Against the Law*. Lee defines the local nature of worker struggles as 'cellular activism' that has occurred in both state owned enterprises and export-oriented manufacturing sectors. In each case, workers are engaged in activism over wages, benefits, and working conditions against employers which have not been expanded to collective claims across communities and regions. In the comparison of the political economies of the north-eastern province of Liaoning, where restructuring of SOEs has expanded job losses, and the south-eastern province of Guangdong, dominated by new migrant workers, Lee argues that labor unrest has been precipitated by economic issues. In Liaoning, workers have opposed privatization, unemployment, and payment of wages, pensions, and other benefits. In Guangdong, new migrant workers in

the 1990s and early 2000s waged protests and legal claims for the payment of wages and improved conditions (pp. 6–9).

13 Pringle, *Trade Unions in China*, p.6.

14 See Pun Ngai, *Made in China: Women Factory Workers in a Global Workplace* (Durham, N.C.: Duke University Press, 2005), for an ethnographic account of on the job resistance among Chinese migrant women who are recent migrants to Shenzhen's SEZ and employees of electronics contractors who manufacture products for export.

15 Pringle, *Trade Unions in China*, p. 42. Pringle explains: 'As private and foreign capital became the engine of China's growth, the rural internal migrant workers who facilitated this realignment faced very high levels of exploitation' (p. 3).

16 Pringle, *Trade Unions in China* , p. 8.

17 Statistical Communiqué of the People's Republic of China on the 2013 National Economic and Social Development, National Bureau of Statistics of China, February 24, 2014. Nearly 62 percent of the 270 million migrant workers in China have moved to urban areas far from their home regions.

18 Zhang Yiwei, 'Wave of strikes shows neglect of labor rights,' *Global Times*, April 22, 2014, www.globaltimes.cn/content/855968.shtml (accessed Nov. 1, 2014).

19 According to NGO reports, the labor protests that have become ubiquitous among manufacturing workers in Guangdong spread to other provinces in 2014.

20 Rena Lau, interview, August 28, 2014.

21 See Tom Mitchell and Demetri Sevastopulo, 'China labour activism: crossing the line,' *Financial Times*, May 7, 2014, www.ft.com/cms/s/0/bb0f1c3a-c953-11e3-99cc-00144feabdc0.html#axzz38gA1DaS9 (accessed June 9, 2015).

22 Interview, May Wong, executive director, Globalization Monitor, Hong Kong, August 28, 2014. Wong notes that salaries are relatively similar among factories at a time when workers are in high demand.

23 ACFTU, *A Brief Introduction to the All-China Federation of Trade Unions (ACFTU)*, 20 September 2007, http://english.acftu.org/template/10002/file.jsp?cid=63&aid=156 (accessed August 14, 2014).

24 During the Cultural Revolution, motivated by unease that state managers of enterprises who were members of the CPC were forming an independent class from 1967 to 1977, the Party suspended the organizational activities of the ACFTU.

25 Article 5 of the agreement states: 'Wal-mart union branches shall support the store administration in exercising its management rights in compliance with the law. They shall mobilize and organize the employees to fulfill their business responsibilities, and shall cooperate on an equal basis with the store administration in mutual support and consultation to work for the enterprise's harmonious development.' On January 1, 2007, *Beijing News* reported the organization of 200,000 workers at Foxconn in Shenzhen a day earlier without comment from the Taiwanese high-technology manufacturer. See http://tech.163.com/07/0101/09/33O9PBJ3000915BD.html (in Chinese) (accessed Nov. 1, 2014).

Notes

26 ACFTU, *Brief Introduction.*

27 The ACFTU has contended that ITUC, the ITO, and international labor organizations are often permeated with foreign agents that seek to subvert the Chinese government, a claim that can be viewed as paranoid, or a means to squash dissent. Still, considering the history of US State Department and labor intervention in the unions of foreign countries and the continued US government funding through the State Department and the National Endowment for Democracy to this day, the claim does have a patina of legitimacy.

28 David Meltcalf and Jianwei Li, 'Chinese unions: nugatory or transforming?' CEP Discussion Paper no. 708, Dec. 2005, Leverhulme Trust, published by Centre for Economic Performance, London School of Economics and Political Science.

29 Data based on the Labour Arbitration Award Committees. See QI Dongtao, 'Progress and dilemmas of Chinese trade unions,' *East Asian Policy*, Vol. 2, No. 3 (Jul./Sep. 2010), pp. 18–22, www.eai.nus.edu.sg/vol2no3_QiDongtau.pdf (accessed August 14, 2014).

30 Dongtau, 'Progress and dilemmas,' p. 19.

31 See Trini Leung, 'ACFTU and union organizing,' *China Labour Bulletin*, April 26, 2002, www.hartford-hwp.com/archives/55/292.html (accessed August 4, 2014).

32 'The Liaoyang protest movement of 2002-03, and the arrest, trial and sentencing of the "Liaoyang Two,"' *China Labor Bulletin*, July 2003, www.clb.org.hk/en/content/liaoyang-protest-movement-2002-03-and-arrest-trial-and-sentencing-liaoyang-two-0 (accessed August 14, 2014).

33 'Laid-off Chinese protest en masse,' Associated Press, March 18, 2002, www.weijingsheng.org/doc/labor/Laid%20-%20Off%20Chinese%20Protest%20en%20Masse.htm (accessed August 14, 2014).

34 Wei Jianxing, 'Conscientiously implement the spirit of the Fifth Plenary Session of the 15th Central Committee and speed up the organising and establishing of trade unions in new enterprises,' speech delivered on November 12, 2000 at the Work Meeting on Organising and Establishing Trade Unions in New Enterprises. Beijing Federation of Trade Unions, www.acftu.org.cn/template/10002/index.jsp. (accessed September 3, 2014).

35 According to a 2002 report on the ACFTU by the *China Labour Bulletin*, Wei Jianxiang, ACFTU chairman, expressed concern that labor unrest posed a risk to stability and placed China at risk to foreign intervention from foreign unions dominated by Western imperial powers: 'When it first breaks out, a labour [action]… will also give our enemies, at home and abroad, who are doing their best to split the Chinese working class, an ideal opportunity. … Their aim is to set up a so-called independent trade union separate from the ACFTU in an attempt to 'westernize' and 'pluralize' us'.

36 Xu Xicheng, 'New trends in the international trade union movement,' *Ban Yue Tan Magazine*, No. 12, June 25, 2001.

37 Labor Contract Law of the People's Republic of China, Order of the President

of the People's Republic of China, No. 65, adopted at the 28th Meeting of the Standing Committee of the Tenth National People's Congress of the People's Republic of the China on June 29, 2007, promulgated and in effect as of January 1, 2008, Hu Jintao, President of the People's Republic of China, June 29, 2007. www.npc.gov.cn/englishnpc/Law/2009-02/20/content_1471106.htm (accessed July 24, 2014). See also Haiyan Wang, Richard P. Appelbaum, Francesca Degliuli, and Nelson Lichtenstein, 'China's new Labour Contract Law: is China moving towards increased power for workers?' *Third World Quarterly*, Vol. 30, No. 30 (2009), pp. 485–501. DOI: 10.1080/01436590902742271.

38   Haiyan Wang et al., 'China's New Labour Contract Law'.

39   For a report on the conditions at Foxconn see 'Foxconn and Apple fail to fulfill promises: predicaments of workers after the suicides,' Students and Scholars against Corporate Misbehavior, May 6, 2011, http://sacom.hk/foxconn-and-apple-fail-to-fulfill-promises-predicaments-of-workers-after-the-suicides/ (accessed September 21, 2014).

40   Rena Lau, 'Restructuring of the Honda Auto Parts Union in Guongdong, China: s 2-year assessment of the 2010 strike,' *Working USA*, Vol. 15, No. 4 (December 2012), pp. 497–515.

41   Tom Mitchell and Demetri Sevastopulo, 'China labour activism: crossing the line,' *Financial Times*, May 7, 2014, www.clb.org.hk/en/content/financial-times-china-labour-activism-crossing-line (accessed October 21, 2014).

42   See Demetri Sevastopulo, 'China sports shoe factory halts production as strike escalates,' *Financial Times*, April 23, 2014, p. 3, www.ft.com/intl/cms/s/0/99c3713e-ca0c-11e3-8a31-00144feabdc0.html#axzz38gA1DaS9 (accessed September 30, 2014).

43   See Yue Yuen Industrial Holdings, 2013 Annual Report, www.yueyuen.com/annual/2013/ew0551.pdf (accessed September 14, 2014); and Wang Feng Fengqian Yu, 'Windsor Dongguan foundries trapped plight of minimum wage labor disputes for 10 years rose 3 times,' *Want News*, www.wantinews.com/news-8046341-Windsor-Dongguan-foundries-trapped-plight-of-minimum-wage-labor-disputes-for-10-years-rose-3-times.html (accessed September 30, 2014).

44   Wang Feng Fengqian Yu, 'Windsor Dongguan foundries.'

45   *World Footwear*. 'Chinese giant manufacturer Yue Yuen with 7.1% decline in profit,' May 6, 2014, http://worldfootwear.com/news.asp?id=271&Chinese_giant_manufacturer_Yue_Yuen_with_71_decline_in_profit (accessed June 17, 2015).

46   Wang Jiangsong of the China Institute for Industrial Relations, quoted by Didi Tang, '30,000 workers are striking at China's biggest shoe factory in one of country's biggest strikes ever,' AP, *Business Insider*, April 17, 2014, www.businessinsider.com/30000-workers-striking-at-chinas-biggest-shoe-factory-2014-4#!HUMat (accessed September 30, 2014).

47   See John Ruwitch, 'China shoe factory strike shoes welfare Achilles' heel,' Reuters, April 18, 2014, http://in.reuters.com/article/2014/04/18/uk-china-la-

bour-welfare-idINKBN0D401R20140418 (accessed January 15, 2015); and May Wong, *Multinational Monitor*, Hong Kong, August 28, 2014.

48 Interviews, Apo Leong, Samuel Li Shing Hong, Hong Kong, August 27–30, 2014.

49 From an unpublished Globalization Monitor report, 'Shoe factory in Dongguan Yue Yuen exposing workers to strike people like slaves,' April 2014.

50 Globalization Monitor, 'Shoe factory in Dongguan.'

51 Interview, Li Shing Hong. AMRC, Hong Kong, August 29, 2014.

52 See Alexandra Harney and John Ruwitch, 'In China, managers are the new labor activists,' Reuters, May 31, 2014 (www.reuters.com/article/2014/06/01/china-labor-strikes-idUSL3N0O929U20140601, accessed July 19, 2014). According to Reuters, the article was based on a previously unpublished account from inside the strike at Yue Yuen which shows that supervisors were the first to challenge senior plant leaders about the underpayment in social insurance contributions that became the focus of the dispute. Yue Yuen Industrial Holdings declined to comment.

53 Typically AFCTU union representatives have little or no stake in the outcome of factory closures.

54 May Wong, interview, August 28, 2014.

55 May Wong, interview, August 28, 2014.

56 As well as Tencent QQ, social networkers used Whatsapp messenger, and Weibo (a social media outlet equivalent to Twitter).

57 Apo Leong, interview, August 29, 2014.

58 'More than ten thousand workers stage strike at massive Dongguan shoe factory,' *China Labour Bulletin*, April 14, 2014, www.clb.org.hk/en/content/more-ten-thousand-workers-stage-strike-massive-dongguan-shoe-factory (accessed July 3, 2014). See also Mimi Lau, 'Yue Yuen shoe factory workers' strike at Dongguan plants continues,' *South China Morning Post*, April 16, 2014, www.scmp.com/news/china/article/1483287/yue-yuen-shoe-factory-workers-strike-dongguan-plants-continues (accessed July 1, 2014).

59 Rina Lau, interview, August 28, 2014.

60 Stephanie Wong, 'Yue Yuen resumes production at Dongguan factory after strike,' Bloomberg News, April 28, 2014, www.bloomberg.com/news/2014-04-28/yue-yuen-resumes-production-at-dongguan-factory-after-strike.html (accessed September 16, 2014). See also Kevin Slaten, 'Government steps up to labor's demands: why the Yue Yuen Shoe factory strike was important,' *China File*, Center on US-China Relations at Asia Society, May 16, 2014, www.chinafile.com/China-Government-Steps-Up-To-Labor-Demands (accessed August 8, 2014).

61 Toh Han Shih, 'Strike's aftermath to lower Yue Yuen's profits by US$112m,' *South China Morning Post*, August 6, 2014, www.scmp.com/business/companies/article/1567408/strikes-aftermath-lower-yue-yuens-profits-us112m (accessed September 30, 2014).

62 See Leah Borromeo, 'How Adidas supported worker rights in China factory

strike,' *Guardian*, June 12, 2014, www.theguardian.com/sustainable-business/sustainable-fashion-blog/adidas-worker-rights-china-factory-strike (accessed September 23, 2014).

63 Yue Yuen worker interview, May 22, 2014, *Chinese Labour Bulletin*, www.clb.org.hk/en/content/defeat-will-only-make-us-stronger-workers-look-back-yue-yuen-shoe-factory-strike (accessed June 27, 2014). The interviews took place between April 24 and 27, and the 13,000-character transcript was published on the blog Worker View Point on April 27, 2014. The interview transcript has been translated and edited by *China Labour Bulletin*.

64 Slaten, 'Government steps up.'

65 During the strike Yue Yuen workers in Jiangxi Province, 500 miles north of Dongguan, protested in their plant in support of the strikers' demands for of social security payments. See also Slaten, 'Government steps up.'

66 'Yue Yuen workers go on strike at Zhuhai plant,' *South China Morning Post*, July 23, 2014, www.scmp.com/business/china-business/article/1557400/yue-yuen-workers-go-strike-zhuhai-plant (accessed August 8, 2014).

67 Hu Huifeng, 'Dongguan cabbies launch strike amid business slowdown,' *South China Morning Post*, April 19, 2014, www.scmp.com/news/china/article/1487693/dongguan-cabbies-launch-strike-amid-business-slowdown (accessed September 30, 2014).

68 Hu Huifeng and Lawrence Chung, 'Workers for Taiwan firm that supplies Apple end strike over cuts to bonus,' *South China Morning Post*, 11 September 2014, www.scmp.com/news/china/article/1590104/16000-chinese-factory-workers-strike-after-receiving-banana-and-chicken (accessed September 15, 2014).

69 According to the *China Labour Bulletin* strike map, the 235 number of strikes recorded in spring 2014 was 49 percent higher than the 158 incidents in spring 2013 and 180 percent higher than the 84 strikes in the second quarter of 2012. The strike wave in spring 2014 included 27 manufacturers employing more than 1,000 workers. In April and May 2014 taxi drivers engaged in escalating slowdowns and strikes in Dongguan to protest against high license fees. See 'Strikes and worker protests gain momentum in China as economy stutters,' *China Labour Bulletin*, July 4, 2014, www.clb.org.hk/en/content/strikes-and-worker-protests-gain-momentum-china-economy-stutters (accessed August 8, 2014).

70 Beverly J. Silver and Lu Zhang, 'China as an emerging epicenter of world labor unrest,' in Ho-fung Hung (ed.), *China and the Transformation of Global Capitalism* (Baltimore, Md.: Johns Hopkins University Press, 2009), soc.jhu.edu/wp-content/uploads/sites/28/2012/02/SilverZhang2009.pdf (accessed September 20, 2014).

6 South Africa: Post-Apartheid Labor Militancy in the Mining Sector

1 Martin Lynch, *Mining in World History* (London: Reaktion, 2009), pp. 322–3.

2 Stuart Kirsch documents the deliberate environmental devastation and the

Notes

associated catastrophic health and social consequences brought about by unregulated copper and gold mining conglomerates from 1970 to the 2010s in Papua New Guinea, in *Mining Capitalism* (Berkeley, Calif: University of California Press, 2014).

3   See Trading Economics, www.tradingeconomics.com/south-africa/exports (accessed January 12, 2014).

4   See Mining Intelligence Database, 'Platinum Mining in South Africa,' www. projectsiq.co.za/platinum-mining-in-south-africa.htm (accessed January 12, 2014).

5   Mining Intelligence Database, 'Platinum Mining in South Africa.'

6   Forrest, 'Marikana,' p. 31.

7   See the International Study Group Report on Africa's mineral regimes, *Minerals and Africa's Development* (Addis Ababa: United Nations Economic Commission for Africa (UNECA), 2011), p. 60. For the effect of liberalization on South African labor and employment, see Southern African Resource Watch (SARW), *Impact of the Global Financial Crisis on Mining in Southern Africa* (Johannesburg: DS Print Media, 2009). For a comparative report on labor input in manufacturing and mining sectors see UNECA, *Economic Report on Africa* (Addis Ababa: UNECA, 2005).

8   Forrest, 'Marikana.' In 2012, in Rustenburg, a platinum mining center in South Africa's North West, permanent rock drillers employed at AmPlats (Anglo-American Platinum) and Implats (Impala Platinum) earned two to three times the monthly wage and allowance of equivalent contracted laborers performing the same work.

9   Nicole Ulrich and Lucien van der Walt, 'South Africa labor movement,' in Immanuel Ness (ed.), *International Encyclopedia of Revolution and Protest*, Vol. 6 (Oxford: Wiley Blackwell, 2009), p. 3,090.

10   See Apollon Davidson, Irina Filatova, Valentin Gorodnov, and Sheridan Johns (eds), *South Africa and the Communist International: A Documentary History, Vol. I, Socialist Pilgrims to Bolshevik Footsoldiers, 1919–1930* (London: Frank Cass, 2003).

11   Ulrich and van der Walt, 'South Africa labor movement,' pp. 3,090–9, document how the banning of the left and passage of racially exclusionary legislation was followed by the fragmentation and declining influence of trade unions through prohibiting Africans from forming new unions, giving rise to the creation of the SACTU as the leading organizational opponent of the apartheid regime in the South African labor movement.

12   John Saul, 'On taming the revolution: the South African case,' in Leo Panitch, Greg Albo, and Vivek Chibber (eds), *Socialist Register 2013: The Question of Strategy* (London: Merlin, 2012), pp.212–40.

13   Saul, 'On taming the revolution'; Ulrich and van der Walt, 'South Africa labor movement,' pp. 3,096–7.

14   See Vishwas Satgar, 'Beyond Marikana: the post-apartheid South African state,' *Africa Spectrum*, Vol. 47, Nos 2–3 (2012), pp. 33–62.

Notes

15 Saul, 'On taming the revolution,' pp. 217–18.

16 Franco Barchiesi, *Precarious Liberation: Workers, the State, and Contested Social Citizenship in Postapartheid South Africa* (Albany, N.Y.: State University of New York Press, 2011)/

17 See the NUM website: www.num.org.za/ (accessed January 2, 2014).

18 Sean Hattingh, 'Exploding anger: workers' struggles and self-organization in South Africa's mining industry,' in Immanuel Ness (ed.), *New Forms of Worker Organization: The Autonomist and Syndicalist Restoration of Class Struggle Unionism* (Oakland, Calif.: PM Press, forthcoming), ch. 7.

19 Jan de Lange, 'The rise and rise of Amcu,' Miningmx.com, August 2, 2012, www.miningmx.com/special_reports/mining-yearbook/mining-yearbook-2012/A-season-of-discontent.htm (accessed January 17, 2014); and Martin Creamer, 'Emerging AMCU mine union favours competitive coexistence,' Miningweekly.com, June 6, 2012, www.miningweekly.com/article/emerging-amcu-mine-union-favours-competitive-coexistence-joseph-mathunjwa-2012-06-06 (accessed January 14, 2014).

20 Saul, 'On taming the revolution,' p. 216.

21 Zanele Sabela, 'Amcu and NUM face off on issues,' Destiny.com, May 13, 2013, www.destinyman.com/2013/05/13/amcu-and-num-face-off-on-issues-2013-05-13/ (accessed January 4, 2014).

22 Chanel de Bruyn, 'Eastplats terminates JIC, Sindele contacts at SA mine,' *Mining Weekly*, July 13, 2009, www.miningweekly.com/article/easplats-2009-07-13 (accessed January 4, 2014).

23 Aquarius Platinum plc is a multinational mining firm headquartered in Bermuda, and Anglo American is based in London, UK.

24 In a press release, Lesiba Seshoka went on to note: 'The National Union of Mineworkers (NUM) is an organization for disciplined cadres and a progressive force involved in the genuine fight for workers (sic) rights. We therefore call on the law enforcement agencies to ensure that those who are involved in all these irregular activities are arrested and no one disguises criminal activity as labour matters. ... Although the NUM has taken their matter legally, the union will review its stance with regard to those who are implicated in criminal deeds.' See '1.2 NUM refutes former Murray & Roberts workers complaints: Lesiba Seshoka, NUM's Head: Media & Communications,' COSATU Today: Our Side of the Story, November 23, 2009, https://groups.google.com/forum/#!msg/cosatu-daily-news/PadcopBapi8/aukJ32VSWsEJ (accessed January 4, 2014).

25 Impala Holdings Limited fact sheet at www.implats.co.za/implats/downloads/2013/Implats_Fact_Sheet_October2013.pdf (accessed January 23, 2014).

26 Greg Marinovich, 'Beyond the chaos at Marikana: the search for the real issues,' *Daily Maverick*, August 17, 2012, www.dailymaverick.co.za/article/2012-08-17-beyond-the-chaos-at-marikana-the-search-for-the-real-issues/# (accessed October 25, 2014).

27   NUM press release, 'NUM, COSATU and Implats agree on reinstatement.' www.cosatu.org.za/docs/cosatu2day/2012/pr0225.html (accessed January 29, 2014).

28   The formation of autonomous workers committees in Marikana is documented by Luke Sinwell, anthropologist at the Centre for Sociological Research at the University of Johannesburg, through extensive ethnographic fieldwork in the Rustenburg mining region of South Africa. See his unpublished research paper, 'Autonomous worker committees in Marikana, South Africa: journey to the mountain.' See also Tito Mzamo, 'South Africa: recent strike at Impala Platinum Mine in Rustenburg, March 6, 2012,' www.marxist.com/south-africa-strike-at-impala-platinum-mine-rustenburg.htm (accessed January 29, 2014).

29   Shawn Hattingh, 'Exploding anger: workers struggles and self-organization in South Africa's mining industry,' in Ness (ed.), *New Forms of Worker Organization.*

30   Mzamo, 'South Africa: Recent strike.'

31   'Modikwa strike ends on wage agreement,' *Mining Journal*, April 11, 2012, www.mining-journal.com/production-and-markets/modikwa-strike-ends-on-wage-agreement (accessed: January 23, 2014).

32   Kwanele Sosibo, 'Amcu treading on NUM territory at Lonmin mine,' *Mail and Guardian*, August 15, 2012, http://mg.co.za/article/2012-08-15-amcu-treading-on-num-territory-at-lonmin-mine/ (accessed January 29, 2014).

33   Marikana Commission of Inquiry. For transcripts see www.marikanacomm. org.za/transcripts.html, October 1, 2012 to January 23, 2014, pp. 1-20,636, days 1-173 (accessed January 2, 2014).

34   Testimony, Marikana Commission of Inquiry, Department of Justice and Constitutional Development, January 25, 2013, www.marikanacomm.org.za/news/2013-01-news.html (accessed January 24, 2014).

35   Peter Alexander, Thapelo Lekgowa, Botsang Mmope, Luke Sinwell, and Bongani Xezwi, *Marikana, Voices from South Africa's Mining Massacre* (London: Bookmarks, 2013), pp. 28–9.

36   Alexander et al. *Marikana, Voices,* pp.25–6. From January 2010 to April 2014, the value of the South African Rand (ZAR) fluctuated from approximately US$.095–0.14.

37   According to Alexander et al. and the South African Marikana Commission of Inquiry, those killed in Marikana included workers' elected representatives who were active in communities in Marikana and in immigrant hometown associations in the Eastern Cape, Lesotho, Swaziland, Mozambique, and beyond, especially workers who organized soccer games and recreational sports. Of equal importance were activists who took responsibility for ensuring respectable funeral arrangements for workers who died on the job, including notification of families, and handling the logistics of funerals in regions of origin, including transport of workers to attend ceremonies. As Alexander et al. note, 'The workers' agency and leadership is no obscure radical rhetoric or

theory of ivory tower academics or non-governmental organisations (NGOs). Rather, it is the unfettered praxis of the working class – which could not be contained, even with national security, the ANC, NUM, and the ideology of the ruling class pitted against it' (*Marikana, Voices*, p. 22).

38 Sosibo, 'Amcu treading on NUM territory.'

39 Marinovich, 'Beyond the chaos at Marikana.'

40 The first authoritative report issued on the Marikana massacre, based on in-depth worker interviews of day-to-day events leading up to August 16, is in Alexander et al., *Marikana, Voices*, pp. 15–46. Hours before the Marikana Massacre by South African State Police, Bishop Jo Seoka of Pretoria urged the striking workers to leave the hill, but they said they would depart only after meeting with Lonmin management. Interview, Bishop Jo Seoka, July 25, 2015.

41 See Marikana Commission of Inquiry, www.marikanacomm.org.za/. For transcripts see www.marikanacomm.org.za/transcripts.html, and for exhibits see www.marikanacomm.org.za/exhibits.html, October 1, 2012 to January 23, 2014, pp. 1–20, 636, days 1–173 (accessed December 18, 2013 to January 25, 2014). On June 25, 2015, President Jacob Zuma issued a statement critical of Lonmin, NUM, and AMCU officials, and the state police, but with no legal consequences. Zuma said that accusations against Cyril Ramaphosa, former NUM leader and trustee of Lonmin, 'were groundless.' Most blame was reserved for the striking workers, who according to Zuma bore responsibility for the events leading up to the massacre and endangered the lives of Lonmin officials and non-striking workers. He made no reference to the killing of the 34 workers on August 16, 2012. See 'Release by President Jacob Zuma of the Report of the Judicial Commission of Inquiry into the events at the Marikana Mine in Rustenburg, Union Buildings, Pretoria': www.thepresidency.gov.za/pebble.asp?relid=19997 (accessed July 25, 2015).

42 See Marikana Commission of Inquiry Exhibits, www.marikanacomm.org.za/exhibits.html, October 1, 2012 to January 23, 2014 (accessed January 25, 2014).

43 Bond, 'The Marikana movement.'

44 See Alexander et al., *Marikana, Voices*, p. 46.

45 Sam Ashman and Nicolas Pons Vignon, 'NUMSA, the working class and socialist politics in South Africa', in Leo Panitch and Greg Albo (eds), *Socialist Register 2015*, Vol. 51 (London: Merlin), p. 94.

46 Ed Stoddard, 'South African strike hits world's top platinum producers,' Reuters, January 23, 2014, www.reuters.com/article/2014/01/23/us-safrica-strikes-idUSBREA0M0AO20140123 (accessed October 22, 2014).

47 Danny Fortson, 'Lonmin threatens to close mines,' *Sunday Times*, May 8, 2014, www.thesundaytimes.co.uk/sto/business/Industry/article1409227 (accessed October 22, 2014); and Sikonathi Mantshantsha, 'Special report: platinum strike – an industry teetering on the precipice,' *Business Day*, June 5, 2014, www.bdlive.co.za/business/trade/2014/06/05/special-report-platinum-strike--an-industry-teetering-on-the-precipice (accessed October 22, 2014).

Notes

48 Leandi Kolver, 'Amplats assures market it will maintain sales volumes despite asset sales,' *Mining Weekly*, July 21, 2014, www.miningweekly.com/article/amplats-to-sell-union-rustenburg-pandore-mines-2014-07-21 (accessed October 22, 2014).

49 For a discussion of the leftist development of NUMSA see Ashman and Pons-Vignon, 2014.

50 See numsa.org.za/admin/assets/articles/attachments/00033_book_4_-_policy_statements.27_may_2012.pdf (accessed September 18, 2014); and Ranjeni Manusamy, 'Profile of a hawk: Numsa's Irvin Jim,' *Daily Maverick*, 15 June 2012, www.dailymaverick.co.za/article/2012-06-15-profile-of-a-hawk-numsas-irvin-jim#.VEgfOxZRUYs (accessed January 19, 2014).

51 Greg Nicolson, 'Numsa, AMCU and the portent of strike-stricken economy,' *Daily Maverick*, 6 June 2014, www.dailymaverick.co.za/article/2014-06-06-numsa-amcu-and-the-portent-of-strike-stricken-economy/#.VEk2fRbtiYU (accessed September 24, 2014).

52 'South African union NUMSA says to intensify metals, engineering strike,' Reuters, July 16, 2014, www.reuters.com/article/2014/07/16/us-safri-ca-strike-idUSKBN0FL1WH20140716 (accessed September 18, 2014).

53 Stafford Thomas, 'News analysis: mining sector suppliers bear brunt of Numsa strike,' *Business Day*, July 15, 2014, www.bdlive.co.za/business/mining/2014/07/15/news-analysis-mining-sector-suppliers-bear-brunt-of-numsa-strike (accessed September 19, 2014).

54 Bond, 'Labour influence.'

55 Following Marikana, as the AMCU's support was growing among rank-and-file miners, the union has been repeatedly disparaged by ANC, SACP, and COSATU leadership. In May 2013, NUM president Senzeni Zokwana and SACP general secretary Blade Nzimande said that AMCU was an organization of 'vigilantes and liars' and not a trade union. See 'ANC alliance members accuse Amcu of being vigilantes and liars,' *Mail and Guardian*, May 18, 2013, http://africajournalismtheworld.com/2013/05/18/anc-alliance-members-accuse-amcu-of-being-vigilantes-and-liars/ (accessed September 24, 2014).

56 NUMSA Press Statement on Expulsion from COSATU, November 9, 2014, www.numsa.org.za/article/numsa-press-statement-expulsion-cosatu/ (accessed November 13, 2014). Also see 'South Africa – COSATU expels NUMSA,' *Mail and Guardian*, http://africajournalismtheworld.com/2014/11/08/south-af-rica-cosatu-expels-numsa/ (accessed December 1, 2014). Zwelinzima Vavi, COSATU general secretary, depicted the expulsion of NUMSA as a 'guillotine of +350,000 workers ... a game changer that will have profound political and organisational implications' on South Africa's labor movement. See Andrew England, 'South Africa crisis deepens after union federation fractures,' *Financial Times*, November 11, 2014, p. 2. After continuing to demand an inclusive union movement committed to the working class of South Africa, Vavi was dismissed as general secretary of COSATU in March 2015.

Notes

7 Conclusion

1   For treatments on the end of the industrial era, see e.g. Stanley Aronowitz and William DeFazio, *The Jobless Future* (Minneapolis, Minn.: University of Minnesota Press, 2nd edn, 2010); Barry Bluestone and Bennett Harrison, *Deindustrialization in America, Plant Closings, Community Abandonment and the Dismantling of Basic Industry* (New York: Basic Books, 1984); Jefferson Cowie, *Stayin' Alive: The 1970s and the Last Days of the Working Class* (New York: New Press, 2012). Judith Stein, *Pivotal Decade: How the United States Traded Factories in the Seventies* (New Haven, Conn.: Yale University Press, 2011).

2   See Jan Breman, *At Work in the Informal Economy of India: A Perspective from the Bottom Up* (New Delhi: Oxford University Press, 2013).

3   Karl Marx, *Capital, Vol. 1* (Chicago, Ill.: Charles H. Kerr, 1921), p. 533.

4   In China, women represent a large and growing share of manufacturing workers in leading sectors of the economy. See Chapter 5 and Pun Ngai, *Made in China: Women Factory Workers in a Global Workplace* (Durham, N.C.: Duke University Press, 2005).

5   Devaluing production of Global South workers in the international system of trade expands profits for the international capitalist class. In addition, this system benefits consumers throughout the North.

6   Giovanni Arrighi, *The Geometry of Imperialism: Limits of Hobson's Paradigm* (London: Verso 1983); Andre Gunder Frank, *Dependent Accumulation and Underdevelopment* (New York: Monthly Review Press, 1998); John A. Hobson, *Imperialism: A Study* (Cambridge, UK: Cambridge University Press, 2010); V. I. Lenin, *Imperialism: The Highest Stage of Capitalism* (New York: Penguin, 2010); Rosa Luxemburg, *Socialism or Barbarism, Selected Writings*, ed. H. C. Scott (London: Pluto Press, 2010); Wolfgang J. Momson, *Theories of Imperialism* (Chicago, Ill.: University of Chicago Press, 1983); Immanuel Wallerstein, *World-systems Analysis: An Introduction* (Chapel Hill, N.C.: Duke University Press, 2004).

7   David Roediger and Elizabeth Esch, *The Production of Difference: Race and the Management of Labor in U.S. History* (New York: Oxford University Press, 2012).

Index

215

Index

Index

217

Index

Index

Index

Index

strikes and stoppages
  in 2011, 1
  in the auto industry, 90–9, 102–3, 134
  banning/restricting of, 155–6, 159
  in China, 108, 115–16, 121, 130–4,
    137–45, 186, 208n69
  in India, 90, 92–4, 96–9, 102–3, 187
  by migrant workers, 3
  in South Africa, 148, 155, 160–75
  in spring 2014, 1
  wildcat, 145–6, 160, 162
strike conduct penalty, 138
structural adjustment policies, 72
structure of book, 22–5
suicide of workers, 134
Suzuki, 91, 95
  ssee also Maruti Suzuki
Syriza, 146

T

taxi drivers, 144, 208n69
technological advances
  and expanded mobility for
    commodity conglomerates, 56
  and reduction in demand for labor, 23
textile industry, 10
Toyota, 175
trade
  19th century, 112–13
  exports from China, 110
  free, 18
  GATS, 75–6
  and mercantilism, 66
  South African exports, 150–1
  South–South, 33
  world's busiest ports, 112, 202n6
Trade Union Advisory Coordinating
  Council (TUACC), 156
trade unions *see* labor unions
Turkey, migration from, 71

U

Ulrich, Nicole, 154

Umkhoto we Sizwe, 156
UNCTAD, 9, 39, 41
underemployment, 87
unemployment, 9, 44, 63, 68, 125, 152,
  153, 203n12
  impact on migrant workers, 78
  unemployed as union members, 51
United Auto Workers, 48
United Democratic Front (South Africa),
  156, 157
United Kingdom, 17, 60
United Nations, 73–4, 153
  Economic Commission for Africa, 153
  UNCTAD, 194n7
United States
  campaigns in, 6
  as contemporary hegemonic power,
    20
  dominant companies, 111
  Federal Reserve, 18
  foreign interventions, 204n27
  Hart–Cellar Act, 68
  Immigration Act (1952), 69
  Immigration and Control Act (1986),
    77
  migrants in, 67–71, 77–8, 198n26
  post Second World War rise of, 15, 18
  poverty in 19
urbanization, 36–7, 65, 72–3, 118, 120,
  122–3

V

value added
  by activity, 8
  forces determining, 37
  by Indian auto manufacturers, 92
  in North and South, 6
van der Walt, Lucien, 154
Vavi, Zwelinzima, 160, 171–2, 213n56
Venezuela, 192n14, 193n22
Vietnam, 136
violence
  and deaths, 100, 169–70, 211n37

Index

World Bank, 15, 18, 19, 25, 42–3, 76
World Economic Forum, 29
World Trade Organization, 25, 75–6, 110

Y
Yates, Michael, 15
Yeros, Paris, 45–6
Yue Yuen, 108, 121, 135–44, 206n52

Z
Zapatistas, 58
Zhong Li, 144
Zokwana, Senzeni, 170, 212n55
Zuma, Jacob, 171, 176